Lecture Notes in Computer Science   11033

Commenced Publication in 1973
Founding and Former Series Editors:
Gerhard Goos, Juris Hartmanis, and Jan van Leeuwen

More information about this series at http://www.springer.com/series/7410

Steven Furnell · Haralambos Mouratidis
Günther Pernul (Eds.)

Trust, Privacy and Security in Digital Business

15th International Conference, TrustBus 2018
Regensburg, Germany, September 5–6, 2018
Proceedings

 Springer

Editors
Steven Furnell ⓘ
University of Plymouth
Plymouth
UK

Günther Pernul
Universität Regensburg
Regensburg
Germany

Haralambos Mouratidis ⓘ
University of Brighton
Brighton
UK

ISSN 0302-9743   ISSN 1611-3349   (electronic)
Lecture Notes in Computer Science
ISBN 978-3-319-98384-4   ISBN 978-3-319-98385-1   (eBook)
https://doi.org/10.1007/978-3-319-98385-1

Library of Congress Control Number: 2018950527

LNCS Sublibrary: SL4 – Security and Cryptology

This Springer imprint is published by the registered company Springer Nature Switzerland AG
The registered company address is: Gewerbestrasse 11, 6330 Cham, Switzerland

Preface

This book presents the proceedings of the 15th International Conference on Trust, Privacy, and Security in Digital Business (TrustBus 2018), held in Regensburg, Germany during September 5–6, 2018. This year's conference continued the tradition of being a forum for disseminating original research results and practical experiences.

TrustBus 2018 brought together academic researchers and industry partners to discuss the state of the art in technology for establishing trust, privacy, and security in digital business.

The conference program included four technical papers sessions covering a broad range of topics, from permission models and cloud, privacy, proactive security measures to cyber-physical systems. In addition to the papers selected by the Program Committee via a rigorous reviewing process (each paper was assigned to four referees for review), the conference program also featured an invited talk delivered by Professor Costas Lambrinoudakis about "The General Data Protection Regulation (GDPR) Era: Ten Steps for Compliance of Data Processors and Data Controllers."

The success of this conference was a result of the effort of many people. We would like to express our appreciation to the Program Committee members and external reviewers for their hard work, and to the members of the Organizing Committee. We would also like to thank Mr. Ludwig Englbrecht for his organizational help and for promoting the conference, and Mrs. Gabriela Wagner for her continuing support of the TrustBus conference series. Special thanks go to the Editorial Director of Springer for including these conference proceedings in the *Lecture Notes in Computer Science* series.

Last but not least, our thanks go to all of the authors who submitted their papers, and to all of the attendees. We hope you find the proceedings stimulating and beneficial for your future research.

September 2018

Steven Furnell
Haralambos Mouratidis
Günther Pernul

Organization

General Chair

Günther Pernul   University of Regensburg, Germany

Program Committee Co-chairs

Steven Furnell   University of Plymouth, UK
Haralambos Mouratidis   University of Brighton, UK

Program Committee

George Aggelinos   University of Piraeus, Greece
Esma Aimeur   University of Montreal, Canada
Nieto Ana   University of Malaga, Spain
Rudolph Carsten   Monash University, Australia
David Chadwick   University of Kent, UK
Cheng-Kang Chu   Huawei International, Singapore
Nathan Clarke   University of Plymouth, UK
Frederic Cuppens   ENST Bretagne, France
José María de Fuentes   University Carlos III of Madrid, Spain
Josep Domingo-Ferrer   Universitat Rovira i Virgili, Spain
Prokopios Drogkaris   University of the Aegean, Greece
Eduardo B. Fernandez   Florida Atlantic University, USA
Simone Fischer-Huebner   Karlstad University, Sweden
Sara Foresti   Università degli Studi di Milano, Italy
Juergen Fuss   University of Applied Science in Hagenberg, Austria
Dimitris Geneiatakis   Aristotle University of Thessaloniki, Greece
Dimitris Gritzalis   Athens University of Economics and Business, Greece
Stefanos Gritzalis   University of the Aegean, Greece
Marit Hansen   Unabhaengiges Landeszentrum fuer Datenschutz
                             Schleswig-Holstein, Germany
Ferrer Josep L.   University Islas Baleares, Spain
Christos Kalloniatis   University of the Aegean, Greece
Maria Karyda   University of the Aegean, Greece
Vasilios Katos   Bournemouth University, UK
Sokratis Katsikas   University of Piraeus, Greece
Spyros Kokolakis   University of the Aegean, Greece
Stewart Kowalski   Norwegian University of Science and Technology,
                             Norway
Costas Lambrinoudakis   University of Piraeus, Greece
Martucci Leonardo   Karlstad University, Sweden

Javier Lopez	University of Malaga, Spain
Stephen Marsh	University of Ontario, Institute of Technology, Canada
Fabio Martinelli	National Research Council, CNR, Italy
Vashek Matyas	Masaryk University, Czech Republic
David Megias	Open University of Catalonia, Spain
Markowitch Olivier	Université Libre de Bruxelles, Belgium
Martin S. Olivier	University of Pretoria, South Africa
Rolf Oppliger	eSECURITY Technologies, Switzerland
Maria Papadaki	University of Plymouth, UK
Andreas Pashalidis	BSI, Germany
Joachim Posegga	Institute of IT-Security and Security Law, Passau, Germany
Panagiotis Rizomiliotis	University of the Aegean, Greece
Rios Ruben	University of Malaga, Spain
De Capitani di Vimer Sabrina	University of Milan, Italy
Pierangela Samarati	University of Milan, Italy
Miguel Soriano	Universitat Politecnica de Catalunya, Spain
Krenn Stephan	AIT Austrian Institute of Technology GmbH, Austria
Stephanie Teufel	University of Fribourg, Switzerland
Aggeliki Tsochou	Ionian University, Greece
Edgar Weippl	SBA, Austria
Christos Xenakis	University of Piraeus, Greece

Additional Reviewers

Agnieszka Kitkowska	Karlstad University, Sweden
Sara Ricci	Universitat Rovira i Virgili, Catalonia
Fadi Hassan	Universitat Rovira i Virgili, Catalonia
Carmen Fernandez	University of Malaga, Spain
Tobias Marktscheffel	University of Passau, Germany
Boutheyna Belgacem	University of Passau, Germany
Ludwig Englbrecht	University of Regensburg, Germany

Contents

Permission Models and Cloud

The General Data Protection Regulation (GDPR) Era: Ten Steps
for Compliance of Data Processors and Data Controllers 3
   Costas Lambrinoudakis

An Inquiry into Perception and Usage of Smartphone Permission Models . . . 9
   Lena Reinfelder, Andrea Schankin, Sophie Russ, and Zinaida Benenson

On the Hardness of Separation of Duties Problems for Cloud Databases 23
   Ferdinand Bollwein and Lena Wiese

Three Tales of Disillusion: Benchmarking Property Preserving
Encryption Schemes 39
   Frank Pallas and Martin Grambow

Privacy

Evaluating the Privacy Properties of Secure VoIP Metadata 57
   João S. Resende, Patrícia R. Sousa, and Luís Antunes

Can Spatial Transformation-Based Privacy Preservation Compromise
Location Privacy? 69
   Anand Paturi and Subhasish Mazumdar

Towards an Effective Privacy Impact and Risk Assessment Methodology:
Risk Assessment 85
   Majed Alshammari and Andrew Simpson

Proactive Security Measures

PERSUADED: Fighting Social Engineering Attacks with a Serious Game . . . 103
   Dina Aladawy, Kristian Beckers, and Sebastian Pape

Developing and Evaluating a Five Minute Phishing Awareness Video 119
   Melanie Volkamer, Karen Renaud, Benjamin Reinheimer, Philipp Rack,
   Marco Ghiglieri, Peter Mayer, Alexandra Kunz, and Nina Gerber

Biometrically Linking Document Leakage to the Individuals Responsible. . . . 135
   Abdulrahman Alruban, Nathan Clarke, Fudong Li, and Steven Furnell

A Decision-Making Approach for Improving Organizations' Cloud
Forensic Readiness 150
   Stavros Simou, Ioannis Troumpis, Christos Kalloniatis,
   Dimitris Kavroudakis, and Stefanos Gritzalis

Cyber Physical Systems

Towards Blockchain-Based Identity and Access Management
for Internet of Things in Enterprises 167
   Martin Nuss, Alexander Puchta, and Michael Kunz

Access Control Requirements for Physical Spaces Protected
by Virtual Perimeters. 182
   Brian Greaves, Marijke Coetzee, and Wai Sze Leung

Towards the Definition of a Security Incident Response
Modelling Language 198
   Myrsini Athinaiou, Haralambos Mouratidis, Theo Fotis,
   Michalis Pavlidis, and Emmanouil Panaousis

An Enhanced Cyber Attack Attribution Framework. 213
   Nikolaos Pitropakis, Emmanouil Panaousis, Alkiviadis Giannakoulias,
   George Kalpakis, Rodrigo Diaz Rodriguez, and Panayiotis Sarigiannidis

A Comprehensive Methodology for Deploying IoT Honeypots 229
   Antonio Acien, Ana Nieto, Gerardo Fernandez, and Javier Lopez

Trustworthiness Cases – Toward Preparation
for the Trustworthiness Certification 244
   Nazila Gol Mohammadi, Nelufar Ulfat-Bunyadi,
   and Maritta Heisel

Author Index 261

Permission Models and Cloud

The General Data Protection Regulation (GDPR) Era: Ten Steps for Compliance of Data Processors and Data Controllers

Costas Lambrinoudakis(✉)

Department of Digital Systems, University of Piraeus,
150 Androutsou St., 18532 Piraeus, Greece
clam@unipi.gr

Regulation (EU) 2016/679 of the European Parliament and of the Council (General Data Protection Regulation (GDPR)) aims at harmonizing the legal framework for the Protection of Personal Data in the EU and, at the same time, strengthening the current regime for the protection of personal data for natural persons. GDPR extends the scope of existing legislation to all EU or non-EU controllers who process personal data of citizens of the EU member states and imposes compliance on a sufficiently rigorous legislative framework.

The Regulation requires controllers to take all appropriate organizational, procedural and technical measures in order to achieve **privacy by default** compliance and the satisfaction of all privacy protection principles during the system design (**privacy by design**). The ultimate goal is to reduce the risks of different probability of occurrence and seriousness for the rights and freedoms of natural persons from processing.

The principle of "risk" for the data subjects' rights and freedoms is a particularly important issue raised by the GDPR. More generally, the regulation adopts a risk-based approach to the protection of personal data [1]. This approach is not new, as GDPR continues and extends the corresponding approach to the concept of risk introduced and described in Directive 95/46/EC of the European Parliament and of the Council.

As "Risk" is defined the possibility that an asset may be damaged due to an unwanted event [2]. Risk assessment is done through risk identification and analysis as well as through the estimation of the impact that the risk may cause for the system/organization (risk evaluation). Risk management aims at adopting all the appropriate technical, organizational and procedural measures required to reduce the risk to acceptable levels (through risk reduction, risk retention, risk sharing and risk avoidance). There are various methods for assessing/measuring and classifying a risk, but most of them are based on the likelihood of a risk being converted into a real event and the consequences (economic or otherwise) that may be caused to the organization. A common method is to score on a numerical scale both the probability of occurrence of an event (P) and the severity/impact of the consequences (I) if the incident occurs - with the most probable and the most serious being higher in scale. In view of this, the risk is quantified in order to obtain a comparative result as follows: Danger = [P] × [I].

The GDPR adopts the principle of risk, while pursuing two different approaches to its endorsement. The first approach concerns the creation of risk categories, and in particular separates the concept of "high risk" from all other categories. This distinction

© Springer Nature Switzerland AG 2018
S. Furnell et al. (Eds.): TrustBus 2018, LNCS 11033, pp. 3–8, 2018.
https://doi.org/10.1007/978-3-319-98385-1_1

is particularly important, since "high risk" cases against the rights and freedoms of the subjects create additional obligations for the controllers. These obligations are mainly related to the requirement to conduct an **impact assessment (PIA)** and the **notification of a data breach** to the data protection authorities and the data subject (Articles 33–36). For the management of "high risk", the Regulation also incorporates the method of **consultation with data protection authorities** in the context of the impact assessment (Article 36).

The second approach considers the risk as continuous of varying likelihood, while its probability and severity for the data subject's rights and freedoms should be determined by reference to the nature, scope, context and the purposes of the processing. More generally, in the GDPR, the concept of risk is one of the "cornerstones" as it is the parameter that will determine the appropriate organizational and technical measures for the data controller. Therefore, in addition to the provisions relating to the conduct of impact assessment (PIA) and the management of data breaches, the GDPR clearly uses the concept of risk to determine the individual **data protection requirements by design** (Article 25), the obligation to **maintain a record of processing activities** (Article 30) and the **adoption of the appropriate technical and organizational measures** for protecting the processing activities (Articles 22, 23, 24 and 32).

In order to address the continuing risk, the Regulation also incorporates the consultation method, seeking to develop guidelines, best practices and building risk categories. Furthermore, the issue of continuing risk is clearly reflected in the key tasks of the **Data Protection Officer (DPO)** (Article 39 (2)), which states that in the performance of his or her tasks have due regard to the risk associated with processing operations, taking into account the nature, scope, context and purposes of processing.

Considering all of the above, we could argue that the ten basic steps to achieve compliance with the requirements of the Regulation are the following:

1. Awareness – Readiness of the Organization

Compliance with the GDPR should be dealt as a systematic action with appropriate planning. Human resources should be aware of the new legal framework and understand the consequences it brings (GDPR may increase the workload of the organization).

The organization should proceed with the assignment of the appropriate roles and responsibilities and assess quickly all important "gaps".

2. Maintain a Record of Processing Activities

The organization should recognize the processing purposes that the organization serves and all related processing activities, paying attention in the fact that many of them nay not be immediately visible (document archive, staff file, customer file, electronic application files, contact files for communication purposes, security files – camera material, online access logs etc.). It is important to distinguish the processing activities per processing purpose.

Then the organization should explore whether there is an obligation to maintain a record of processing activities, although it is certainly a good practice to do it. An obligation exists if the organization employs more than 250 persons or if processing poses a risk to the rights of the data subjects or if it involves special data categories ('sensitive' data) or data relating to criminal convictions.

The record of processing activities should provide the answers to the following questions:

- Who? (identity the person responsible, way of communication, representative and DPO)
- Why? (purpose of processing)
- What? (categories of data subjects, data categories)
- To whom? (categories of recipients)
- Transfers? (in non-EU countries)
- For how long? (deletion deadline for each data category)
- How? (general description of security measures)

3. Designate a Data Protection Officer (DPO)

An obligation to designate a Data Protection Officer (DPO) have all public authorities as well as organizations that perform regular and systematic monitoring of subjects on a large scale, or large-scale processing of special data categories.

The role of the DPO is to advice the data controller/processor, organize training/ awareness programs, act as an internal auditor on personal data issues and monitor compliance with legal requirements. Furthermore the DPO is the point of contact with the data protection authorities as well as with the data subjects.

4. Consent

If the legal basis for the processing of personal data is the consent, the controller must be able to prove that:

- he has obtained the consent of the data subjects.
- the consent was 'free'
- the consent is specific and explicit for a well-defined processing purpose
- the consent has been obtained with a clear positive action (e.g. filling in a box when visiting a web site, selecting desired technical settings for a service etc.). Silence, pre-filled boxes or inactivity should not be taken as consent
- for underage persons the consent is considered to be "valid" when the child is at least 16 years of age. Otherwise consent must be given by the person who has parental responsibility.

5. Privacy -by Design and -by Default

Privacy by design is an approach that requires the integration of the key protection parameters by the controller into existing wider project management and risk management methodologies and policies. GDPR provisions facilitate to this direction by requiring controllers (companies, organizations, etc.) to ensure that the protection of users' privacy is a basic parameter in the early stages of each project and then throughout its life cycle. To achieve that it is important to consider issues like: state of the art technology developments, cost of implementing the protection measures, nature – scope - context and purposes of processing, minimization of threats against the rights and freedoms of individuals from processing.

As far as the privacy by default approach, it requires to ensure that the initial settings of applications/services are set to the most privacy-friendly ones.

6. Protection (Security) of Processing – Risk Management/Data Protection Impact Assessment (DPIA)

While Directive 95/46/EC implies the requirement for risk management procedures, GDPR clearly proposes the implementation of management processes that will facilitate the objective assessment of risks in order to determine whether the data processing operations involve a risk or a high risk. Furthermore, the concept of risk management becomes even more clear in GDPR since it imposes the requirement for an impact assessment (when a type of processing, in particular using new technologies and taking into account nature, scope, context and processing purposes, is likely to cause a high risk to the rights and freedoms of natural persons), a very risk-centric process.

In general, Impact Assessment is one of the most useful tools for identifying and assessing risks to privacy when a controller employs new technologies, products or services. To this end, a variety of methodologies have been proposed, several of which are also included in the guidelines of the Article 29 Working Party [3]. However, data protection impact assessment processes are not included in most risk management standards, they are often not embedded in an organization's broader risk management framework, and are even less relevant to an organization's internal business processes [4].

An integrated risk management process should support the ability to control and limit the risk at all levels, while assessing how the impact of a specific risk compares with the consequences that may be caused by some other risk. Risk management, in the framework of privacy protection, can have many common elements with risk management for the protection of personal data in an organization (e.g., security, information systems, etc.). Their successful combination allows optimization of resources (human and technical) and better risk management [5].

The Data Protection Impact Assessment (DPIA) should provide:

- a systematic description of the processing activities envisaged, the purposes of the processing and its legal basis
- an assessment of the necessity and proportionality of the processing activities
- a risk assessment on the rights and freedoms of data subjects
- the anticipated risk mitigation measures

while in terms of the protection (security) of the processing activities it is necessary for the organization to propose the appropriate/suitable technical and organizational measures. Indicatively:

- Pseudo-anonymization and encryption
- Ensuring Privacy, Integrity, Availability, and Reliability
- Restoration of availability and access in the event of an incident
- Testing, assessing and continually evaluating the effectiveness of the protection measures

7. Data Protection Policy

The organizations need to update/enhance their data protection policies in relation to the existing legal framework, and thus provide information on:

- the legal basis for the processing (which "complicates" the information as it requires legal analysis)
- the time frame that the processing/storage will take place
- the existence of any automated decision making process, including profiling, with information on possible consequences
- data collected from other sources
- the Data Protection Officer's data
- the procedures employed in order to satisfy all data subjects' rights

8. Data Breaches

The timely detection and evaluation of a data breach incident is extremely crucial. A prerequisite to achieve that is to make clear what constitutes a data breach, since the term may be broader from what we originally think.

As soon as an incident has been detected the organization must notify, within 72 h, the data protection authority providing all available information. Furthermore the organization should notify the data subjects if the specific incident may expose their rights and freedoms at high risk.

9. Organizations Acting in Several EU Member States

If the controller is active in more than one member state, the country of the main establishment should be designated. The data protection authority of this country is the Lead Supervisory Authority for the organization.

It is therefore important for the organization to clearly address the following questions:

- Which is the place/country of the main establishment (headquarters)?
- Are there other facilities within EU?
- Are the basic decisions for processing taken in the headquarters or not?
- Are there any joint data controllers?

10. Transferring Data to Non EU Countries

In cases where the controller must transfer data to non EU countries it is necessary to ensure that it is legal to do so (Binding Corporate Rules –BCRs, Standard Contract Clauses SCCs etc.). Then it is important to assess and select an appropriate transmission mechanism and also to explore whether it has an obligation to inform the persons whose data will be is transferred.

References

1. Fisher, J.: How to Adopt the GDPR Risk-Based Approach, 25 April 2017. https://www.linkedin.com/pulse/how-adopt-gdpr-risk-based-approach-james-fisher
2. "Risk" & "Risk Management", Wikipedia. https://en.wikipedia.org/wiki/Risk_management. Accessed 7 Aug 2017

3. 17/EN WP248, Guidelines on Data Protection Impact Assessment (DPIA) for the Purposes of Regulation 2016/679, Article 29 Data Protection Working Party, 4 April 2017
4. Wright, D., et al.: Integrating privacy impact assessment in risk management. Int. Data Priv. Law 4(2), 155–170 (2014)
5. Notario, N., et al.: PRIPARE: integrating privacy best practices into a privacy engineering methodology. In: IEEE Security and Privacy Workshops 2015, May 2015

An Inquiry into Perception and Usage of Smartphone Permission Models

Lena Reinfelder[1]([✉]), Andrea Schankin[2], Sophie Russ[1],
and Zinaida Benenson[1]

[1] Computer Science Department,
Friedrich-Alexander-Universität Erlangen-Nürnberg, Erlangen, Germany
{lena.reinfelder,sophie.russ,zinaida.benenson}@fau.de
[2] Computer Science Department, Karlsruhe Institue of Technology,
Karlsruhe, Germany
schankin@teco.edu

Abstract. Initially, Android and iOS took different approaches to protect users' privacy from third-party apps by means of permissions. The old Android permission model has been repeatedly criticized for its poor usability, whereas the runtime permission model of iOS received relatively low attention in the usable security community. Since October 2015, Android also implements the runtime permission model. We compare perception and usefulness of the respective permission models by three groups: users of old Android, runtime Android and iOS permissions. To this end, we conducted a survey with over 800 respondents. The results indicate that both permission types are reportedly utilized by users for decision making regarding app usage. However, runtime permissions in Android and iOS are perceived as more useful than the old Android permissions. Users also show a more positive attitude towards the runtime permission model independently of the smartphone operating system.

Keywords: Runtime permissions · Android · iOS · User perception

1 Introduction

Smartphones store and process a large amount of sensitive personal data. Until recently, Android and iOS took different approaches to protect this information from unwanted access by third-party apps. Following the terminology by Bonne et al. [4], we call these approaches *old Android permission model* and *runtime permission model*, respectively.

Runtime permission model was introduced in iOS 6 in September 2012.[1] If an installed app needs access to sensitive data for the first time, the user is presented with a permission request for this data type and can grant or refuse access.

---

[1] Previous iOS versions asked for runtime permissions for location data, but most other data types could be accessed freely by the apps.

© Springer Nature Switzerland AG 2018
S. Furnell et al. (Eds.): TrustBus 2018, LNCS 11033, pp. 9–22, 2018.
https://doi.org/10.1007/978-3-319-98385-1_2

Moreover, users can adjust (grant or revoke) permissions in the smartphone's settings. Thus, the runtime permission model allows for fine-grained control over the data access by the apps.

The old Android permission model was used by Android prior to the introduction of Android 6.0 (Marshmallow). During the installation process of any app, Android users are shown permission requests by this app. If the users do not want an app to access one or more of the required data types, they have to cancel the installation process. However, if users install the app, they permanently grant all permissions. This permission model has been repeatedly criticized for its poor usability. User studies have shown that many users do not notice and do not understand permissions. Moreover, the users are required to take an "all-or-nothing" decision at a psychologically inconvenient time point, as they are shown the permission screen after they already decided to install an app [6,7,9].

Maybe in response to the above critique, the old Android permission model was changed to the runtime permission model starting with Android 6.0 in October 2015. Referring to Android's permission model before and after version 6.0 (Marshmallow), researchers have used different terminology, as presented in Table 1. We use the terminology of Bonne et al. [4] and thus refer to the Android permission model before the version 6.0 as the old Android permission model and to the permission model for version 6.0 and later as the runtime permission model.

Table 1. Various terminology used for Android permission models

	Before Android 6.0	After Android 6.0
Tsai et al. [15]	Ask-on-install (AOI)	Ask-on-first-use (AOFU)
Bonne et al. [4]	Old permission model	Runtime permission model
Micinski et al. [12]	Install-time permission lists	Run-time dialog boxes
Andriotis et al. [2]	Binary model (accept-reject)	Runtime permission model

It seems that the runtime permission model is considered to be "better" by both, Google and Apple. However, it is not clear whether users also perceive the runtime permission model to be "better", and whether these perceptions differ for different smartphone operating systems, Android and iOS. The goal of this work is to investigate these questions.

Currently, some users have smartphones with the old Android permission model, whereas others already use the new one. Thus, we have a unique opportunity to compare usage and perception of permissions of these two user groups. Additionally, if we capture the same data from iOS users, we may be able to see whether usage and perception of runtime permissions are similar across both smartphone operating system. More precisely, we consider the following research questions:

- *RQ1:* How are different permission models reportedly used in practice?[2]
- *RQ2:* How are different permission models perceived by the users?

To answer RQ1, we consider the reported role of the old Android permissions in the installation process and the reported behavior of users when they encounter runtime permissions: how they usually react and whether they adjust permissions in the smartphone's settings.

To specify RQ2 more concretely, we formulate the following hypotheses:

- *RQ2-H1:* Runtime permissions are perceived as more useful than old Android permissions.
- *RQ2-H2:* Runtime permissions are perceived more positively than old Android permissions.

To answer these research questions, we conducted an online survey with 864 participants: 339 users of old Android permissions, 211 users of runtime Android permissions and 314 iOS users. We found that both permission types are reportedly utilized by users for decision making regarding app installations and usage. However, runtime permissions in Android and iOS are perceived as more useful than the old Android permissions. Users also show a more positive attitude towards the runtime permission model.

Outline. This paper is organized as follows. We discuss related work in the next section, and outline study design and participants' demographics in Sect. 3. Study results are presented in Sect. 4 and discussed in Sect. 5. We conclude in Sect. 6.

2   Related Work

User perceptions, attitudes and behavior concerning various aspects of smartphone security and privacy has been an active research topic in the last decade. Here we focus on research regarding permissions.

iOS runtime permissions have received limited research attention so far. Tan et al. [13] investigated how developer-specified reasons for iOS permission requests influence user behavior. They found that users are significantly more likely to grant permission requests when an explanation was available, even if the content of that explanation was not relevant for the app usage.

Previous research mainly focused on Android permissions. We provide an overview of research on perception of the old Android permission model and possible design improvements. We then consider research on alternative presentation forms and extensions of the old Android permission model, and finally on the runtime permissions.

Regarding the old Android permission model, users are confronted with making privacy related decisions at installation time of an app by either granting all

---

[2] "Reportedly" means that we ask users how they utilize permissions, but do not measure their actual behavior, which is out of scope of this study.

requested permissions or aborting the app installation. This process often induces users to grant all permissions without reading them or without understanding the consequences [6,9]. Android users seem also unaware of the frequency of apps collecting personal data e.g. regarding tracking data points [8] and of apps continuing to access smartphone's resources when running in the background [14]. Kelley et al. [9] report that the permission display is read in general, but rarely understood. Even text-based warnings which explain the access of an app do not show a strong effect on decisions about app installations [3].

In order to improve the comprehension of applications accessing and changing data and settings on users' smartphones, many alternative interfaces and extensions to existing permission systems have been developed [10,11,15].

Some research efforts tried to increase understanding and usage of permissions for decision making by providing additional information next to the permission screen. Kelley et al. [10] designed a display with privacy information to help users to make better decisions on security and privacy in choosing applications with fewer permissions. As a result, they could support users in selecting apps with less permissions. Kraus et al. [11] supplied users with statistical information: the number of permissions compared to other apps with similar functionality. Tsai et al. [15] argue that the Android permission privacy interfaces are insufficient in helping users making informed decisions about privacy desires and needs because they disregard contextual factors. Therefore, they present TurtleGuard, a privacy feedback interface based on machine-learning techniques. Overall, Android users have consistently expressed surprise about apps' data access and a desire to have more control over it [1,7,16].

The first study on the adaptation of Android users to the runtime permission model was conducted by Andriotis et al. [2]. They designed an application which was installed by 50 Android Marshmallow users. This app gathered smartphone's current information about permission settings for each installed app. Additionally, participants were asked six multiple choice questions about their understanding and perception of the new model. This study shows that the majority of users prefer the new permission system as it enabled them to better control their data being accessed by apps. Bonne et al. [4] examine reasons why Android users install or remove apps from their smartphones in the runtime permission model. The authors collected data using questionnaires and observed real app usage behavior through the use of an Android app. They conclude that requested permissions are less important for user's app choice and that 15% of users uninstalled apps due to permissions. We further discuss the work of Andriotis et al. and Bonne et al. in Sect. 5.

To summarize, usage and usefulness of Android permissions have been a very active research topic, whereas iOS permissions have not received much attention. Although runtime permissions have been positively received by the Android users, it is not clear whether research results concerning Android runtime permissions can be generalized to the iOS runtime permissions as well, and to possible future uses of runtime permissions in other systems. We take the first step in closing this research gap by comparing usage, usefulness and attitude to permissions by the three major smartphone user groups available today: users of old Android permissions and users of runtime permissions for both, Android and iOS.

3 Method

In the following we describe the survey design, data analysis approach, the recruiting process and the characteristics of the participants.

3.1 Survey Design

The survey focused on users' reported handling of permissions at installation and during runtime, on perception of permissions' usefulness and on positive or negative attitude to them. It consisted of the following question groups:

1. Smartphone usage: OS version, duration of usage, OS of the previous smartphone[3], number of self-installed apps, frequency of app installations;
2. Usage of permissions: important factors in the app choice process, canceling of installations due to permissions requests, handling of runtime permissions;
3. Usefulness of permissions and attitude towards permissions;
4. Demographics: age, sex, education, occupation, affinity towards technology. The latter was measured using the psychometric scale by Zawacki-Richter et al. [17] (in German). This scale rates eight statements by using a 5-point Likert scale (from "disagree" to "agree"). The statements cover experience, competence, attitude, knowledge, interest and acceptance towards technology.

In the questions about *usage of permissions* users were first shown a screenshot of the respective app store and asked to indicate which interface elements are important to them when choosing an app. The participants were shown the list of interface elements (e.g., app name, app size, price, reviews) in randomized order and asked to order the elements by importance. For the users of the old Android model, this list contained the item *Requested permissions* and was used to establish the role of the old Android permission model in the app choice process. We also asked whether users sometimes cancel installation of apps and for what reason. Afterward, we explicitly asked about canceling of app installations due to permissions.

With respect to runtime permissions, we first showed to the users example situations that arise if an app asks for permissions. We asked whether the users are familiar with similar situations, and how they usually react to them (latter as a free-text question). Furthermore, we asked users of runtime permissions whether they have ever changed permissions in the settings of their smartphones.

---

[3] We were concerned that users that recently switched from Android to iOS or vice versa might confound both permission models in their answers, and thus might not be able to provide consistent answers regarding permissions. However, this threat to validity was later mitigated by the data analysis, see Sect. 3.3.

The *usefulness of permissions* was assessed with the statement "I find permissions useful". It was rated on a 5-point Likert scale from 1 = "disagree" to 5 = "agree". To assess users' *attitude towards permissions*, they were asked to complete the following statements on a 5-point Likert scale (from 1 = "negative" to 5 = "positive"):

- My attitude toward permissions is generally ...
- My overall experience with permission requests is ...

We conducted several pretest runs with Android and iOS users during the survey design process. We first tested individual questions with users of both operating systems and adjusted them accordingly. Finally, the complete questionnaire was tested by five Android and two iPhone users.

3.2   Data Analysis

We calculated Chi-squared tests (χ^2) for nominally scaled variables or Analyses of Variance (ANOVA) for interval scaled variables, respectively. Significant differences are indicated if $p < .05$. Because of the large sample size, even small effects reach statistical significance. Therefore, we also report η^2 as estimate of effect size in ANOVAs, and Cramer's V (φ_c) for χ^2 tests. According to Cohen [5], effect size is considered to be small at $\eta^2 = 0.01$ or $\varphi_c = 0.07$, medium at $\eta^2 = 0.09$ or $\varphi_c = 0.21$, and large at $\eta^2 = 0.25$ or $\varphi_c = 0.35$.

The reliability of the scale "affinity for technology" was assessed by Cronbach's α as a measurement for internal consistency. With a Cronbrach's $\alpha = 0.85$, the reliability is good.

The survey also contained open-ended questions, which were categorized using MAXQDA. We applied an inductive approach, meaning that categories were derived from the data material. A given answer could be assigned to more than one category. As the most free-text answers were very short and unambiguous, the categorization codebook was compiled by one researcher. The resulting categories were then discussed by the research team, and thereafter one researcher coded all answers.

3.3   Participants

The questionnaire was available online for 30 days in October 2016. It was approved by the data protection office of the Friedrich-Alexander University of Erlangen-Nuremberg (FAU). We advertised the study on the mailing lists of the economics and the social sciences departments and at the official Facebook group of the FAU. To avoid self-selection and priming issues, the recruitment message stated that the study was about smartphone usability.

The average completion time of the questionnaire was fifteen minutes. The users did not receive any compensation for participation. Overall 1164 people took part in the study. 208 answers were sorted out because these participants did not complete the survey. Additionally, 92 participants either did not have a

Table 2. Demographics of the participants ($N = 864$), σ denotes standard deviation. Some values are missing in the dataset, therefore values do not always add up to 864.

	All users	Old Android	Runtime Android	iOS
Participants	864	339	211	314
	68% female	71% female	61% female	69% female
Average age	23 ($\sigma = 6.2$)	23 ($\sigma = 6.3$)	23 ($\sigma = 5.7$)	23 ($\sigma = 6.5$)
Educational degree				
High school	612 (71%)	238 (70%)	149 (71%)	225 (72%)
Bachelor's degree	167 (19%)	73 (22%)	44 (21%)	50 (16%)
Master's degree	64 (7%)	20 (6%)	12 (6%)	32 (10%)
Other	19 (2%)	8 (2%)	4 (2%)	7 (2%)
Occupation				
Student	773 (89%)	314 (93%)	186 (88%)	273 (87%)
Employee	63 (7%)	17 (5%)	18 (9%)	28 (9%)
Other	24 (3%)	8 (2%)	5 (2%)	12 (4%)
Affinity towards technology	2.86 ($\sigma = 0.76$)	2.67 ($\sigma = 0.76$)	3.05 ($\sigma = 0.82$)	2.93 ($\sigma = 0.77$)

smartphone with Andorid or iOS, or did not provide their Android version in the questionnaire.[4] Both types of participants were not asked any further questions. This yielded a dataset of 864 utilizable responses.

Consistency of Smartphone Usage. As described in Sect. 3.1, we asked participants how long they have been using their current smartphone, and which kind of smartphone they had before (if any). We did this in order to identify users that recently switched from Android to iOS or vice versa, as we were afraid that they might confound both permission systems in their answers. However, this fear was not justified by the data, as we discuss below.

We define users that consistently used operating system $OS \in \{$Android, iOS$\}$ if and only if they satisfy one of the following conditions:

- currently use OS & it is their first smartphone;
- have been using OS since 2014[5] or earlier;
- currently use OS & previous smartphone had OS.

---

[4] We took special care to guide participants through the process of finding out the version of their operating system, accounting for different interfaces of various Android manufacturers.

[5] The study was conducted in October 2016, such that users that have been using OS since 2014 have more than 1,5 years of experience with it.

Out of 864 users, 760 users (88%) used their operating system consistently. Comparing their answers with the answers of all 864 users, we found no statistically significant differences in any of the results that we present in Sect. 4 (mostly, the descriptive statistics were exactly the same). Thus, we conclude that the answers of "inconsistent" users did not influence the results. This may be due to the low number of these users, or possibly consistency of usage is not important for our research questions. In any case, in the following we present results based on the dataset of all 864 users.

Demographics. The sample characteristics are presented in Table 2. Two-thirds of participants are female, most of them are students in the lower semesters, before Bachelor's degree. On average, their affinity for technology is low (under 3).

Our research questions include statistical comparison of the three user groups with the permission model as independent variable and usefulness of permissions (RQ2-H1) and attitude towards them (RQ2-H2) as dependent variable. Therefore, we need to make sure that the results of the analysis are not confounded by the differences in the demographic characteristics of the three groups. To determine whether the three groups differ in their demographic characteristics, we calculated the corresponding statistic measures with permission model as between-subjects factor and a demographic characteristic as dependent variable.

In rare cases, some values are missing in the dataset, therefore we report sample sizes for each statistic result separately. The groups were similar in their average age ($F(2, 860) < 1$), educational degree ($\chi^2(6, N = 862) = 8.315$, $p = .216$, $\varphi_c = .07$), and occupation ($\chi^2(4, N = 861) = 6.084$, $p = .193$, $\varphi_c = .06$). However, their affinity towards technology significantly correlated with operating system (and thus permission model) they used, $F(2, 863) = 17.150$, $p < .001$, $\eta^2 = .04$. It was lowest for participants with the old Android permission model, $p < .001$, whereas participants with runtime Android permissions or iOS did not differ, $p = .233$. As men in the sample were more affine towards technology than women, $F(1, 862) = 221.227$, $p < .001$, we also observed a small but not significant effect of sex, $\chi^2(2, N = 863) = 5.256$, $p = .072$, $\varphi_c = .08$.

Because this difference in the affinity towards technology might confound the effects of the permission model, we controlled for this variable statistically. In the following, we calculated Analyses of Covariance (ANCOVA) with affinity for technology as covariate. Because this was not possible for Chi-squared tests, we calculated the correlation between the affinity for technology and the respective dependent variable to assess whether there was a confound. This was not the case (all $r < .10$).

App Usage. All three user groups have similar experiences with app installations: most installed 30 or less apps. The majority of participants installs apps several times per month or per year. Overall, users of old Android versions install less apps than the other groups.

4   Results

We present the findings of our study according to the two research questions in the following.

4.1   RQ1 – Usage of Permission Models

To answer RQ1, we consider the role of the old Android permissions in the installation process, and the reported behavior of the users when they encounter runtime permissions: how they usually react, and whether they adjust permissions in the smartphone's settings.

Usage of Permissions for Installation Decisions. When asked to place some elements of user interfaces of the respective app stores in the order of their importance for app choice, the three user groups reported similar behavior. Top 3 elements in all groups were "Price", "Reviews" and "App Description". Both groups of Android users put "Permissions" at the fourth place (iOS users do not have this interface element in their app store). 9% of old Android permissions users and 10% of runtime Android users put "Permissions" into the first place. We also asked the participants an open question about additional factors that they consider when choosing an app. Permissions were mentioned by 5% of iOS users, including three users that never used an Android smartphone.

Waiving of App Usage Due to Permissions. When asked whether they have ever canceled app installations or usage because of permissions, 45% of old Android permissions users, 46% of new Android permissions users, and 31% of iOS users answered in the affirmative. The close similarity between the answers of the users of old Android permissions and runtime Android permissions may be due to the fact that, according to the survey results, all but 11 Android users encountered both permission models.

In an open-ended question about the canceling reasons, users across all permission models most often reported that they waive app usage when there is no understandable reason why an app should access certain resources. Users expressed concerns about data security and privacy, and criticized lack of transparency why apps need certain permissions. Users often hesitate to use apps if they require permissions that are obviously not related to the functionality, e.g., a calculator app requiring access to the contact list. Furthermore, the participants mentioned specific sensitive data types which, when being accessed by apps, lead to their non-usage or deinstallation. Permissions such as location, photos and contact lists were mentioned most often by users of all permission models.

Usage of Runtime Permissions. Survey participants were shown examples of runtime permission requests and asked whether they are familiar with such situations (see Sect. 3.1). Overwhelming majority of runtime Android and iOS users (99%) answered in the affirmative.

The participants were subsequently asked an open question about how they usually react in these situations. Their strategies can be subdivided into three categories (see Table 3). The majority of runtime permission users say that they usually take situational decisions. This means that they decide on whether to allow or decline permissions based on the necessity for the app or depending on the permissions type. Some users feel that some permissions, such as location, camera, contact list or microphone, are more sensitive than the others. Some users reported the strategy of first denying all runtime permissions and then granting them if the app does not work as expected.

A notable minority of users (around 20%) report that they usually grant permissions. In this case, some users commented that as they download apps from the official stores, they trust these apps.

Table 3. Usual behavior towards runtime permissions requests (211 runtime Android users and 314 iOS users; percentages not always add up to 100% due to rounding)

	Runtime Android	iOS
Allow	38 (18%)	62 (20%)
Decline	58 (27%)	60 (19%)
Depends on the situation	100 (47%)	157 (50%)
No answer provided	15 (7%)	35 (11%)

Users were furthermore asked whether they use the possibility to change their permission decisions in the settings of their smartphones. Strong majority of users, 83% for iOS and 71% for Android, answered in the affirmative. The difference between user groups may be due to the fact that the Android users have not fully adapted to the new permissions model yet.

4.2   RQ2 – Perception of Permission Models

Both hypotheses formulated in Sect. 1 could be supported:

- *RQ2-H1:* Runtime permissions are perceived as more useful than old Android permissions.
- *RQ2-H2:* Runtime permissions are perceived more positively than old Android permissions.

The usefulness of permissions was assessed by asking the participants to rate the statement "I find permissions useful" on a 5-point Likert scale from 1 = "disagree" to 5 = "agree". The results are shown in Table 4. The permissions model correlates significantly with the perceived usefulness of the permissions, $F(2, 860) = 5.987$, $p = 0.003$, $\eta^2 = 0.014$. In particular, users with runtime

Android or iOS systems rated permissions similarly useful, and as more useful than users with the old Android system.

Table 4. Results of participants' ratings on a 5-point Likert scale from $1 =$ "disagree" to $5 =$ "agree" ($N = 864$)

	Old Android	Runtime Android	iOS
I find permissions useful	3.39 ($\sigma = 1.15$)	3.74 ($\sigma = 1.14$)	3.74 ($\sigma = 1.17$)

Table 5. Attitude and experiences with permissions on a 5-point Likert scale from $1 =$ "negative" to $5 =$ "positive" ($N = 864$)

	Old Android	Runtime Android	iOS
General attitude towards permissions	2.40 ($\sigma = 0.88$)	2.76 ($\sigma = 1.00$)	2.87 ($\sigma = 0.94$)
Overall experience with permissions	3.01 ($\sigma = 0.67$)	3.23 ($\sigma = 0.75$)	3.23 ($\sigma = 0.76$)

Attitude to permissions was assessed by two items, both rated on a 5-point Likert scale from $1 =$ "negative" to $5 =$ "positive". The results are shown in Table 5. The permission model is significantly correlated with the attitude, i.e., with the general attitude, $F(2, 860) = 15.309$, $p < 0.001$, $\eta^2 = 0.034$, as well as with the overall experience, $F(2, 860) = 5.233$, $p = 0.006$, $\eta^2 = 0.012$. Although, users perceive permissions as slightly negative on average, this emotion is weaker for runtime permissions, nearing the neutral attitude. Moreover, the overall experience with permissions is reported as neutral, but with more positive reaction from the runtime permissions users.

5   Discussion

According to the reported usage of permissions, both permission types are utilized by the users when they decide on installation and usage of apps. Old Android permissions seem to play an important role in the app choice process for a notable amount of Android users: they put permissions at the fourth place in the app choice process (after price, reviews and app description), and almost half of them (45%) reported that they canceled app installations because of permissions.

Users of the runtime permissions report that they cancel usage of apps that request unreasonable (from the user's point of view) permissions. The request for unreasonable permissions could diminish trust into the app. Another possible explanation might be that if the app is not important for the users, they may decide that additional effort required for management of runtime permissions is not worth the benefit they get from the app. However, users of runtime permissions cancel app usage less frequently. This may be due to the fact that many apps still work as expected if the users are free to manage the permissions.

Andriotis et al. [2] found in a within-subjects study that Android users encountering both permission models prefer the runtime permission model to the old Android model. The authors used an Android app to collect data from participants' smartphones regarding permission settings for each installed application. Additionally, participants were asked six multiple choice questions about their understanding and perception of the new model. In comparison to Andriotis et al. we used a more extensive questionnaire including also open questions, analyzed a larger user sample and included iOS users in our data collection process. Therefore, we were able to investigate the perception of permission systems independent of the smartphone operating system. However, we did not ask our participants to download an app, and therefore we could not observe their actual behavior. Our results confirm the findings of Andriotis et al. Corroborating their evidence, we find in a between-subject study with Android and iOS users that runtime permissions are perceived more useful and more positively than the old Android permissions. A more extended study that uses both, Android and iOS apps, could build on our findings and provide further insights into permission perception and usage.

Bonne et al. [4] examine how Android users of version 6.0 or higher decide on installing or removing apps from their smartphones. They also logged grant and denial rates of permissions. The authors used data from questionnaires as well as data from observed real app usage behavior through the use of an Android app. Regarding app choice, requested permissions were found to play the least important role in the survey results. This is in contrast to our survey where permissions were ranked fourth after app price, reviews and app description. However, logged data revealed that 15% of all users uninstalled apps due to permissions. In our survey, 30% of iOS and 46% of Android runtime model users stated that they at least once canceled app usage because of permission requests. As our question was formulated without time boundaries, but Bonne et al. observed their users for a limited amount of time, we think that our survey results are reasonably close to reality, corroborating the results by Bonne et al.

To summarize, we find that the runtime permissions provide users with both, the benefits of the old Android permissions (as they can decide to cancel app usage in case of unreasonable permissions requests), and with more control over apps that they want to use despite some unwelcome permissions requests.

6   Conclusion

We conducted a survey with over 800 respondents comparing perception and reported usage of the respective permission models by three groups: users of old Android, runtime Android and iOS permissions. Both permission types are reportedly utilized in users' decision making concerning app installation and usage. However, runtime permissions in Android and iOS are perceived as more useful and evoke a more positive emotional attitude than the old Android permissions.

Our study has several limitations. We use a convenience sample, mostly consisting of students, and two-thirds of participants are female. Furthermore, the three user groups differ in their affinity towards technology (we control for the latter in our statistical analysis). Therefore, it is not clear how our results can be generalized to other population groups. Additionally, as we used an online survey, we could not assess the actual behavior of the users, but only their reported behavior.

Future work is especially needed to understand the actual effectiveness of the runtime permission model, that is, how well it prevents users from unintended installation of privacy-invasive or malicious apps.

References

1. Almuhimedi, H., et al.: Your location has been shared 5,398 times!: A field study on mobile app privacy nudging. In: Proceedings of the 33rd Annual ACM Conference on Human Factors in Computing Systems, pp. 787–796. ACM (2015)
2. Andriotis, P., Sasse, M.A., Stringhini, G.: Permissions snapshots: assessing users' adaptation to the android runtime permission model. In: IEEE International Workshop on Information Forensics and Security (WIFS) (2016)
3. Benton, K., Camp, L.J., Garg, V.: Studying the effectiveness of android application permissions requests. In: 2013 IEEE International Conference on Pervasive Computing and Communications Workshops (PERCOM Workshops), pp. 291–296, March 2013
4. Bonné, B., Peddinti, S.T., Bilogrevic, I., Taft, N.: Exploring decision making with android's runtime permission dialogs using in-context surveys. USENIX Association (2017)
5. Cohen, J.: Statistical Power Analysis for the Behavioral Sciences, pp. 20–26. Lawrence Earlbaum Associates, Hillsdale (1988)
6. Felt, A.P., Ha, E., Egelman, S., Haney, A., Chin, E., Wagner, D.: Android permissions: user attention, comprehension, and behavior. In: Proceedings of the Eighth Symposium on Usable Privacy and Security, SOUPS 2012, pp. 3:1–3:14. ACM, New York (2012)
7. Harbach, M., Hettig, M., Weber, S., Smith, M.: Using personal examples to improve risk communication for security & privacy decisions. In: Proceedings of the 32nd Annual ACM Conference on Human Factors in Computing Systems, pp. 2647–2656. ACM (2014)
8. Jung, J., Han, S., Wetherall, D.: Short paper: enhancing mobile application permissions with runtime feedback and constraints. In: Proceedings of the Second ACM Workshop on Security and Privacy in Smartphones and Mobile Devices, pp. 45–50. ACM (2012)
9. Kelley, P.G., Consolvo, S., Cranor, L.F., Jung, J., Sadeh, N., Wetherall, D.: A conundrum of permissions: installing applications on an Android smartphone. In: Blyth, J., Dietrich, S., Camp, L.J. (eds.) FC 2012. LNCS, vol. 7398, pp. 68–79. Springer, Heidelberg (2012). https://doi.org/10.1007/978-3-642-34638-5_6
10. Kelley, P.G., Cranor, L.F., Sadeh, N.: Privacy as part of the app decision-making process. In: Proceedings of the SIGCHI Conference on Human Factors in Computing Systems, CHI 2013, pp. 3393–3402. ACM, New York (2013)

11. Kraus, L., Wechsung, I., Möller, S.: Using statistical information to communicate android permission risks to users. In: 2014 Workshop on Socio-Technical Aspects in Security and Trust, pp. 48–55, July 2014

12. Micinski, K., Votipka, D., Stevens, R., Kofinas, N., Mazurek, M.L., Foster, J.S.: User interactions and permission use on android. In: Proceedings of the 2017 CHI Conference on Human Factors in Computing Systems, pp. 362–373. ACM (2017)

13. Tan, J., et al.: The effect of developer-specified explanations for permission requests on smartphone user behavior. In: Proceedings of the SIGCHI Conference on Human Factors in Computing Systems, pp. 91–100. ACM (2014)

14. Thompson, C., Johnson, M., Egelman, S., Wagner, D., King, J.: When it's better to ask forgiveness than get permission: attribution mechanisms for smartphone resources. In: Proceedings of the Ninth Symposium on Usable Privacy and Security, p. 1. ACM (2013)

15. Tsai, L., et al.: Turtle Guard: helping android users apply contextual privacy preferences. In: Symposium on Usable Privacy and Security (SOUPS) (2017)

16. Wijesekera, P., Baokar, A., Hosseini, A., Egelman, S., Wagner, D., Beznosov, K.: Android permissions Remystified: a field study on contextual integrity. In: Proceedings of the 24th USENIX Conference on Security Symposium, SEC 2015, pp. 499–514. USENIX Association, Berkeley (2015)

17. Zawacki-Richter, O., Hohlfeld, G., Müskens, W.: Mediennutzung im studium. Schriftenreihe zum Bildungs-und Wissenschaftsmanagement 1(1) (2014)

On the Hardness of Separation of Duties Problems for Cloud Databases

Ferdinand Bollwein[1] and Lena Wiese[2(✉)]

[1] Institute of Applied Stochastics and Operations Research, TU Clausthal,
Clausthal-Zellerfeld, Germany
ferdinand.bollwein@tu-clausthal.de
[2] Institute of Computer Science, University of Göttingen, Göttingen, Germany
wiese@cs.uni-goettingen.de

Abstract. Using cloud databases puts confidential data at risk. We apply vertical fragmentation of data tables in order to obtain insensitive data fragments. These fragments can then be hosted in databases at different cloud providers. Under the assumption that the cloud providers do not communicate, we then obtain a separation of duties such that each provider is unable to recombine the original confidential data set. In this paper, we view this separation of duties as an optimization problem. We show that it is a combination of the two famous NP-hard problems bin packing and vertex coloring. We analyze the complexity of the problem in the standard case (when only confidentiality is required) and the extended case (when also utility is a requirement).

1 Introduction

Cloud databases are a convenient solution for solving data management problems. However, when outsourcing data to a cloud service, the users (the so-called data owners) transfer the control of the data to the cloud service provider. The here presented separation of duties approach aims at protecting confidentiality of data stored in cloud databases. Consistent with [1,8] cloud service providers are assumed to be *honest-but-curios*: the cloud database servers answer queries correctly and do not manipulate the stored data – but they try to analyze the data and the queries in order to gain as much information as possible from them. Our work is based on the so-called *keep-a-few* approach which was introduced in [8]; we extend this basic approach in several ways – in particular, by allowing more than one external server. Like in [1], we assume that cloud service providers are *non-communicating* – otherwise servers could collaborate to reestablish sensitive information from their insensitive portions of data. The non-communication assumption can be avoided by encrypting tuple identifiers or replacing them by different placeholders in every fragment.

The separation of duties approach is based on the assumption that often the association of data is sensitive, while individual values are insensitive; under this assumption confidentiality can be protected by distributing the data among multiple servers and thereby breaking these associations. However, there is of course

S. Furnell et al. (Eds.): TrustBus 2018, LNCS 11033, pp. 23–38, 2018.
https://doi.org/10.1007/978-3-319-98385-1_3

the possibility that certain values themselves are too sensitive to be exposed to a cloud database provider. For this problem, there are basically two possible solutions. Either the sensitive values are encrypted before storing them in the cloud database – or the sensitive data are not outsourced at all and instead stored locally at the user's site (called the *owner* site). While the encryption approach is certainly more beneficial for the user from the storage consumption point of view (no local storage at the owner site is needed), there is only a limited possibility to perform queries on the encrypted data; encryption also involves a non-negligible overhead when encrypting and decrypting the data. A comparison of *property-preserving* encryption schemes (that support sorting and range queries on encrypted data as well as searching for encrypted keywords) is given in [21] including an assessment of the encryption overhead.

We want to emphasize the point that we are addressing the problem of outsourcing data *storage* into the cloud so that the data have to retain their original quality and accuracy. This is opposed to data *publishing* approaches, that – in order to achieve privacy-preserving statistical evaluations – distort or modify data so that the original data set is not recoverable without additional metadata that could undo the distortion or modification. Prominent approaches that include data distortion are k-anonymity [19,20] and differential privacy [14].

To summarize our contributions, we use vertical fragmentation as a technique to protect data confidentiality from honest-but-curious cloud database servers. Consistent with related work, the confidentiality requirements are modeled as subsets of columns of the individual relations – the so-called confidentiality constraints. The resulting fragments are linkable by a common attribute but it is assumed that they are stored on separate non-communicating servers. The problem of finding such fragmentations is modeled as a mathematical optimization problem and it is one of the main objectives to minimize the number of involved servers. In this paper we extend the work in [4,5]: we analyze the theoretical complexity of the standard separation of duties problem (that enforces confidentiality constraints) by polynomial reduction of the NP-hard problem vertex coloring. Moreover, extended requirements (visibility constraints and closeness constraints) are introduced to improve the utility of the resulting fragmentations and to enable efficient query processing. Those constraints are modeled as soft constraints – in contrast to the confidentiality requirements. We also show NP-hardness of this *extended* separation of duties problem.

Organization of the Article. Related work is presented in Sect. 2. Section 3 introduces the main notions used in this article. Section 4 analyzes the standard variant of separation of duties under confidentiality constraints. Section 5 treats the more involved case of visibility as well as closeness constraints to enforce data locality for more performance of distributed query answering. Section 6 concludes this article with suggestions for future work.

2   Related Work

The major component of our separation of duties approach is the concept of *vertical fragmentation*. This concept is part of many standard textbooks like [18]. Basically, the term vertical fragmentation refers to the process of dividing a relation (see Sect. 3.1 for a formal definition of the relational data model) into smaller units called (relation) fragments. Usually, as described in [18], this is done to speed up database systems. In related work, several approaches apply vertical fragmentation and consider attribute affinity in a given workload of transactions as an optimization measure. A recent comparative evaluation of vertical fragmentation approaches is provided in [17]; however all of these approaches do not consider fragmentation as a security mechanism.

In this paper, we apply vertical fragmentation as a powerful technique to set up a confidentiality-preserving cloud database environment. Two approaches can be seen as starting points for using vertical fragmentation to achieve confidentiality in distributed databases:

- The "two can keep a secret" approach [1] considers distribution of a single table between two database servers and leverages encryption whenever necessary to maintain confidentiality of data stored at the external servers.
- The "keep a few" approach [8] ensures confidentiality by storing highly confidential data at the owner site (in a so-called "owner fragment") and only outsourcing the remaining data to an external server.

Several extensions have spawned off these two basic approaches covering different extensions like visibility constraints and dependencies [2,6,7,9–13]. In particular, in [8,13] Hypergraph Coloring is applied to show hardness of the underlying problems. We complement these approaches by explicitly allowing more than two external servers. We formalize this as an optimization problem such that the amount of necessary cloud database providers is minimized. In our problem formulation visibility and confidentiality constraints may be in conflict (a problem that we solve by treating visibility constraints as soft constraints) – and we additionally consider closeness constraints (that improve data locality).

In general our approach is applicable to databases with multiple relations; this setting was formalized in [5]. Unlike [3] where inter-table constraints involving two relations require that no combination of attributes from these relations are stored in the same fragment, we model confidentiality constraints as subsets of the whole set of attributes from all relations of the database. With this approach the inter-table constraints from [3] can be modeled as pairwise confidentiality constraints for the attributes of the involved relations but it also allows modeling more fine-grained confidentiality concerns.

3   Background and Example

3.1   Relational Data Model

This work uses the notations of the *relational database model* which was first introduced by Codd in 1970 [15] and has become one of the most commonly used models in the context of databases. The main concept in the relational model is the notion of a *relation schema*. A relation schema $R(a_1, \ldots, a_n)$, consists of a *relation name* R and a finite set of *attributes* $\{a_1, \ldots, a_n\}$ with $n \geq 1$. Each attribute a_i is associated with a specific domain of possible values which is accounted for by the expression $dom(a_i)$. Next, a *relation (instance)* r on the relation schema $R(a_1, \ldots, a_n)$, also denoted by $r(R)$, is defined as an ordered set of *n-tuples* $r = (t_1, \ldots, t_m)$ such that each *tuple* t_j is an ordered list $t_j = \langle v_1, \ldots, v_n \rangle$ of values $v_i \in dom(a_i)$ or $v_i = $ NULL. The NULL value is a special constant which is used whenever a certain value of the attribute is unknown or does not apply for a certain tuple. For sake of simplicity we only discuss the theory of Separation of Duties in the context of a single relation r on schema $R(A)$ for a set A of attributes. Lastly, two relational operations are introduced. Let $r = (t_1, \ldots, t_m)$ denote a relation over the relation schema $R(A)$. The projection $\pi_f(r)$ for any $f \subseteq A$ is defined as the mapping that assigns a relation r to the set of tuples:

$$\pi_f(r) := \{t_1[f], \ldots, t_m[f]\}.$$

This corresponds to the set of tuples of r restricted to the subset $f \subseteq A$. Projection is used to obtain the resulting relation fragments from the relation instance. The second important operation is the *equi-join*. To define this operation, let r_1 and r_2 denote relations over the relation schemes $R_1(A_1)$ and $R_2(A_2)$ respectively. The *cartesian product* of r_1 and r_2 is defined as the set of tuples $r_1 \times r_2 := \{(t_1, t_2) \mid t_1 \in r_1, \ t_2 \in r_2\}$. If $A_1' \subseteq A_1$ and $A_2' \subseteq A_2$ denote subsets of attributes of the relation schemes $R_1(A_1)$ and $R_2(A_2)$, the equi-join of r_1 and r_2 on A_1' and A_2' is defined as the operator that returns the set:

$$r_1 \bowtie_{A_1' = A_2'} r_2 := \{t \in r_1 \times r_2 \mid t[A_1'] = t[A_2']\}$$

In the context of vertical fragmentation, the equi-join operation is used to reconstruct the original relation from the obtained fragments by including common attributes in the fragments and performing equi-joins on those attributes.

3.2   Fragmentation

When fragmenting a relation vertically, there are two main requirements. The *first* property (completeness) is that every attribute must be placed in at least one fragment. The *second* property (reconstruction) requires that it must be possible to reconstruct the original relation from the fragments. This is usually achieved by placing a set of common attributes – the *tuple identifier* – into every fragment which makes it possible to link the individual tuples of each fragment. Equi-join operations on those attributes can then be used to reconstruct the original relation. Note that, due to the non-communicating server assumption applied in this work, linkability of fragments is not a security issue. It is further worth noting that the tuple identifier is required to form a proper subset of the fragments which prohibits fragments consisting of the tuple identifier attributes only. This requirement is due to the fact that the tuple identifier's sole purpose should be to ensure the reconstruction property. There is also a *third* property (disjointness) which is often required. This property demands that every non-tuple identifier attribute is placed in exactly one vertical fragment. A *correct vertical fragmentation* of a single relation is formally defined as follows:

Definition 1 (Vertical Fragmentation, Cardinality). *Let r be a relation on the relation schema $R(A)$. Let $tid \subset A$ be the* tuple identifier *of r. A tuple $\mathbf{f} = (f_0, \ldots, f_k)$ where $f_j \subseteq A$ for all $j \in \{0, \ldots, k\}$ is called a* correct vertical fragmentation *of r if the following conditions are met:*

1. **Completeness:** $\bigcup_{j=0}^{k} f_j = A$
2. **Reconstruction:** $tid \subset f_j$, *if* $f_j \neq \emptyset$
3. **Disjointness:** $f_i \cap f_j \subseteq tid$ *(for $f_i \neq f_j$ and $f_i, f_j \neq \emptyset$).*

The cardinality $\mathrm{card}(\mathbf{f})$ *of a correct vertical fragmentation of r is defined as the number of nonempty fragments of $\mathbf{f}$ as* $\mathrm{card}(\mathbf{f}) = \sum_{\substack{j=0 \\ f_j \neq \emptyset}}^{k} 1$. *At physical level, the relation fragment* derived from fragment f_j *is given by the projection $\pi_{f_j}(r)$.*

A fragmentation that satisfies the completeness and the reconstruction but not necessarily the disjointness property is called a *lossless fragmentation* of r.

3.3 Motivating Example

This section provides a motivating example to illustrate the ideas behind the separation of duties approach. Similar to [8], a hospital environment is considered that stores the patients' medical records in a relation as illustrated in Table 1; the patient identifiers (called PID) act as tuple identifiers.

Table 1. Database table storing medical records

PID	Name	DoB	ZIP	Diagnosis	Doctor
1	J. Doe	07.01.1986	12345	Flu	H. Bloggs
2	W. Lee	12.08.1974	23456	Broken Leg	G. Douglas
3	F. Jones	05.09.1963	23456	Asthma	H. Bloggs
4	G. Miller	10.02.1982	12345	Cough	H. Bloggs

Clearly, storing such data in a cloud database and exposing it to the provider violates the patients' privacy. Hence, this is definitely not an option for the hospital. However, it is only the association of the attributes which makes this relation problematic. This observation encourages the idea that it is possible to vertically divide the relation into multiple insensitive fragments which can be distributed among different cloud databases. The hospital develops the following confidentiality constraints to protect their patients' identities:

Table 2. One owner fragment f_0 and two server fragments f_1 and f_2

f_0:

PID	Name
1	J. Doe
2	W. Lee
3	F. Jones
4	G. Miller

f_1:

PID	DoB
1	07.01.1986
2	12.08.1974
3	05.09.1963
4	10.02.1982

f_2:

PID	ZIP	Diagnosis	Doctor
1	12345	Flu	H. Bloggs
2	23456	Broken Leg	G. Douglas
3	23456	Asthma	H. Bloggs
4	12345	Cough	H. Bloggs

- The patients' names must not be stored in plaintext by an untrusted server.
- The date of birth and the ZIP-Code leak too much information about a patient's identity; they must not be stored by a single untrusted server.

A vertical fragmentation consisting of two server fragments and one owner fragment is considered confidentiality-preserving by the hospital. Both server fragments f_1 and f_2 (see Table 2) are insensitive and can therefore be placed on two separate cloud database providers. As long as the respective database providers are not collaborating to reestablish the sensitive associations, the confidentiality requirements imposed by the hospital are met. Because the names of the patients of a hospital are considered to be sensitive on their owns, fragment f_0 (see, Table 2) has to be treated differently. Basically, there are two options: Encrypting the names before outsourcing – or storing them locally in an owner fragment and not in a cloud database. In this work, the second option is chosen: no encryption – limiting the execution of queries involving patients' names – is necessary.

3.4 Data Distribution as Optimization Problems

We will later on combine two different NP-hard problems to obtain our Separation of Duties problem formulation. We now introduce the two underlying problems: Bin Packing and Vertex Coloring.

When outsourcing the data to cloud databases, it might be required that certain capacities in terms of storage space are not exceeded – otherwise the cloud provider could for example charge more usage fees. A famous NP-hard problem considering capacities is Bin Packing; this well-known NP-hard problem is for example stated in [16] (we adapt the notation to our purposes):

Definition 2 (Bin Packing). *Given a set $B = \{b_1, \ldots, b_k\}$ of bins (each with a maximum capacity W_j) and a set $O = \{o_1, \ldots, o_n\}$ of objects (each with a capacity consumption w_i), find the minimum number K such that all objects in O are placed in some bin, the set of used bins $U \subseteq B$ is of cardinality K (that is, $|U| = K$) and the capacities are not exceeded (that is, for each $b_j \in U$ it holds that $\sum_{o_i \in b_j} w_i \leq W_j$).*

The data distribution problem with capacity constraints is basically a Bin Packing Problem (BPP) in the following sense:

- k servers correspond to k bins
- each server b_j has a maximum capacity W_j
- n attributes correspond to n objects
- each attribute has a capacity consumption w_i
- attributes have to be placed into a minimum number of servers K without exceeding the maximum capacities W_j.

On the other hand (to later on ensure confidentiality) we have to express that certain attributes should *not* be placed on the same server. This can be achieved by a graph coloring problem – more precisely Vertex Coloring; this well-known NP-hard problem is also stated in [16] (we again slightly adapt the notation):

Definition 3 (Vertex Coloring). *Given an undirected graph $\mathcal{G} = (N, E)$ consisting of nodes $N = \{n_1, \ldots, n_n\}$ and edges $E \subseteq N \times N$ with $n_i \neq n_{i'}$ for all $(n_i, n_{i'}) \in E$, find the minimum number K such that there exists a K-coloring $\varphi : N \longrightarrow \{1, \ldots, K\}$ that satisfies $\varphi(n_i) \neq \varphi(n_{i'})$ for every edge $(n_i, n_{i'}) \in E$.*

The data distribution problem with pairwise confidentiality constraints is basically a Vertex Coloring Problem (VCP) in the following sense:

- k available servers correspond to the amount k of available colors
- n attributes correspond to n nodes
- if a confidentiality constraint requires that two attributes a_i and $a_{i'}$ should be assigned to different fragments, there should be an edge $(n_i, n_{i'}) \in E$ between the two nodes n_i and $n_{i'}$ corresponding to the attributes; in effect, the two nodes will be colored with two different colors which corresponds to placing them on different servers.
- finding the minimum number K of occupied servers corresponds to finding the minimum number of colors.

In this paper we extend these basic data distribution problems into separation of duties problems that take confidentiality constraints into account and furthermore consider several additional optimization goals and settings. In particular, we consider the capacities and weights in the bin packing problem as one component of our overall optimization problem while confidentiality constraints are enforced by the constraints of the vertex coloring problem.

4   Standard Separation of Duties Problem

We now move on to the formal specification of our Separation of Duties problems. The security requirements are at attribute level, i.e. certain attributes or combinations of attributes are considered sensitive and must not be stored by a single untrusted database server. This can – consistently with related work [1] – be modeled with the notion of *confidentiality constraints*.

Definition 4 (Confidentiality Constraints). *Let $R(A)$ be a relation schema over the set of attributes A. A confidentiality constraint on $R(A)$ is defined by a subset of attributes $c \subseteq A$ with $c \neq \emptyset$. Two types of constraints are distinguished:*

- **Singleton Constraint:** *A singleton constraint is a confidentiality constraint c with* $|c| = 1$*. This means that the confidentiality constraint consists of a single sensitive attribute which should not be exposed to any untrusted server.*
- **Association Constraint:** *An association constraint satisfies* $|c| > 1$*. This means that a server is not allowed to store the combination of attributes contained in c. However, any proper subset of c may be revealed.*

Because attributes contained in a singleton constraint are not allowed to be accessed by an untrusted server, they cannot be outsourced in plaintext at all. Hence, because our approach works without encryption, those attributes have to be stored locally at the owner site. On the other hand, association constraints can be satisfied by distributing the respective attributes among two or more database servers. More precisely, a correct vertical fragmentation $\mathbf{f} = (f_0, \ldots, f_k)$ has to be found in which one fragment stores all the attributes contained in singleton constraints and all other fragments are not a superset of any confidentiality constraint. As a common convention throughout the rest of this work, fragment f_0 will always denote the *owner fragment* which stores all the attributes contained in singleton constraints. This fragment is stored by a local, trusted database. The other fragments $f_1, \ldots, f_k$ denote the *server fragments* and each of those is stored by a different untrusted database server. This leads to the formal definition of a *confidentiality-preserving vertical fragmentation*:

Definition 5 (Confidentiality-preserving Vertical Fragmentation). *For a relation r on the relation schema $R(A)$ and a set of confidentiality constraints C, a correct vertical fragmentation $\mathbf{f} = (f_0, \ldots, f_k)$ is confidentiality-preserving with respect to C if $c \not\subseteq f_j$, for all $c \in C$ and $j \geq 1$.*

The condition requires that no attributes contained in a confidentiality constraint are simultaneously stored in a server fragment and hence, exposed to an untrusted cloud database provider. On the one hand, this ensures that no confidentiality constraint is violated for any server fragment f_j for $j \in \{1, \ldots, k\}$. On the other hand, this means that all attributes contained in singleton constraints must be placed in the owner fragment f_0.

It is necessary to introduce some reasonable restrictions to the set of confidentiality constraints. These restrictions are of theoretical nature and will not restrict its expressiveness. These requirements are summarized by the following definition of a *well-defined* set of confidentiality constraints:

Definition 6 (Well-defined Set of Confidentiality Constraints). *Given a relation r on the relation schema $R(A)$ and a designated tuple identifier $tid \subset A$. A set of confidentiality constraints C is well-defined if it satisfies:*

1. *For all $c, c' \in C$ with $c \neq c'$, it holds that $c \not\subseteq c'$.*
2. *For all $c \in C$, it holds that $c \cap tid = \emptyset$.*

The first condition requires that no confidentiality constraint c is a subset of another confidentiality constraint c'. By the definition of a confidentiality-preserving vertical fragmentation, the satisfaction of c' would be redundant because $c \not\subseteq f_j$ for $j \in \{1, \ldots, k\}$ implies that $c' \not\subseteq f_j$ for $j \in \{1, \ldots, k\}$ if $c \subseteq c'$. The second condition requires that the tuple identifier attributes are considered insensitive: the tuple identifier's sole purpose is to ensure the reconstruction of the fragmentation by placing it in every nonempty fragment.

Space requirements might also be an important factor for the vertically fragmented relation and the owner and the server fragments may not exceed certain storage capacities. Hence, the concept of attribute weight is introduced:

Definition 7 (Weight Function). *Let r be a relation over the relation schema $R(A)$ and let $\mathcal{P}(A)$ denote the power set of the set of attributes A. A weight function for r is defined as a function $w_r : \mathcal{P}(A) \longrightarrow \mathbb{R}_{\geq 0}$ that satisfies:*

- *$w_r(f) = 0$, if and only if $f = \emptyset$*
- *$w_r(f) = \sum_{a \in f} w_r(\{a\})$ for all $f \subseteq A$.*

To denote the weight of a single attribute $a \in A$, the notation $w_r(a)$ is used instead of $w_r(\{a\})$.

Due to the second condition such a weight function is fully defined by the values $w_r(a)$ for all attributes $a \in A$: any subset of A is a combination of these attributes and its weight is defined by the sum of the weights of its elements.

Keeping the number of involved server as low as possible will reduce the user's costs, lower the complexity of maintaining the vertically fragmented relation and also increase the efficiency of executing queries. Therefore, in the following problem statement, the objective is to find a confidentiality-preserving correct vertical fragmentation of minimal cardinality. Additionally, the capacities of the involved servers must not be exceeded.

Definition 8 (Standard Separation of Duties Problem). *Given a relation r over the relation schema $R(A)$, a well-defined set of confidentiality constraints C, a tuple identifier $tid \subset A$, a weight function w_r, servers $S_0, \ldots, S_k$ (where S_0 denotes the owner's trusted server and $S_1, \ldots S_k$ denote the untrusted external servers) and maximum capacities $W_0, \ldots, W_k \in \mathbb{R}_{\geq 0}$, find a correct confidentiality-preserving fragmentation $\mathbf{f} = (f_0, \ldots, f_k)$ of minimal cardinality such that the capacities are not exceeded, i.e. $w_r(f_j) \leq W_j$ for all $0 \leq j \leq k$.*

One should note that in this general formulation the owner fragment can possibly contain all of the attributes if W_0 is sufficiently large. Yet, the purpose of the owner fragment is to store the attributes contained in singleton constraints. Therefore, in a variation of this problem, the capacity of the owner fragment is chosen such that it cannot hold any attribute other than the most sensitive ones and, of course, the tuple identifier; all other attributes are actually distributed among the server fragments. If there are singleton constraints, this can be achieved by choosing W_0 as $w_r(\text{tid}) + \sum_{c \in C : |c| = 1} w_r(c)$.

4.1 Complexity Analysis

In this section, the complexity of the Standard Separation of Duties Problem is analyzed. The problem can be viewed as a combination of two famous NP-hard problems, the Bin Packing Problem due to the capacity constraints and the Vertex Coloring Problem due to the confidentiality constraints. Both problems can easily be modeled as a Separation of Duties Problem to prove NP-hardness of the latter. In real life scenarios however, the capacity constraints might often be less important because cloud storages can generally be enlarged on demand. Therefore, the proof is based on the Vertex Coloring Problem. The following theorem is proven by a polynomial reduction of an instance of the Vertex Coloring Problem to an instance of the Standard Separation of Duties Problem. For simplicity, the former is denoted by VC and the latter by SSoD. The proof proceeds by finding a fragmentation of minimal cardinality K for SSoD which can then define a coloring for VC; lastly, we show that if K is a minimal fragmentation, there can be no coloring for VC with $K' < K$ colors.

Theorem 1. *The Standard Separation of Duties Problem is NP-hard.*

Proof. Let VC be defined by a graph $\mathcal{G} = (N, E)$ with nodes $N = \{n_1, \ldots, n_k\}$ and edges $E = \{e_1, \ldots, e_m\} \subseteq N \times N$. Without loss of generality, it is assumed that if E contains the edge $(n_i, n_{i'})$, it does not contain the equivalent edge $(n_{i'}, n_i)$. Then, SSoD is defined as follows for all $a \in A$ and $j = 1, \ldots, k$:

- For every node $n_i \in N$, an attribute a_{n_i} is defined. Additionally, an artificial tuple identifier tid $:= \{a_{\text{tid}}\}$ is introduced. Overall, the set of attributes is therefore defined by $A := \text{tid} \cup \{a_{n_i} \mid n_i \in N\}$.
- $R(A)$ is a relation schema over A and r is a relation on $R(A)$.
- The weight function $w_r : \mathcal{P}(A) \longrightarrow \mathbb{R}_{\geq 0}$ is defined by $w_r(\emptyset) := 0$, $w_r(a) := 1$.
- There is an owner server S_0 and external servers S_j for each node n_j.
- The capacity of the owner's server W_0 equals zero and the servers' capacities are all large enough to potentially hold all the attributes, i.e. $W_j := w_r(A)$.
- For every edge $(n_i, n_{i'}) \in E$, a confidentiality constraint $\{a_{n_i}, a_{n_{i'}}\} \subseteq A \times A$ is introduced. The set of confidentiality constraints is hence defined by $C := \{\{a_{n_i}, a_{n_{i'}}\} \subseteq A \times A \mid (n_i, n_{i'}) \in E\}$. This set is well-defined because $a_{\text{tid}} \cap c = \emptyset$ for all $c \in C$ and it is assumed that if E contains $(n_i, n_{i'})$, it does not contain $(n_{i'}, n_i)$ which ensures that $c \not\subseteq c'$ for all $c, c' \in C$.

By definition, for both instances of VC and SSoD a feasible solution exists: In the former, there always exists a k-coloring which assigns each of the k nodes to a different color. In the latter, the number of servers is the same as the number of non-tuple-identifier attributes and each servers' capacity is sufficiently large to hold such an attribute together with the tuple identifier. Hence, the correct vertical fragmentation $\mathbf{f} = (f_0, \ldots, f_k)$ with $f_0 = \emptyset$ and $f_j = \{a_{\text{tid}}, a_{n_j}\}$ for $j \in \{1, \ldots, k\}$ satisfies the capacity constraints and is thus a feasible solution.

Hence, a correct privacy-preserving vertical fragmentation $\mathbf{f} = (f_0, \ldots, f_k)$ of *minimal* cardinality $\text{card}(\mathbf{f}) := K$ of SSoD can be assumed. Without loss of generality, for this fragmentation it can be assumed that $f_0 = \emptyset$, $f_1, \ldots, f_K \neq \emptyset$ for $K \leq k$ and $f_{K+1}, \ldots, f_k = \emptyset$ because all the servers' capacities are the same and hence, the server fragments can be permuted such that the fragmentation satisfies this property. In the definition of SSoD, every non-tuple-identifier attribute

$a_{n_i} \in A$ corresponds to a node n_i which allows the definition of a K-coloring $\varphi : N \longrightarrow \{1, \ldots, K\}$ from that fragmentation as $\varphi(n_i) \mapsto j$, if $a_{n_i} \in f_j$: if the attribute n_i is contained in fragment $f_j \in \mathbf{f}$, then the color j is chosen. This coloring is well-defined due to the disjointness and the completeness property of $\mathbf{f}$. More precisely, because each a_{n_i} is contained in exactly one server fragment f_j, each n_i is assigned exactly one color j. Because the confidentiality constraints are derived from the edges of the graph, it is not possible that attributes a_{n_i} and $a_{n_{i'}}$ are in the same fragment if there exists an edge $(n_i, n_{i'}) \in E$. Therefore, no adjacent nodes are assigned the same color. This coloring uses $\mathrm{card}(\mathbf{f}) = K$ colors – one for each nonempty fragment.

It remains to show that the numbers of colors used is in fact minimal. For that, it is assumed that there exists a K'-coloring ϕ of $\mathcal{G}$ with $K' < K$. Then, for every color $j' \in \{1, \ldots, K'\}$ in the image of ϕ, define the set $f'_{j'}$ as follows:

$$f'_{j'} := \{a_{n_i} \in A \mid n_i \in N \text{ and } \phi(n_i) = j'\} \cup \mathrm{tid}$$

Additionally, $f'_0 := \emptyset$ and $f'_{K'+1}, \ldots, f'_k := \emptyset$ is defined. Then, $\mathbf{f}' = (f'_0, \ldots, f'_k)$ forms a confidentiality-preserving correct vertical fragmentation of cardinality K': Every node n_i is assigned exactly one color $j' \in \{1, \ldots, K'\}$ and hence, every attribute a_{n_i} is contained in exactly one fragment, namely $f_{j'}$. Thus, $\mathbf{f}'$ satisfies the completeness and the disjointness property. Additionally, as the tuple identifier is included in every nonempty fragment, those fragments form a correct vertical fragmentation of r. The confidentiality constraints of SSoD are derived from the edges of $\mathcal{G}$ and therefore, there is a confidentiality constraint $\{a_{n_i}, a_{n_{i'}}\}$ if $(n_i, n_{i'}) \in E$. Moreover, the coloring satisfies $\phi(n_i) \neq \phi(n_{i'})$ if $(n_i, n_{i'}) \in E$ which means that attributes a_{n_i} and $a_{n_{i'}}$ are placed in different fragments and therefore, the corresponding confidentiality constraint is satisfied. This proves that the fragmentation is indeed confidentiality-preserving. This, however, contradicts the assumption that the cardinality K of $\mathbf{f}$ is minimal. This means, that the previously defined coloring φ is in fact minimal and a solution to the vertex coloring problem which concludes the proof of the theorem.

5   Extended Separation of Duties Problem

While the problem formulation for the Standard Separation of Duties Problem is suitable to preserve confidentiality, several enhancements will now be presented to make it applicable for practical purposes. These enhancements are mainly concerned with the distribution of the attributes to allow efficient query processing. In many scenarios, it is desirable that certain combinations of attributes are stored by a single server or in other words, these combinations are visible on a single server, because they are often queried together. This can be accounted for with the notion of *visibility constraints*:

Definition 9 (Visibility Constraint). *Let $R(A)$ denote a relation schema over the set of attributes A and let r be a relation over $R(A)$. A visibility constraint over $R(A)$ is a subset of attributes $v \subseteq A$. A fragmentation*

$\mathbf{f} = (f_0, \ldots, f_k)$ satisfies v if there exists $0 \leq j \leq k$ such that $v \subseteq f_j$. In this case, define $\mathrm{sat}_v(\mathbf{f}) := 1$ and $\mathrm{sat}_v(\mathbf{f}) := 0$ otherwise. Furthermore, for any set V of visibility constraints define $\mathrm{sat}_V(\mathbf{f}) := \sum_{v \in V} \mathrm{sat}_v(\mathbf{f})$ to count the number of satisfied visibility constraints.

In contrast to confidentiality constraints, the fulfillment of visibility constraints is not mandatory, i.e. confidentiality constraints are *hard constraints* while visibility constraints are *soft constraints*. While we require the resulting fragmentation to satisfy the completeness property, breaking the disjointness property can help increase the number of satisfied visibility constraints. Hence, in the upcoming problem definition only a lossless fragmentation will be required.

In case a visibility constraint cannot be satisfied (because otherwise a confidentiality constraint will be violated), the distribution of the visibility constraint attributes is arbitrary.

Therefore, it is reasonable to provide constraints to ensure that certain attributes be distributed among as few servers as possible. Moreover, as in the following problem statement a lossless fragmentation will be required, those constraints can also be used to limit the number of copies of any individual attribute. We introduced so-called *closeness constraints* in [4]:

Definition 10 (Closeness Constraint [4]). *Let r be a relation over relation schema $R(A)$. A closeness constraint over $R(A)$ is a subset of attributes $\gamma \subseteq A$. Let $\mathbf{f} = (f_0, \ldots, f_k)$ be a correct/lossless vertical fragmentation of r, the distribution $\mathrm{dist}_\gamma(\mathbf{f})$ of γ is defined as the number of fragments that contain one of the attributes in γ: $\mathrm{dist}_\gamma(\mathbf{f}) := \sum_{f_j \cap \gamma \neq \emptyset} 1$ (for $j = 0 \ldots k$). Moreover, for any set Γ of closeness constraints, the distribution $\mathrm{dist}_\Gamma(\mathbf{f})$ is defined as the sum of distributions of $\gamma \in \Gamma$: $\mathrm{dist}_\Gamma(\mathbf{f}) := \sum_{\gamma \in \Gamma} \mathrm{dist}_\gamma(\mathbf{f})$.*

The minimization of the distribution of the closeness constraints is the third goal in the following problem formulation. However, minimizing the cardinality of the fragmentation, maximizing the number of satisfied visibility constraints and minimizing the distribution of the closeness constraints are three separate, non-complementary goals. Hence, a balance has to be found between them. Therefore, the objective stated in the problem definition is expressed as a weighted sum of these three goals using weights α_1 (for the cardinality), α_2 (for visibility) and α_3 (for closeness). Note that satisfying the confidentiality constraints is still mandatory. The *Extended Separation of Duties Problem* is defined as follows:

Definition 11 (Extended Separation of Duties Problem). *Given a relation r over a relation schema $R(A)$, a well-defined set of confidentiality constraints C, a set of visibility constraints V, a set of closeness constraints Γ, a tuple identifier $tid \subset A$, a weight function w_r, servers $S_0, \ldots, S_k$, maximum capacities $W_0, \ldots, W_k \in \mathbb{R}_{\geq 0}$ and weights $\alpha_1, \alpha_2, \alpha_3 \in \mathbb{R}_{\geq 0}$. Find a lossless confidentiality-preserving fragmentation $\mathbf{f} = (f_0, \ldots, f_k)$ of minimal cardinality which satisfies $w_r(f_j) \leq W_j$ for all $0 \leq j \leq k$ such that the weighted sum $\alpha_1 \mathrm{card}(\mathbf{f}) - \alpha_2 \mathrm{sat}_V(\mathbf{f}) + \alpha_3 \mathrm{dist}_\Gamma(\mathbf{f})$ is minimal.*

Generally the choice of the weights α_1, α_2 and α_3 depends on the application. Yet, a reasonable choice is to assign priorities to the three different objectives. In most scenarios, the overall number of necessary servers will have the highest impact on the utility and therefore, minimizing it should have the highest priority. The satisfaction of visibility constraints has the second highest priority. Finally, among those solutions, the distribution of the closeness constraints should be minimized. Under the assumption that $|V| > 0$ and $|\Gamma| > 0$, one possible solution is given by $\alpha_1 = 1$, $\alpha_2 = \frac{0.9}{2|V|}$ and $\alpha_3 = \frac{0.87}{2(k+1)|V||\Gamma|}$.

5.1   Complexity Analysis

Next, NP-hardness of the Extended Separation of Duties Problem is shown. To accomplish this, the similarity to the standard version is used.

Theorem 2. *The Extended Separation of Duties Problem is NP-hard.*

Proof. The proof is by reducing an instance of the Standard Separation of Duties Problem, denoted by SSoD, on an instance of the Extended Separation of Duties Problem, denoted by ESoD. This is done by canonically adopting the provided parameters and additionally defining the set of visibility constraints $V := \emptyset$ and the set of closeness constraints $\Gamma := \emptyset$. Formally, let SSoD be defined by a relation r over a relation schema $R(A)$, a tuple identifier tid $\subset A$, a set of well-defined confidentiality constraints C, a weight function w_r, servers $S_0, \ldots, S_k$ and maximum capacities $W_0, \ldots, W_k \in \mathbb{R}_{\geq 0}$. Then, ESoD is defined as follows:

- The relation r over the relation schema $R(A)$
- The tuple identifier tid
- The weight function $w_r : \mathcal{P}(A) \longrightarrow \mathbb{R}_{\geq 0}$
- The servers S_j for $0 \leq j \leq k$
- The server capacities W_j for $0 \leq j \leq k$
- The set of confidentiality constraints C
- A set of visibility constraints $V := \emptyset$
- A set of closeness constraints $\Gamma := \emptyset$
- Weights $\alpha_1 := 1$, $\alpha_2 := 1$ and $\alpha_3 := 1$.

Let a solution of ESoD be given by a lossless confidentiality-preserving fragmentation $\mathbf{f} = (f_0, \ldots, f_k)$. As V and Γ are empty, this fragmentation must be of minimal cardinality. For SSoD however, a correct fragmentation is required and therefore, to establish the disjointness property, duplicate attributes must be eliminated from some fragments in $\mathbf{f}$ to obtain a correct fragmentation $\mathbf{f}'$. This can be achieved in polynomial time. The correct fragmentation $\mathbf{f}'$ then solves both the standard and the extended version of the Separation of Duties Problem. To conclude the proof, the case that one of the instances is not solvable must be discussed. Due to the fact that every correct vertical fragmentation is also lossless and that every lossless fragmentation can be transformed into a correct one by removing duplicate attributes, it is clear that there exists a correct vertical fragmentation of r if and only if there exists a lossless vertical fragmentation of r. Hence, SSoD is solvable if and only if ESoD is also solvable.

6   Conclusion and Future Work

In this work we have presented a practical approach for preserving confidentiality in cloud databases which does not require encryption. Our separation of duties approach is based on the observation that by vertical fragmentation and by distribution of fragments among multiple non-communicating cloud database servers, sensitive associations among columns can be broken such that each of these servers only stores an insensitive portion of the database. To model the confidentiality concerns, confidentiality constraints were introduced. Visibility constraints and closeness constraints were introduced to increase the utility of the resulting vertically fragmented database. The problem of finding such confidentiality-preserving vertical fragmentations was shown to be NP-hard.

Our approach was studied in this paper for a single database relation. However it more generally applies as well to databases consisting of many relations as studied previously in [5] to make the theory applicable in practical scenarios. Moreover, because certain combinations of attributes often reveal sensitive information about others, data dependencies can be introduced, too – this setting was also considered in [5]. Together, the confidentiality constraints and data dependencies are capable of expressing a wide range of confidentiality concerns that appear in the context of cloud databases.

One possibility to expand this work is to develop heuristics for solving the Separation of Duties Problem. The evaluation in [5] has shown that modern ILP solvers are capable of quickly finding confidentiality-preserving fragmentations of minimal cardinality. However, the introduction of visibility constraints can increase the time for finding an optimal solution significantly. Therefore, heuristics can be beneficial in situations where a long runtime is expected. Furthermore, as sensitive associations could not only occur between columns but also between rows of a database, another interesting extension of this work is to additionally explore horizontal fragmentation [22] which means that database tables are fragmented by rows. In combination with vertical fragmentation this leads to the problem of finding confidentiality-preserving hybrid fragmentations.

Last but not least, it might be worthwhile to study separation of duties also for non-relational data models (as for example surveyed in [23]).

References

1. Aggarwal, G., et al.: Two can keep a secret: a distributed architecture for secure database services. In: The Second Biennial Conference on Innovative Data Systems Research (CIDR 2005) (2005)
2. Biskup, J., Preuß, M., Wiese, L.: On the inference-proofness of database fragmentation satisfying confidentiality constraints. In: Lai, X., Zhou, J., Li, H. (eds.) ISC 2011. LNCS, vol. 7001, pp. 246–261. Springer, Heidelberg (2011). https://doi.org/10.1007/978-3-642-24861-0_17
3. Bkakria, A., Cuppens, F., Cuppens-Boulahia, N., Fernandez, J.M., Gross-Amblard, D.: Preserving multi-relational outsourced databases confidentiality using fragmentation and encryption. JoWUA 4(2), 39–62 (2013)

4. Bollwein, F., Wiese, L.: Closeness constraints for separation of duties in cloud databases as an optimization problem. In: Calì, A., Wood, P., Martin, N., Poulovassilis, A. (eds.) BICOD 2017. LNCS, vol. 10365, pp. 133–145. Springer, Cham (2017). https://doi.org/10.1007/978-3-319-60795-5_14

5. Bollwein, F., Wiese, L.: Separation of duties for multiple relations in cloud databases as an optimization problem. In: Proceedings of the 21st International Database Engineering and Applications Symposium, pp. 98–107. ACM (2017)

6. Ciriani, V., De Capitani di Vimercati, S., Foresti, S., Jajodia, S., Paraboschi, S., Samarati, P.: Fragmentation and encryption to enforce privacy in data storage. In: Biskup, J., López, J. (eds.) ESORICS 2007. LNCS, vol. 4734, pp. 171–186. Springer, Heidelberg (2007). https://doi.org/10.1007/978-3-540-74835-9_12

7. Ciriani, V., De Capitani di Vimercati, S., Foresti, S., Jajodia, S., Paraboschi, S., Samarati, P.: Fragmentation design for efficient query execution over sensitive distributed databases. In: ICDCS, pp. 32–39. IEEE Computer Society (2009)

8. Ciriani, V., De Capitani di Vimercati, S., Foresti, S., Jajodia, S., Paraboschi, S., Samarati, P.: Keep a few: outsourcing data while maintaining confidentiality. In: Backes, M., Ning, P. (eds.) ESORICS 2009. LNCS, vol. 5789, pp. 440–455. Springer, Heidelberg (2009). https://doi.org/10.1007/978-3-642-04444-1_27

9. Ciriani, V., De Capitani di Vimercati, S., Foresti, S., Jajodia, S., Paraboschi, S., Samarati, P.: Combining fragmentation and encryption to protect privacy in data storage. ACM Trans. Inf. Syst. Secur. (TISSEC) **13**(3), 22 (2010)

10. Ciriani, V., De Capitani di Vimercati, S., Foresti, S., Jajodia, S., Paraboschi, S., Samarati, P.: Selective data outsourcing for enforcing privacy. J. Comput. Secur. **19**(3), 531–566 (2011)

11. Ciriani, V., De Capitani di Vimercati, S., Foresti, S., Livraga, G., Samarati, P.: An OBDD approach to enforce confidentiality and visibility constraints in data publishing. J. Comput. Secur. **20**(5), 463–508 (2012)

12. De Capitani di Vimercati, S., Erbacher, R.F., Foresti, S., Jajodia, S., Livraga, G., Samarati, P.: Encryption and fragmentation for data confidentiality in the cloud. In: Aldini, A., Lopez, J., Martinelli, F. (eds.) FOSAD 2012-2013. LNCS, vol. 8604, pp. 212–243. Springer, Cham (2014). https://doi.org/10.1007/978-3-319-10082-1_8

13. De Capitani di Vimercati, S., Foresti, S., Jajodia, S., Livraga, G., Paraboschi, S., Samarati, P.: Fragmentation in presence of data dependencies. IEEE Trans. Depend. Secur. Comput. **11**(6), 510–523 (2014)

14. Dwork, C.: Differential privacy: a survey of results. In: Agrawal, M., Du, D., Duan, Z., Li, A. (eds.) TAMC 2008. LNCS, vol. 4978, pp. 1–19. Springer, Heidelberg (2008). https://doi.org/10.1007/978-3-540-79228-4_1

15. Codd, E.F.: A relational model of data for large shared data banks. Commun. ACM **13**(6), 377–387 (1970)

16. Garey, M.R., Johnson, D.S.: Computers and Intractability: A Guide to the Theory of NP-Completeness. W. H. Freeman & Co., New York (1979)

17. Jindal, A., Palatinus, E., Pavlov, V., Dittrich, J.: A comparison of knives for bread slicing. Proce. VLDB Endow. **6**(6), 361–372 (2013)

18. Ozsu, M.T.: Principles of Distributed Database Systems, 3rd edn. Prentice Hall Press, Upper Saddle River (2007)

19. Samarati, P.: Protecting respondents identities in microdata release. IEEE Trans. Knowl. Data Eng. **13**(6), 1010–1027 (2001)

20. Sweeney, L.: k-anonymity: a model for protecting privacy. Int. J. Uncertain. Fuzziness Knowl. Based Syst. **10**(05), 557–570 (2002)

21. Waage, T., Wiese, L.: Property preserving encryption in NoSQL wide column stores. In: Panetto, H., et al. (eds.) OTM 2017. LNCS, vol. 10574, pp. 3–21. Springer, Cham (2017). https://doi.org/10.1007/978-3-319-69459-7_1
22. Wiese, L.: Horizontal fragmentation for data outsourcing with formula-based confidentiality constraints. In: Echizen, I., Kunihiro, N., Sasaki, R. (eds.) IWSEC 2010. LNCS, vol. 6434, pp. 101–116. Springer, Heidelberg (2010). https://doi.org/10.1007/978-3-642-16825-3_8
23. Wiese, L.: Advanced Data Management for SQL, NoSQL, Cloud and Distributed Databases. DeGruyter, Berlin (2015)

Three Tales of Disillusion: Benchmarking Property Preserving Encryption Schemes

Frank Pallas[1]([✉]) and Martin Grambow[2]

[1] Information Systems Engineering Research Group, TU Berlin, Berlin, Germany
`fp@ise.tu-berlin.de`
[2] Mobile Cloud Computing Research Group, TU Berlin, Berlin, Germany
`mg@mcc.tu-berlin.de`
`http://ise.tu-berlin.de, http://mcc.tu-berlin.de`

Abstract. Property preserving encryption mechanisms have repeatedly been proposed for ensuring confidentiality against cloud providers. However, the performance overhead introduced by such mechanisms has so far only been estimated theoretically or in overly simple settings. In this paper, we present results of first experiments corresponding to realistic scenarios. The results are noteworthy: The Boldyreva scheme for order preserving encryption generates an overhead of approx. 400% for write operations and a 480-fold overhead for substantial range queries. Partial order preserving encoding introduces a 300% overhead for inserts and fast-growing query times of approx. 9 s for queries over just 30.000 items. With Fully Homomorphic Encryption, in turn, we observed a runtime of 4,5 h for just one simplified payroll calculation. These results allow for a more deliberate application of respective schemes in real-world business scenarios.

Keywords: Property preserving encryption · Privacy
Confidentiality · Cloud computing · Benchmarking
Order preserving encryption · Partial order preserving encoding
Fully homomorphic encryption

1 Introduction

Modern information systems are increasingly based on cloud services, ranging from plain virtual instances and hosted databases to higher-order services for data analytics or machine learning. From the business perspective, employing such services provides significant benefits in matters such as availability, elastic scalability, or pace of development.

On the other hand, the model of cloud computing requires strong trust in the employed provider, especially when the data that are to be stored and processed raise – for regulatory reasons or to protect business secrets – confidentiality requirements. While techniques and mechanisms for data in transit encryption are widely established and used in the context of cloud computing to achieve

© Springer Nature Switzerland AG 2018
S. Furnell et al. (Eds.): TrustBus 2018, LNCS 11033, pp. 39–54, 2018.
https://doi.org/10.1007/978-3-319-98385-1_4

confidentiality against external eavesdroppers, these leave data fully readable to the provider, posing risks of large-scale data leakage and provider-side data exploitation. Methods for client-side data at rest encryption based on established ciphers like AES, in turn, may be used for ensuring confidentiality against the provider but entail significant drawbacks in matters of implementable functionality: When data are encrypted with established algorithms before being stored in a cloud-hosted database, for example, these data cannot be meaningfully queried or processed on the provider side anymore, rendering the approach of client-side encryption useless for many application scenarios.

In order to resolve this contradiction between confidentiality and functionality, several schemes for so-called property preserving encryption have been proposed in the past, ranging from order-preserving [1] to fully homomorphic encryption [2]. All these mechanisms allow certain functionalities – sorting, querying, or even calculating – to be realized on top of encrypted data and thus eliminate the need for clear text to be known by a cloud provider at all. Given these characteristics, property preserving encryption schemes attracted significant attention in security research as well as in the policy domain [3–6].

Like every security mechanism, however, property preserving encryption comes at a cost in the form of overheads. A reasonable decision on the application of respective schemes in real information systems must therefore be based on a conscious weighing between these overheads and the benefits gained in matters of risk reduction or, respectively, realizable functionality. Even though the fact that property preserving encryption raises significant overheads is often recognized [7], the actual magnitude of these overheads has so far only been estimated on a purely theoretical basis [8–10] or through experiments with overly simplistic and thus unrealistic settings [11–13]. Without sound knowledge on the overhead to be expected in practice, in turn, business decisions on the practical application of property preserving encryption schemes lack solid grounding.

For similar reasons, gathering experiment-based evidence on the performance overhead of security mechanisms that is to be expected in realistic scenarios has established as a valuable source of insights relevant for making well-founded, rational, and reproducible trade-offs in the design and implementation of information systems with reasonable security or privacy requirements. For instance, it has been shown that HBase, one of the most important datastores used in the Big Data context, suffers a throughput drop of up to 47% as soon as its native data in transit encryption is used in a realistic setting [14], while other datastores like Cassandra or Amazon's database as a service (DBaaS) DynamoDB exhibit lower (ca. 20–30%) or even no measurable impact [15]. Client-side encryption with traditional symmetric schemes on top of Cassandra and HBase, in turn, has been shown to significantly affect achievable throughput in a single-client setting, given the additional computational load induced [16]. With explicit regard to property preserving encryption schemes, first benchmarks applying different schemes on top of NoSQL stores suggest an overhead of up to 500% for inserts and up to 1.800% for queries [13], albeit under explicit exclusion of schemes that require additional components on the provider side, for one particular type of payload, and, most importantly, under lab conditions intentionally eliminating network traffic, clearly motivating further experiments in realistic cloud settings.

In this paper, we thus empirically examine the practical applicability of different property preserving encryption schemes through experiments resembling realistic use cases of cloud computing. In particular, we determine the performance overhead generated by three schemes: the Boldyreva scheme for order-preserving encryption, the POPE (Partial Order Preserving Encoding) scheme of partially order-preserving encoding, and the FHEW (Fastest Homomorphic Encryption in the West) scheme for fully homomorphic encryption. To properly assess these schemes in line with their intended applications, we apply each scheme to a different realistic scenario specifically tailored to the respectively provided functionality. On this basis, our results provide clear indications about the limitations as well as viable use cases of the considered schemes and, thus, a valuable basis for reasoning about their practical applicability.

For this aim, we proceed as follows: In Sect. 2, we present our general experimentation approach. Sections 3, 4, and 5 are then dedicated to our experiments conducted for the three mentioned schemes, respectively. For each of these cases, we briefly introduce the scheme and its provided capabilities, describe our experiment setting, present our benchmarking results, and discuss implications for its practical application in concrete, cloud-based information systems. Section 6 provides some common insights and concludes.

2   Experimentation Approach

We conducted experiments for three established property preserving encryption schemes. Each of these experiments represents a realistic application scenario particularly fitted to the respective scheme, thus providing insights about the performance impact to be expected when the employed scheme is well-chosen based on the particular application requirements. The conducted benchmarks therefore had to differ between the experiments to match the specifics of the different encryption schemes.

Beyond this, our experiments follow established design objectives and practices for benchmarking cloud services in general [17] and with particular regard to security overheads [18]. In order to ensure reproducibility and to eliminate random side effects as far as possible, we deployed provider-side components on Amazon EC2 instances particularly fitted for the respective use case (e.g., db.m3.medium for a MySQL database), thus reflecting real application scenarios. For similar reasons, we also deployed the client-side components on Amazon EC2, using a m3.medium instance. Especially in matters of reproducibility and random side-effects, this leads to significant benefits over other approaches, even though we are aware that doing so limits realisticness to a certain extent. Client- and provider-side were always deployed in different regions (eu-central and eu-west) to reflect real use cases and to avoid unintended side effects of co-location.

Instead of implementing encryption schemes by ourselves, we used existing and well-established reference implementations. In every scenario, we wrapped these implementations within an en- and decryption service which was used from our Java-based benchmarking application via a local socket interface. This model allowed us to use one benchmarking application independently from the language in which the employed libraries are programmed and, importantly, properly resembles potential real-world applications of respective schemes. We ensured that the overhead resulting from this architecture is negligible.[1] The application-specific loads representing real use cases, in turn, were provided in separate scripts to enhance the flexibility of our benchmarking application.[2]

We always aligned our experiments to the particular characteristics of the benchmarked scheme to avoid misaligned bottlenecks. For example, when a scheme raises significant portions of the overhead on the client side, we avoided to actually benchmark the provider side using multiple clients. Insofar, the benchmarking approach pursued herein differs from typical cloud security benchmarking practices where the usual approach is to employ multiple clients to ensure a low workload on the client while stressing the provider side [14,15]. Based on these core considerations, we can now proceed with our three experiments:

3   Order Preserving Encryption (OPE)

Order preserving encryption (OPE) schemes preserve the order of encrypted values. If a plain value a is smaller than a second value b, the encrypted value $enc(a)$ is also smaller than $enc(b)$. Some examples of deterministic and symmetric OPE schemes are given by Agrawal et al. [19], Boldyreva et al. [8] and Kerschbaum [20].

OPE enables range queries over encrypted data, which is sufficient for several realistic scenarios, and can be easily applied to existing databases or key value stores. To request all datasets in a given range from x_1 to x_2, the client encrypts both values and queries from $enc(x_1)$ to $enc(x_2)$. Because of the order preserving property, it is possible to sort and group values. Moreover, OPE schemes allow joins of tables and counting values but eliminate the possibility to aggregate values (e.g., add, calculate average, etc.) [21]. These properties make OPE schemes particularly suitable for DBaaS applications which do not require computations on the provider side. Our experiment setting therefore resembles the scenario of a small crafting company which outsources their database with employee and customer information, order details and resource requirements to a cloud provider.

In line with our experimentation approach laid out above, we applied the prominently discussed OPE scheme given by Boldyreva et al. [8] to this DBaaS scenario. Expecting only limited load on the database itself, we used a

---

[1] Respective experiments indicated a performance overhead of approximately 0.5 ms per call as compared to a native implementation. For the tested encryption schemes, this results in a maximum relative overhead of 2% (in most cases, it was significantly below that), which we deemed acceptable.

[2] The whole sourcecode employed for our experiments is available at https://github.com/martingrambow/ppe.

db.m1.medium RDS instance running a current version (5.6) of MySQL. Due to the functioning of the Boldyreva scheme, no further components or adaptations had to be made on the provider side. On the client side, we used an existing and well-established Python implementation[3] of the Boldyreva OPE scheme as the basis for our local en- and decryption service. To heighten the validity of our results even further, we also implemented a corresponding dummy service without actual encryption to avoid adulterated results. The complete setup of our experiment is illustrated in Fig. 1.

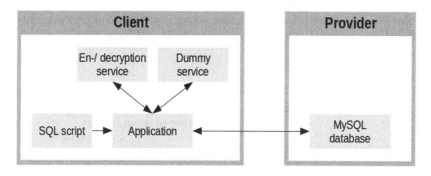

Fig. 1. Setup of OPE benchmarking experiment

As the employed library only supports integer values, we had to convert strings into sufficiently small integers within our encryption service first. For this, we initially translated any single character into a two-digit integer[4] and then concatenated them in groups of five, thus leading to integer values between 0 and 9.999.999.999 ($10^{10} - 1$). We then fed these integers into the Boldyreva encryption scheme, resulting in larger but similarly ordered integers, which we then splitted back into two-digit integers and converted back into characters. After joining these single characters, we received encrypted strings which are typically longer than the original ones but which still have the same ordering as the original plaintext strings. These OPE-encrypted strings are then used in the respective database operations.

To reflect realistic workloads for this application scenario, the external scripts fed into our application performed the following operations: First, the whole database is deleted and a new database with a representative relational schema comprising customers, orders, etc. (see above) is created. Second, the database is filled with 50.000 data items in total. Finally, seven selections, which request 41.500 data rows in total and also include sorting specifications and joins over multiple tables, are executed. Given the mode of operation of Boldyreva, we expected no significant additional insights from executing updates and therefore

---

[3] https://github.com/rev112/pyope.

[4] For reasons of simplicity, we explicitly decided against more complex character encodings here.

did not benchmark them separately. Database deletion and creation were also not benchmarked at all, while filling and selection were benchmarked separately.

Table 1 summarizes our results. In the filling phase, the overall runtime is mainly determined by transportation (including the insertion process in the database itself) for the baseline setting with only the dummy-service being used. Here, inserting the 50.000 items took around 27 min overall. With Boldyreva-based order preserving encryption turned on, the same operations took more than 132 min (an increase by approx. 400%), of which around 106 min (or 128 ms per value) fell upon the encryption service, while transportation time (including database inserts) stayed virtually constant. Within the encryption service, in turn, the impact of the above-mentioned conversions between text and integer was negligible: the raw Boldyreva encryption itself took more than 99,8% of the service's overall runtime.

Table 1. Experimental results of OPE setup

| Script / Part | Runtime of setup (in ms) | | | |
| | Baseline | | Boldyreva | |
	All	Per value	All	Per value
Create	–	–	–	–
Fill ($n = 50.000$)				
Encryption service	12.396	0, 25	6.382.946	127, 66
Transportation (incl. DB)	1.581.543	31, 63	1.569.455	31, 39
Total	**1.593.939**	**31, 88**	**7.952.401**	**159, 05**
Select ($n = 41.500$)				
Decryption service	36.197	0, 87	18.667.941	449, 83
Transportation (incl. DB)	2.507	0, 06	2.663	0, 06
Total	**38.704**	**0, 93**	**18.670.604**	**449, 89**

For the selection part of the experiment, results were even more devastating. While the time required for data transfer and executing the query itself increased only slightly (approx. 6,5%), the decryption service took more than five hours with Boldyreva encryption as opposed to the baseline of 36 s required by the dummy service, thus confirming our assumption that the limiting factor will mainly be on the client side for this experiment.[5] Using order preserving encryption thus led to a more than 480-fold overall runtime in the selection part of the experiment.

On the provider side, consumed disk space increased by more than 75%, which can, like the slight increase in time for transportation and query execution, be explained by the larger values resulting from the Boldyreva scheme. For settings

---

[5] Again, conversions between text and integers within the decryption service were negligible, accounting for less than 0,2% of the overall service runtime.

with many clients, this size increase would presumably also affect achievable throughput on the provider side, but compared to the significant overheads on the client side, this effect will only be decisive in few real-world settings.

Overall, the Boldyreva scheme of order preserving encryption is easily applicable to existing DBaaS offers and allows a limited set of operations, particularly including range queries, to be performed on encrypted data. The overhead of approximately 400% for database inserts might be deemed acceptable for certain scenarios because of the achieved increase in confidentiality against the cloud provider. However – and even leaving aside further weaknesses of the scheme with regard to ciphertext-only attacks, which shall not be discussed in detail here – the massive decrease in query performance observed in our experiment with many query results will presumably disqualify the Boldyreva scheme of order preserving encryption for many practical use cases. If at all, Boldyreva-based order preserving encryption should thus only be applied in use cases where expectable query results are rather small and can thus be decoded on the client side in reasonable time.

4   Partial Order Preserving Encoding (POPE)

Partial Order Preserving Encoding was introduced by Roche et al. [12]. The general idea of this approach is to encrypt values in a semantically secure way and to store the ordering information in a tree structure. To insert a new item, the client simply has to encrypt the value with an arbitrary scheme and send the ciphertext to a POPE server on the provider side which stores all values in a buffered tree.

Put briefly, this tree consists of nodes which have an unlimited buffer of unsorted encrypted values and a sorted list of child nodes. If a new encrypted value is received, the POPE server inserts it into the buffer of the root node, which grows until a range query occurs. Before processing and answering such a query, the POPE server initiates a communication protocol with a comparison oracle on the client side: For every buffered value, it requests the proper child node and moves the value according to the answer from the oracle. Next, it similarly iterates recursively over all child nodes until all necessary buffers are cleared. Moreover, the POPE server inserts new nodes or rebalances the tree if necessary. For answering a range query, the provider can then identify the two nodes representing the start and the end of the requested range and return all (encrypted) values between them.

On this basis, POPE enables secure range queries over encrypted data which only reveal some information about the ordering of stored values to the provider. This makes POPE more secure than classical order preserving encryption schemes like Boldyreva. On the other hand, POPE requires additional communication between the POPE server on the provider side and the comparison oracle deployed on the client side, which leads to slower range queries when transportation time increases. Moreover, the oracle has to be continuously reachable, limiting POPE's applicability for use cases with high availability requirements.

Like classical OPE schemes, POPE is particularly targeted to DBaaS scenarios which do not require computations on the provider side. However, data storage must be done within a dedicated POPE server and cannot be delegated to a standard database application. Furthermore, a separate tree structure must be maintained for every dimension that range queries should be executed upon.

To experimentally investigate the practical applicability of POPE, we assumed a database which maintains photo information, whereas the storage of the photos themselves was explicitly out of scope. We implemented the POPE client, server, and comparison oracle based on the python reference implementation given by Roche et al. [12].[6] We furthermore assumed five searchable dimensions providing typical query functionality for photos (year, month, hourOfDay, city, tag). For each of these dimensions, we instantiated a separate POPE server, POPE client, and comparison oracle.

Our benchmarking application used the POPE clients as proxies via local network interfaces. As provided by the reference implementation, inserts as well as queries (including the en- and decryption of values) were then handled by the POPE clients and forwarded to the respective POPE servers, each of which communicated with a corresponding comparison oracle. Update operations were not separately considered here because they are not yet supported by the established POPE library. To avoid unintended side-effects, we refrained from making own extensions. POPE clients and comparison oracles used standard AES-128 encryption in ECB mode as provided by the employed PyCrypto library and shared the secret key through the benchmarking application.[7]

Given the higher processing load we expected on the provider side for this setting, we used a m3.medium instance – the same instance type used on the client side – running all POPE servers. As a baseline for comparing our POPE results to, we used a db.m3.medium RDS instance with default configuration and MySQL 5.6 against which our benchmarking application executed the same workloads. Figure 2 illustrates this setup.

We used different repeatable workloads each of which alternated between a fixed number i of inserts and a fixed number q of range queries until a target number of 30.000 inserted items was reached. Range queries targeted either one or combined two dimensions. We performed experiments with different settings for i and q, using random as well as fixed queries to uncover potential side effects of the POPE-specific approach of query-triggered sorting.

Basically, our results are similar for different sequences of inserts and queries: Inserts into POPE servers always took between 200 and 300 ms and did not change significantly with growing datasets. Range queries to POPE, in turn, got significantly slower with increasing dataset size and had substantial runtime variance for random queries. Basically, however, we observed query times to grow linearly with increasing datasets, resulting in query times of up to 9 s for a dataset of just 30.000 items with random queries. Linear growth of query times was also confirmed in fixed query experiments, which showed significantly lower variance

---

[6] https://github.com/dsroche/pope.
[7] A critical evaluation of the ECB mode in this scenario was not part of our focus.

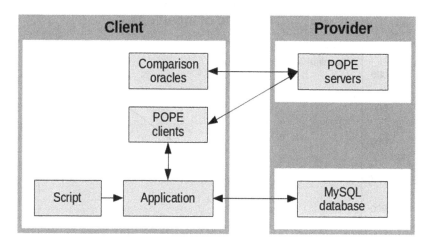

Fig. 2. Setup of POPE benchmarking experiment

and query times around 7 s for queries on 30.000 items. Given the approach taken by POPE, these runtimes can be attributed to the process of sorting recently added items into the tree structure only before answering queries. For every item, this process requires repeated interaction with the respective comparison oracle on the client side, leading to significant overheads.[8] In contrast, the baseline setting using a standard MySQL database always took around 60 ms (ca. 25% of POPE) per insert and queries were always faster than 100 ms for all workloads.

For our experiment with one random query following 10 inserts, 30.000 inserts overall, and nearly 13 million queried items in total, these differences summed up to a cumulated insert runtime of ca. 120 min for POPE as opposed to ca. 30 min required with MySQL and without any optimizations (see Fig. 3). Depending on the use case, this increase might be deemed acceptable for achieving confidentiality against the provider. For queries, however, numbers are rather disastrous: With POPE, the cumulated query runtime was above 130 min while plain MySQL served the same queries within less than 140 s (see Fig. 4). Other experiments with different settings for i and q resulted in similar relations.

Even leaving aside further downsides like the need for maintaining a separate tree for every attribute that should be queried, POPE thus already becomes impractical for use cases with several thousands of repeatedly inserted items and with many different queries to be executed over these items. However, POPE might be suitable for scenarios with a small number of inserts and a larger number of queries over the same range. In such cases, only few items have to be sorted into the POPE trees – leading to fewer interactions with the comparison oracles – before queries can be answered. In practice, POPE should thus only

---

[8] Client-side en- and decryption of values itself, however, took less than 100 µs per value and can thus be considered rather irrelevant for the overall runtimes observed.

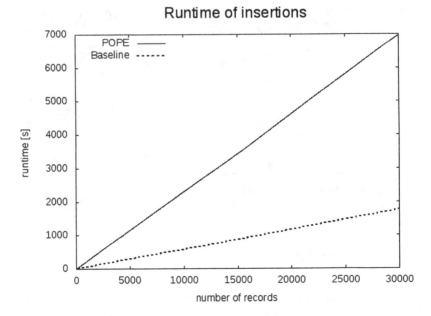

Fig. 3. Total runtime of insertions for POPE

be applied to few, highly specific use cases. As a broadly applicable scheme for achieving confidentiality against cloud providers, however, it largely disqualifies.

5   Fully Homomorphic Encryption (FHE)

As opposed to order-preserving encryption, homomorphic encryption schemes allow mathematical operations to be executed on encrypted data, ensuring that the decrypted result of these operations is similar to the result of respective operations being executed on unencrypted data, e.g., $dec(enc(a) + enc(b)) = a + b$. The supported operations vary among different schemes, whereas the most powerful homomorphic encryption schemes – called "fully homomorphic" – typically support multiplication *and* addition. By choosing binary values as plain messages, addition and multiplication can then be used to simulate logical AND and XOR gates, thus allowing to calculate *any* mathematical function [22].

Obviously, FHE's capability to compute with encrypted information makes it particularly interesting for our problem of ensuring confidentiality against cloud providers while still providing functionality beyond mere raw data storage. Being able to perform arbitrary operations on encrypted data would thus be a door-opener for applying the concept of cloud computing to domains and scenarios that have so far been abstaining from it because of particularly strict confidentiality requirements. Consequently, FHE schemes have been suggested for application domains like e-health [10] or smart metering [23,24].

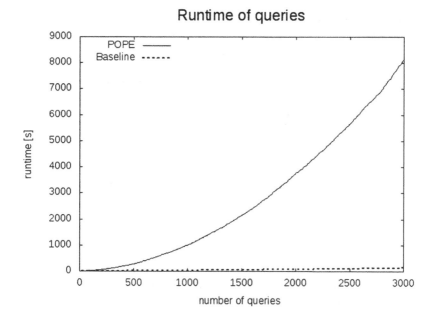

Fig. 4. Total runtime of range queries for POPE

We therefore explicitly wanted to benchmark the performance of real implementations of the "arbitrary operations" functionality of FHE based on simulated logical gates. Being aware that the performance overhead to expect would be substantial, we strove for a scenario with minimal viable complexity for our experiment and chose a simplified payroll calculation scheme that should be executed within the cloud, resembling a cloud-hosted and FHE-enabled salary calculation service. For this purpose, we built a basic service application (called EFHE) based on the well-established FHEW library.[9] FHEW implements the FHE scheme by Ducas et al. [25] which is broadly known for its superior performance as compared to other FHE schemes like the BGV scheme [26] implemented in HElib [11].

Our service application consists of a client and a server component, which encapsulate fundamental FHEW operations and make the scheme easily usable: The client encrypts and decrypts given integer values. The server part, in turn, simulates multiple combined gates and on this basis performs basic arithmetic functions over the encrypted values, thus implementing FHE's core concept for executing arbitrary mathematical functions. Both components communicate with the core FHEW functionality via local network services and offer a simple socket interface which enables component-specific interactions. Given the comparably simple benchmarks that we used in this case, we abstained from implementing a dedicated benchmarking application but rather used direct parameterized

---

[9] https://github.com/lducas/FHEW.

executions of the EFHE client here. Again, both components were deployed on separate m3.medium instances. Figure 5 illustrates this setup.

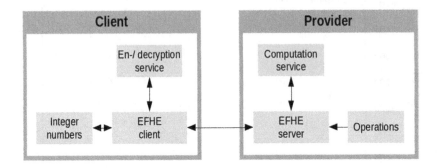

Fig. 5. Setup of EFHE benchmarking experiment

In an initial, rather explorative experiment, we performed additions, subtractions, multiplications and divisions for integers of 3 different dimensions (8, 16, and 24 bit). Next, we applied a simplified payroll calculation which comprises 3 additions, 1 subtraction, 4 multiplications and 4 divisions. Even this basic set of operations cannot be completely realized through plain FHE and therefore requires the above-mentioned approach of function implementation through simulated logical gates.

Table 2 shows the results of our first experiment. We performed each operation 10 times and converted each total runtime to the average time per operation. Because of the linear complexity of addition and subtraction circuits, respective runtime grows with the number of bits per integer value. In our experiment, addition and subtraction of 24-bit integers each took about 65 s on the employed m3.medium instance. The runtime of multiplications and divisions, in turn, grows exponentially with increasing bit length. We measured a runtime of about 18 min for the multiplication of two 24-bit integers, whereas respective divisions took almost one hour. Moreover, we performed 5 simplified payroll accounting calculations which comprise 12 operations each. On average, any such payroll calculation ran almost 4,5 h, which corresponds to a price of 0.33 USD at the time of writing just for the instance performing the computation on the provider side. The additional effort generated by local network services and the conducting applications consumed less than 0,6% of the total runtime and is thus negligible.

Besides computation, massive overheads also arose in terms of storage space and transfer volume. In the default configuration, FHEW consumes 2.004 bytes (16.032 bits) of disk space per bit of raw data or, respectively, 47 kByte per 24 bit integer value. This obviously also disqualifies it for applications with reasonable volumes of data to be processed.

As it already becomes clear from these numbers, implementing arbitrary functions through simulated logical gates on top of FHE should currently only

Table 2. Runtime of basic arithmetic operations of n-bit integers

| | Runtime per op | | |
Bits	8	16	24
Addition	18.621ms	38.832ms	66.096ms
	($\sim 18s$)	($\sim 39s$)	($\sim 66s$)
Subtraction	18.656ms	38.775ms	65.222ms
	($\sim 19s$)	($\sim 39s$)	($\sim 65s$)
Multiplication	87.942ms	405.838ms	1.055.858ms
	($\sim 1,5min$)	($\sim 6,8min$)	($\sim 17,6min$)
Division	316.534ms	1.311.147ms	3.299.631ms
	($\sim 5min$)	($\sim 22min$)	($\sim 55min$)

be considered a theoretical concept. Given the massive overhead generated in terms of time and, notably, costs to be borne, we do not even see single realistic use cases. As a basis for realizing cloud services with arbitrary functionality while still providing confidentiality against the provider, the approach of simulated logical gates on top of FHE is, by all means, far from being a realistic option. This might, of course, be different for use cases that can be implemented through plain FHE without the need for simulated logical gates or where schemes for "somewhat" homomorphic encryption are sufficient [10] in matters of functionality *and* confidentiality. Even in these cases, any consideration of practical applications should nonetheless be accompanied by sustainable benchmarks of arising overheads to avoid futile development paths as early as possible.

6 Conclusion

Property preserving encryption schemes have repeatedly been suggested for resolving the conflict between realizing functionality and achieving confidentiality against the provider in cloud-based information systems. In this paper, we experimentally evaluated three well-established property preserving encryption schemes with regard to the expectable overhead when applied in realistic scenarios.

The covered schemes achieve the goal of functionality preservation through different approaches: The Boldyreva scheme uses a highly specific encryption algorithm that has order preservation as a core characteristic and thus allows for comparisons, range queries, etc. even when used on top of a standard database or a DBaaS service. The POPE scheme, in contrast, is used together with standard encryption algorithms like AES and achieves functionality through a highly specific, tree-based approach for data handling and a more complex interplay between different components on the client- and the provider-side.

Based on our experiments, we see only limited reasonable applications in concrete business information systems for both: The Boldyreva scheme produces acceptable overheads for inserts but should – if at all – only be applied in scenarios with comparably few query results, given the overhead arising from costly client-side decryption. The more complex POPE scheme, in turn, exhibits acceptable overheads for scenarios with few inserts but performs poorly as soon as new values must repeatedly be sorted into its data trees. Furthermore, POPE requires significant implementation efforts on the provider side, limiting reasonable scenarios for its practical application even further. In select use cases, however, both might represent a rational choice for bringing together confidentiality against the provider and functionality.

Finally, the approach of realizing arbitrary functions through simulated logical gates based on the FHEW scheme for fully homomorphic encryption, which significantly differs from the aforementioned ones, turned out to be technically possible but to raise tremendous overheads. Its application will therefore hardly be justifiable in any realistic use case.

Besides providing valuable insights for rational weighing decisions on the application of covered schemes in real-world information systems, our experiments also highlight the importance of empirical experiments resembling realistic application scenarios in general. Applying a similar approach to other property preserving encryption schemes beyond those covered herein would thus presumably help to better understand reasonable fields of application for these schemes, too. In any case, property preserving encryption schemes should not be applied blindly without experimentally evaluating their suitability for a given business scenario to prevent later disillusions.

Acknowledgments. Parts of the work presented herein have been supported by the European Commission through the Horizon 2020 Research and Innovation program under contract 731945 (DITAS project).

References

1. Moghadam, S.S., Gavint, G., Darmonti, J.: A secure order-preserving indexing scheme for outsourced data. In: IEEE International Carnahan Conference on Security Technology (ICCST 2016), pp. 1–7. IEEE (2016)
2. Gentry, C., Halevi, S.: Implementing gentry's fully-homomorphic encryption scheme. In: Paterson, K.G. (ed.) EUROCRYPT 2011. LNCS, vol. 6632, pp. 129–148. Springer, Heidelberg (2011). https://doi.org/10.1007/978-3-642-20465-4_9
3. Spindler, G., Schmechel, P.: Personal data and encryption in the European general data protection regulation. JIPITEC **7**(2), 163–177 (2016)
4. Bonfanti, M.E.: Let's go for new or emerging security technologies!... what about their impact on individuals and the society? In: Democrazia e Sicurezza-Democracy and Security Review, no. 2 (2017)

5. Schulz, W., van Hoboken, J.: Human Rights and Encryption. UNESCO, Paris (2016)
6. Acquisto, G.D., Domingo-Ferrer, J., Kikiras, P., Torra, V., de Montjoye, Y.A., Bourka, A.: Privacy by design in big data - an overview of privacy enhancing technologies in the era of big data analytics. ENISA (2015)
7. Danezis, G., et al.: Privacy and data protection by design - from policy to engineering. ENISA (2014)
8. Boldyreva, A., Chenette, N., Lee, Y., O'Neill, A.: Order-preserving symmetric encryption. In: Joux, A. (ed.) EUROCRYPT 2009. LNCS, vol. 5479, pp. 224–241. Springer, Heidelberg (2009). https://doi.org/10.1007/978-3-642-01001-9_13
9. Damgård, I., Jurik, M.: A generalisation, a simplification and some applications of paillier's probabilistic public-key system. In: Kim, K. (ed.) PKC 2001. LNCS, vol. 1992, pp. 119–136. Springer, Heidelberg (2001). https://doi.org/10.1007/3-540-44586-2_9
10. Naehrig, M., Lauter, K., Vaikuntanathan, V.: Can homomorphic encryption be practical? In: Proceedings of the 3rd ACM Workshop on Cloud Computing Security, pp. 113–124. ACM, New York (2011)
11. Halevi, S., Shoup, V.: Bootstrapping for HElib. In: Oswald, E., Fischlin, M. (eds.) EUROCRYPT 2015. LNCS, vol. 9056, pp. 641–670. Springer, Heidelberg (2015). https://doi.org/10.1007/978-3-662-46800-5_25
12. Roche, D.S., Apon, D., Choi, S.G., Yerukhimovich, A.: POPE: partial order preserving encoding. In: Proceedings of the 2016 SIGSAC Conference on Computer and Communications Security, pp. 1131–1142. ACM (2016)
13. Waage, T., Wiese, L.: Property preserving encryption in NoSQL wide column stores. In: Panetto, H., et al. (eds.) OTM 2017. LNCS, vol. 10574, pp. 3–21. Springer, Cham (2017). https://doi.org/10.1007/978-3-319-69459-7_1
14. Pallas, F., Günther, J., Bermbach, D.: Pick your choice in HBase: security or performance. In: IEEE International Conference on Big Data, pp. 548–554 (2016)
15. Müller, S., Bermbach, D., Tai, S., Pallas, F.: Benchmarking the performance impact of transport layer security in cloud database systems. In: IEEE International Conference on Cloud Engineering (IC2E), pp. 27–36 (2014)
16. Waage, T., Wiese, L.: Benchmarking encrypted data storage in HBase and Cassandra with YCSB. In: Cuppens, F., Garcia-Alfaro, J., Zincir Heywood, N., Fong, P.W.L. (eds.) FPS 2014. LNCS, vol. 8930, pp. 311–325. Springer, Cham (2015). https://doi.org/10.1007/978-3-319-17040-4_20
17. Bermbach, D., Wittern, E., Tai, S.: Cloud Service Benchmarking: Measuring Quality of Cloud Services from a Client Perspective. Springer, Heidelberg (2017). https://doi.org/10.1007/978-3-319-55483-9
18. Pallas, F., Bermbach, D., Müller, S., Tai, S.: Evidence-based security configurations for cloud datastores. In: Proceedings of the Symposium on Applied Computing, SAC 2017, pp. 424–430. ACM (2017)
19. Agrawal, R., Kiernan, J., Srikant, R., Xu, Y.: Order preserving encryption for numeric data. In: Proceedings of the 2004 ACM SIGMOD International Conference on Management of Data, pp. 563–574. ACM (2004)
20. Kerschbaum, F.: Frequency-hiding order-preserving encryption. In: Proceedings of the 22nd ACM SIGSAC Conference on Computer and Communications Security, pp. 656–667. ACM (2015)
21. Malkin, T., Teranishi, I., Yung, M.: Order-preserving encryption secure beyond one-wayness. IACR Cryptology ePrint Archive (2013)
22. Armknecht, F., et al.: A guide to fully homomorphic encryption. IACR Cryptology ePrint Archive, p. 1192 (2015)

23. Tonyali, S., Saputro, N., Akkaya, K.: Assessing the feasibility of fully homomorphic encryption for smart grid AMI networks. In: International Conference on Ubiquitous and Future Networks, pp. 591–596 (2015)

24. Deng, P., Yang, L.: A secure and privacy-preserving communication scheme for advanced metering infrastructure. In: IEEE PES Innovative Smart Grid Technologies (ISGT), pp. 1–5 (2012)

25. Ducas, L., Micciancio, D.: FHEW: bootstrapping homomorphic encryption in less than a second. In: Oswald, E., Fischlin, M. (eds.) EUROCRYPT 2015. LNCS, vol. 9056, pp. 617–640. Springer, Heidelberg (2015). https://doi.org/10.1007/978-3-662-46800-5_24

26. Brakerski, Z., Gentry, C., Vaikuntanathan, V.: (Leveled) fully homomorphic encryption without bootstrapping. In: Proceedings of the 3rd Innovations in Theoretical Computer Science Conference, pp. 309–325. ACM (2012)

Privacy

Evaluating the Privacy Properties
of Secure VoIP Metadata

João S. Resende$^{(\boxtimes)}$, Patrícia R. Sousa , and Luís Antunes

Department of Computer Science, Faculty of Science,
University of Porto, Porto, Portugal
{jresende,psousa,lfa}@dcc.fc.up.pt

Abstract. Some governments do not consider metadata as personal data, and so not in the scope of privacy regulations. However, often, metadata gives more relevant information than the actual content itself. Metadata can be very useful to identify, locate, understand and manage personal data, i.e., information that is eminently private in nature and under most privacy regulation should be anonymized or deleted if users have not give their consent. In voice calls, we are facing a critical situation in terms of privacy, as metadata can identify who calls to whom and the duration of the call, for example. In this work, we investigate privacy properties of voice calls metadata, in particular when using secure VoIP, giving evidence of the ability to extract sensitive information from its ("secure") metadata. We find that ZRTP metadata is freely available to any client on the network, and that users can be re-identified by any user with access to the network. Also, we propose a solution for this problem, suitable for all the ZRTP-based implementations.

Keywords: Metadata · VoIP · Privacy

1 Introduction

Nowadays, voice calls are so common that we carry on our pockets a device that we use mainly for this purpose. In the recent years, it has been disclosed that some countries can massively tap this calls, staging the pave for secure voice calls. However, often despite the privacy of the "content" of the data "being preserved", the metadata has serious implications on privacy. Metadata leakage is not about the information content of published data but the properties of it that makes disclosures of sensitive personal information [7]. The properties can be size or location (in the case of an image, for example, modern smartphones (and many digital cameras) embed GPS coordinates in the photos) [8]. The user's privacy can be compromised through metadata as the information can identify the user (directly or indirectly). NSA General Counsel Stewart Baker has said, *"metadata absolutely tells you everything about somebodys life. If you have enough metadata, you dont really need content."* [10]. In fact, even the indirect information, the interconnection between metadata can provide a complex profile of the person in question.

© Springer Nature Switzerland AG 2018
S. Furnell et al. (Eds.): TrustBus 2018, LNCS 11033, pp. 57–68, 2018.
https://doi.org/10.1007/978-3-319-98385-1_5

A recent study by *Gruber* [1] presents an application that characterizes the behavioral patterns of suspect users versus non-suspect users based on metadata usage such as call duration, call distribution, interaction time preferences and text-to-call ratios, while avoiding any access to the content of calls or messages. This was based on the traditional communications and the metadata provided by the smartphone.

However, with the evolution of the communications industry, many alternatives have been offered to the business market. Among these options are the telephone exchanges, corporate cell phones, conventional telephones and Internet Protocol (IP). The options offered by telephones, came to simplify and streamline organizational communications. The costs of communication between people from different countries by telephone connection are very high, in addition to the cost with the subscription and the costs with the additional minutes. Not only for these reasons, but in this sense, the technologies currently available can help save money and Voice over Internet Protocol (VoIP) technology is becoming more popular. VoIP transforms analog audio signals into digital data that can be transferred over the internet. With the spread of the internet, this technology has become increasingly common and we can easily see it in tools like Whatsapp, Skype, Facebook Messenger, among others.

The goal of this work, is to analyze a sub-field of metadata based on a protocol used in some well known secure VoIP applications (such as Linphone [3], Silent Phone [4,5]) called ZRTP [6] ("Z" is a reference to its inventor, Zimmermann; "RTP" stands for Real-time Transport Protocol).

This paper is organized as follows: Sect. 2 describes the related work with some attacks already discovered of ZRTP and some literature about the metadata information extraction and how privacy is concerned with this type of information leak. Section 3 describes the problem that we are addressing. Section 4 state the implementation, setup and demonstration of the information extracting by metadata and ZRTP identifier (ZID). In Sect. 5, we present a possible solution for the problem of the information leakage. Finally, the last section presents the conclusions of the work and some future work in this area.

2   State of the Art

This section provides an overview of the literature, focusing on ZRTP attacks and metadata analysis in general, with special focus on private information leakage.

ZRTP is a end-to-end secure communication protocol that contains a session set-up phase used to agree on key exchange and parameters for establishing Secure Real-time Transport Protocol (SRTP) sessions. The Diffie-Hellman (DH) method is a specific cryptographic algorithm for key exchange based on discrete logarithms. These keys contribute to the generation of the session key and parameters for the SRTP sessions. Although ZRTP initially needs to use a signalling protocol, such as a Session Initiation Protocol (SIP)[1], the key negotiation

---

[1] SIP is a third party server that allows the peer discovery and negotiation, in the case of ZRTP does not interact with the key negotiation.

is performed only by ZRTP. The DH algorithm, alone, does not provide protection against Man-in-the-Middle (MitM) attacks. In order to authenticate both peers in the key exchange on ZRTP, a Short Authentication Strings (SAS) is used that is distributed to both phones and compared verbally by both ends. If the SAS is the same, both users must press a button in order to accept the key. The SAS is destroyed in the end of the call, but if the users don't verbally compare the SAS, after the first call the media stills with authentication against a MiM attack based on a form of key continuity, if both ends have in a previously call accepted the SAS, so after the first call the users don't need to continuously check the SAS.

The ZRTP provides the user two important features to become more efficient and robust: Preshared mode and key continuity. In the Preshared mode, both party can skip the DH calculation if they have established a ZRTP media session before, and both users have verified if the SAS displayed in the previous call matched in both ends. Preshared mode uses the previous shared secret, to establish the next call and holds forward secrecy. Forward secrecy assures that, if one attacker gains access to the keys present in one device, he is not able to decrypt previous communications, as the shared secret is replaced in each new call from the same pair of users. So, if the attacker gains access to the cached secret, he can gains access to all future communication while the Preshared mode remain to be used if he can intercepts all the call from that moment on. The key continuity features, caches some hashed key information to be used in the future call and, exchange with each session. If Mallory is capable of steal shared secrets caches from one user, the user just have one opportunity to perform a MiM/eavesdropping attack in the next session. If Mallory misses the interception the shared secret is updated and the opportunity to intercept all the calls from their on is lost.

As the ZRTP is used in many secure call applications, it is critical to know if there is a possibility of perceiving which calls are being made by the user, who the calls are to be made to, call duration, etc. Often this subject is addressed only at the content level of the call, but sometimes realizing these call patterns between users is also critical to the privacy of each of them. This analysis will allow to see if it is possible to re-identify people and their communications.

2.1 Attacks on ZRTP

As presented in [16], it is possible to perform a MiTM attack on ZRTP. Instead of cracking the DH key exchange, Mallory - the malicious attacker, tries to force Alice and Bob (the honest participants) connect directly to her, without knowledge. This way, Alice and Bob have two different connections with Mallory and she just needs to relay the packets from one connection to the other. There are different session keys and different SAS in these two connections, meaning that if Alice or Bob decide to exchange the SAS, Mallory will be detected (because the SAS will be different in both devices). To solve this, the same document [16] suggest that Mallory can avoid this detection by Direct relay + Imitation SAS, Direct relay + Slide-stepping SAS and Masquerade. To be able to perform these attacks, Mallory always needs to perform a new DH key exchange and for that, the authors use different ZID to make the end users exchange new keys. The authors also suggest that a different ZID in a new call is normal, it can be originated by a new installation on the device or by one exchange of device, that always will end with a new ZID.

The most recent attack on ZRTP presented by *Schürmann et al.* [15] is focused on both implementation and theoretical analyses by applying practical usage to applications such as *Linphone* and *CSipSimple*. They present some security breaches starting by a *CVE-2016-6271* that overcome the security limitations imposed by the ZRTP protocol because it does not implement the packet verification of some parameters. However, the paper also addresses the protocol structure from the ZRTP where the authors explore a vulnerability from the ZID. In this vulnerability, it is possible explore a MiTM after the first call, so, an attacker just needs to perform a call for the victim beforehand. To solve this issue, the authors use the SIP URI along with the ZID of the client to lock that attack. *Alvanos et al.* [24] also present a document with analysis on security features of ZRTP VoIP clients, more specifically, *Linphone* client.

2.2 Metadata Information Extraction

There are several studies evaluating the privacy impact of metadata information extraction. Smart services and experiences are based on high-dimensional metadata from users. For example, in Netflix or Amazon, metadata is used by commercial algorithms to help users become more connected, productive, and entertained [2].

There exist several algorithms to re-identifying people based on metadata, namely based on human behavior, such as the credit-card metadata [12], *Like credit card and mobile phone metadata, Web browsing or transportation data sets are generated as side effects of human interaction with technology, are subjected to the same idiosyncrasies of human behavior, and are also sparse and high-dimensional (for example, in the number of Web sites one can visit or the number of possible entry-exit combinations of metro stations).* In another example, *Narayanan et al.* [13] apply de-anonymization algorithms to a Netflix Prize database that anonymizes the movie ratings of 500,000 Netflix subscribers. They have demonstrated that they can re-identify the subscribers only knowing little about each subscriber.

These are some examples of re-identification based on human behavior. This motivates our work, as we are interested, in some way, with human behaviours. To the best of our knowledge, the metadata of VoIP was never studied, and by nature it may be quite sensitive if leaking information about the calls and participants.

Still, there are some work done on telephone metadata [19–23]. *Mayer et al.* [9] study the privacy properties of telephone metadata to assess the impact of policies that distinguish between content and metadata. They claim that there are significant privacy flaws associated with telephone metadata because it *is densely interconnected, easily re-identifiable, and trivially gives rise to location, relationship, and sensitive inferences. Furini* [11] *also states that the high availability of geolocation technologies is changing the social media mobile scenario and is exposing users to privacy risks. Alexandre Pujol et al.* analyze the metadata of instant messaging services in order to retrieve sensitive knowledge. The work assumes that the attacker has a full access to the server, in order to retrieve metadata. Also, this work proposes a solution for this metadata leak based on Oblivious RAM model.

3   Problem Statement

The privacy risk, as we have already mentioned, is not only concerned with the ciphered content of the voice call, but rather with the care taken with the metadata. Often, metadata reveals more information than the content itself (about the name, location, etc.), these are the data that lead us to profile the participant and to re-identify him.

VoIP calls have not yet been analyzed at the metadata level, and so, we decided to analyze the ZRTP, where calls are encrypted in both ends, however, does the metadata give us some sensitive information or is possible to infer information that should be anonymized?

ZRTP is a cryptographic key-agreement protocol meant to negotiate the keys for encryption between two end points in VoIP telephony. This key agreement (Fig. 1a) can be divided into four steps: Discovery, Hash Commitment, DH exchange and Key Derivation and Confirmation.

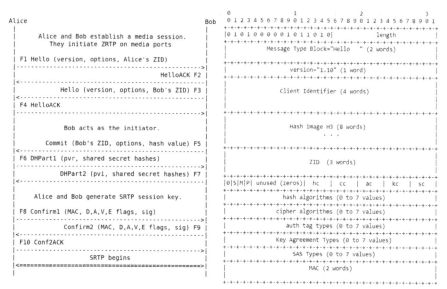

(a) ZRTP Key Agreement Packet Flow [8]   (b) "Hello" Message Packet Format [8]

Fig. 1. ZRTP

These phases are described in the RFC of ZRTP [6], and we focus on the discovery phase, that exchange some information that is sensible. In this phase, the initiator and the responder exchange their ZRTP identifiers, as well as information about each others supported ZRTP versions, hash functions, ciphers, authorization tag lengths, key agreement types, and SAS algorithms through the packet Hello (Fig. 1b). One important field is the unique 96-bit random ZID that is generated once at installation time. This field is important because it is used to index the cryptographic materials used by the key continuity and forward secret properties of the protocol in each device.

By having an identifier such as the ZID, it is possible to perceive call patterns with network sniffing, as the ZID is unique and is shared with both the callers (receiver and sender ZIDs). In addition, the ZID can be combined with metadata (such as the duration of the call) to know how long the call between the parties lasted. So far, even though we infer from the ZID which calls exist and between whom, as well as the duration of the call, we could not connect the ZID to the physical person. Note that, the ZRTP packets are used without extra encryption, meaning that a content of a packet *Hello* can be seen by any person while the transfer is being processed from the origin to the destination through the server. The reason is that ZRTP is a protocol design for end-to-end communication, so, this should not exchange crypto material by a third party server unless needed. This attack can be conducted by an attacker on the same network of the victim, by having specially authorizations to access to the network, by an ISP or governance agencies.

4   Extracting the Information

This section focuses on the study of how this information can increase the risk of re-identification or profiling users, creating a traceability problem regarding the privacy of the users.

4.1   Implementation

To test VoIP communications based on ZRTP, we use the *Linphone* [3] client (available on the Google Play).

To simulate the real environment, we start by using a public SIP server (*sip.linphone.org*). However, during the tests, we detect that all the communications are made with the server and not peer-to-peer. The Fig. 2 represents a normal call between Alice and Bob where the packets are sent/receive by the server that brings an extra problem regarding security, because users communicate always with the server, so the eavesdropping process can be taken not only on the local network (similar to our setup) but also during the handling of the packet up to and from the server.

In order to create a communication pattern dataset, we first started by implementing a sniffer. We use the *tcpdump* to collect the information from all the network packets that contain all the communications between the users and

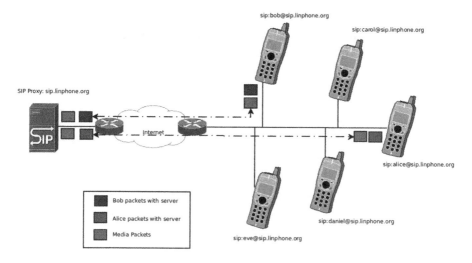

Fig. 2. ZRTP peer-to-peer communication

the SIP server to establish a peer-to-peer connection. Then, we use the *scapy* tool [14] to process the information (packets) stored by *tcpdump* and detect the ZID's of a given connection between two users. The creation of the dataset was based on the following steps:

1. Using *scapy*, we receive and manipulate the packets from *tcpdump* starting by search for the field *"Message Type Block"* to see if we got the packet "Hello" (Fig. 1b);
2. Then, with the tool, we select the field ZID of both ends of the communication and store it in the dataset;
3. During the transmission of the packets, we also use *scapy* to store the initial and final time of the transmission, in order to get the duration of the call;
4. Finally, we store in the dataset a field of each communication with this format: <Alice's ZID, Bob's ZID, Initial Call Time, Call Duration Time>.

4.2 Setup

We deployed a laboratory environment simulating a company with five employees, where one of them just arrived to the company. The employees are represented by five mobile devices (with Android operating systems from version 19 to 27) connected to a wireless device. Also, an external sniffing network device (represented by the *tcpdump* that just dumped the information to a *Wireshark* type file) is on the network.

4.3 Demonstration

For demonstration purposes we assume the following scenario: In a company there are four employees and a new one arriving to the company. The new employee wants to know more than he should about communications within the company (who communicates with whom, and for how long each call was made). Figure 3 illustrates this scenario. In this case, each phone has the ZIDs of the caller.

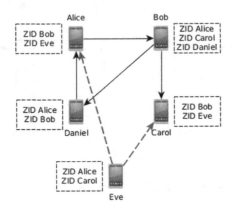

Fig. 3. ZRTP communication

When Eve arrives at the company, despite seeing the communications and the ZID of each one with a network sniffer, it can not identify each user. However, assuming that Eve calls Alice and Carol because once she gets each of the ZIDs from these two people, she automatically can identify the history of these two users. The history contains the number of calls and the duration of the calls between these two users or between these users and the remaining. From there, the privacy of Alice and Carol are compromised, as Eve gets to know too much about the communications that each of them perform.

With this example of Eve, we can assume that if the users in the network (all employees) want to do network sniffing, they will get the same information about other employees. Therefore, the privacy of these users is compromised. In addition, for the purposes of forensics, we know that it is enough to know that two persons have communicated with each other and their respective duration of the call. Therefore, it is critical to have ZID privacy so that there is no such information leakage, as well as the metadata that is generated over the duration of the call.

Finally, we can also identify users by the behaviour in the real life. This way, Eve can get the match of the ZID with the physical person by searching patterns for example, isolating by the employee in vacations or time of the day.

5   Proposed Solution

To be able to solve the information leakage, we can follow two possible solutions. Both need to use the SIP URI, that is a string used to identify the user towards a SIP server (an example can be *sip:alice@sip.linphone.org*). In any possible solutions, this SIP URI is needed to fix the problem as stated by *Schürmann et al.* [15].

5.1   Scenario 1

We create the first scenario to solve the privacy issue in all the calls after the first one with each peer. To encrypt the ZID, we propose the use of the derivation of the cryptography material stored on the local phone. However, in the first call between two peers, we do not have the cryptographic material. For this reason, the ZID is not encrypted in the first call.

With this solution, the attacker can only trace the first call between each communication between two users. This protects the privacy (after the first call) of users by mitigating the problem of leakage of the duration of the calls and also the number of calls between each pair of users, improving the protection against traceability.

5.2   Scenario 2

The second scenario is focused essentially on the use of SIP URI. As we already describe in the Related Work Section, there are a vulnerability related to MiTM where the proposed solution is the use of SIP [15]. In order to secure all the protocol, and as we have to use SIP to be secure, we can use it to discover the peers instead of use ZID. So, SIP URI is used to look up retained shared secrets from previous ZRTP sessions with the endpoint, to replace the functionality of ZID. In brief, it is used as an index into a cache of shared secrets that were previously negotiated and retained between the two parties.

Note that, we use SIP URI only for identification of peers, that is, we are only dependent of a third party in the discover phase.

5.3   Implementation

Based on the two proposed scenarios, we decide to follow Scenario 2 and implement it. This decision is mainly focused on the mitigation of the metadata leakage problem even at the first call.

In order to test the proposed solution, we implement a prototype/patch based on *ZRTPCPP* [17] library with *PJSIP* [18]. However, we must ensure that the users of *ZRTPCPP* can communicate with the users of *Linphone* for example, or any other application that supports ZRTP. As a requirement we consider also that the implementation must be compliant with the RFC of the ZRTP [6], in order to be suitable to all the implementations of the protocol. For this reason, it is important to follow the protocol and the packets format presented in the RFC, making the implementation interoperable. Also, the implementation must be secure and privacy by design, where we block the traceability issue and not leak any other information maintaining the communications secure and private.

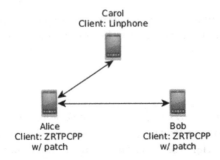

Fig. 4. Different ZRTP client communications

Our patch propose the replacement of ZID by the SIP URI. In a normal call between two users using our scenario (Fig. 4), it will be granted that both clients will store the SIP URI from the SIP layer in order to store the credentials values and maintain the preshared mode. One of the most important features of preshared mode is the key continuity, that is important because the validation of the SAS is not necessary after the first call. However, if we have a call between two different clients (Alice and Carol - Fig. 4), the ZID field is required by Carol (she is not using our scenario). For this reason, we keep this field with a random value to be compliant with the RFC of ZRTP. In the communication between Alice and Carol, the users do not have the key continuity/preshared mode properties, so, it will be used the DH key agreement in all calls. This means that it is required the validation of the SAS in all the communications, even after the first call (it looses the key continuity because the ZID is random, and therefore, the ZID is different in all the calls).

The traceability problem is mitigated with our solution because what the attacker sees on the network is that Alice is always calling a "different" user in each call to Bob. So, the attacker does not know that Alice is calling Bob and so, it is impossible to trace their behaviour. Regarding Carol, the problem of traceability is still there but mitigated because she is speaking with a patched client that will always produce a different ZID value, so, it is impossible to see who is she calling to.

6 Conclusion

In this paper, we described a metadata vulnerability in secure VoIP calls. We stress that this finding is of utmost importance as these users are looking not only for secure communications but also for privacy guarantees. To make our findings clear we developed a laboratory demonstration of how to explore this vulnerability, along with a state of the art regarding similar problems both in terms of metadata in voice communication and others. Given the high privacy risk, we proposed two solutions. Finally we implement also a VoIP client that implements this security properties based on ZRTPCPP.

The insights and results gained throughout this work highlights the necessity of using open-source resources where researchers can study and deploy this type of approach, in an effort to build a secure open-source ecosystem. The future work will focus in the analyzes of other VoIP protocols and in the exploration of this metadata in a real environment, to understand communications patterns.

Acknowledgements. This work is partially funded by the ERDF through the COMPETE 2020 Programme within project POCI-01-0145-FEDER-006961, and by National Funds through the FCT as part of project UID/EEA/50014/2013.

The work of João S. Resende was supported by a scholarship from the Fundação para a Ciência e Tecnologia (FCT), Portugal (scholarship number PD/BD/128149/2016).

The work of Patrícia R. Sousa and Luís Antunes was supported by Project "NanoSTIMA: Macro-to-Nano Human Sensing: Towards Integrated Multimodal Health Monitoring and Analytics/NORTE-01-0145-FEDER-000016", financed by the North Portugal Regional Operational Programme (NORTE 2020), under the PORTUGAL 2020 Partnership Agreement, and through the European Regional Development Fund (ERDF).

References

1. Gruber, A., Ben-Gal, I.: Using targeted Bayesian network learning for suspect identification in communication networks. Int. J. Inf. Secur. **17**(2), 169–181 (2018)
2. de Montjoye, Y.-A., et al.: openPDS: protecting the privacy of metadata through safeanswers. Plos One **9**(7), e98790 (2014)
3. LinPhone Open source VOIP project (2017). http://www.linphone.org/. Accessed 29 Mar 2018
4. Moscaritolo, V., Belvin, G., Zimmermann, P.: Silent circle instant messaging protocol protocol specification. Online, White Paper (2012)
5. Silent Circle (2018). https://www.silentcircle.com/. Accessed 29 Mar 2018
6. Zimmermann, P., Johnston, A., Callas, J.: ZRTP: media path key agreement for unicast secure RTP. No. RFC 6189 (2011)
7. Greschbach, B., Kreitz, G., Buchegger, S.: The devil is in the metadata—new privacy challenges in decentralised online social networks. In: 2012 IEEE International Conference on Pervasive Computing and Communications Workshops (PERCOM Workshops). IEEE (2012)
8. Tesic, J.: Metadata practices for consumer photos. IEEE MultiMed. **12**(3), 86–92 (2005)
9. Mayer, J., Mutchler, P., Mitchell, J.C.: Evaluating the privacy properties of telephone metadata. Proc. Nat. Acad. Sci. **113**(20), 5536–5541 (2016)
10. Cole, D.: We kill people based on metadata. New York Rev. Books **10**, 2014 (2014)
11. Furini, M., Tamanini, V.: Location privacy and public metadata in social media platforms: attitudes, behaviors and opinions. Multimed. Tools Appl. **74**(21), 9795–9825 (2015)
12. de Montjoye, Y.-A., Radaelli, L., Singh, V.K.: Unique in the shopping mall: on the reidentifiability of credit card metadata. Science **347**(6221), 536–539 (2015)
13. Narayanan, A., Shmatikov, V.: Robust de-anonymization of large sparse datasets. In: IEEE Symposium on Security and Privacy, SP 2008. IEEE (2008)

14. Scapy: the Python-based interactive packet manipulation program and library (2015). https://github.com/secdev/scapy/
15. Schrmann, D., et al.: Wiretapping end-to-end encrypted VoIP calls: real-world attacks on ZRTP. Proc. Priv. Enhanc. Technol. **2017**(3), 4–20 (2017)
16. Petraschek, M., et al.: Security and usability aspects of man-in-the-middle attacks on ZRTP. J. UCS **14**(5), 673–692 (2008)
17. Werner Dittmann, ZRTPCPP (2018). https://github.com/wernerd/ZRTPCPP
18. PJSIP version, teluu. http://www.pjsip.org/
19. Toole, J.L., et al.: Tracking employment shocks using mobile phone data. J. Roy. Soc. Interface **12**(107), 20150185 (2015)
20. Arai, A., et al.: Understanding user attributes from calling behavior: exploring call detail records through field observations. In: Proceedings of the 12th International Conference on Advances in Mobile Computing and Multimedia. ACM (2014)
21. de Montjoye, Y.-A., Quoidbach, J., Robic, F., Pentland, A.S.: Predicting personality using novel mobile phone-based metrics. In: Greenberg, A.M., Kennedy, W.G., Bos, N.D. (eds.) SBP 2013. LNCS, vol. 7812, pp. 48–55. Springer, Heidelberg (2013). https://doi.org/10.1007/978-3-642-37210-0_6
22. Chittaranjan, G., Blom, J., Gatica-Perez, D.: Mining large-scale smartphone data for personality studies. Pers. Ubiquit. Comput. **17**(3), 433–450 (2013)
23. Zhong, E., et al.: User demographics prediction based on mobile data. Pervasive Mobile Comput. **9**(6), 823–837 (2013)
24. Alvanos, D., Limniotis, K., Stavrou, S.: On the cryptographic features of a VoIP service. Cryptography **2**(1), 3 (2018)

Can Spatial Transformation-Based Privacy Preservation Compromise Location Privacy?

Anand Paturi[✉] and Subhasish Mazumdar[✉]

Computer Science and Engineering Department,
New Mexico Institute of Mining and Technology, Socorro, NM, USA
{anand,mazumdar}@cs.nmt.edu

Abstract. While mobile users would like to pose location-based queries such as "find me the nearest service of type S" or "find me k nearest services of type S," they are increasingly aware of the underlying privacy concerns and threats. One of the two main approaches suggested by researchers for countering this threat involves spatial transformation via Hilbert curves. This scheme transforms a two-dimensional coordinate space into a one-dimensional space such that adjacency in the latter space implies contiguity in the former. A Trusted Server (TS) provides a Location-Based Server (LBS) with Points of Interest (POIs) indexed by the one-dimension Hilbert indices obtained by transforming their two-dimensional coordinates; mobile users query the LBS using the Hilbert index corresponding to their two-dimensional coordinates; the LBS finds the nearest Hilbert indices with appropriate POIs and returns them to the users. Owing to the large number of possible Hilbert transformations using different parameters, the attempt by an LBS to invert the transformation, i.e., compute a two-dimensional coordinate of the target user (or the POIs) is generally considered infeasible. In this paper, we ask to what extent and by which methods can a rogue LBS squeeze a privacy compromise from this scheme? We model the adversary and examine the possibilities of an attack based on semantic factors such as the distribution of POI categories and variations in POI density as well as collusion and exploitation of weaknesses in the mobile system software architecture. Finally, we point out limitations of such attacks and suggest strategies to strengthen defences against them.

Keywords: Mobile computing · Location privacy
Spatial transformation · Hilbert curves · Location-based queries
Location-based service

1 Introduction

The importance to mobile users of location-based queries of the form "find me the nearest service of type S" or "find me k nearest services of type S," cannot

© Springer Nature Switzerland AG 2018
S. Furnell et al. (Eds.): TrustBus 2018, LNCS 11033, pp. 69–84, 2018.
https://doi.org/10.1007/978-3-319-98385-1_6

be overestimated. Unfortunately, their satisfaction is tempered by the underlying threat to their privacy. One of the two main approaches suggested by researchers for countering this threat involves spatial encoding via Hilbert curves. The idea is that the server handling these user queries can be made unaware of the actual geographical coordinates of users, of the points of interest (POIs), and the categories of POIs like restaurant, gas station, etc., by being provided encoded spatial coordinates instead of actual geographic coordinates and encrypted identifiers instead of plaintext categories by another server, a trusted one. The spatial encoding seems infeasible to break (invert) because of the large number of possibilities. In this paper, we show that by following a step-by-step approach based on semantic considerations among others, it is possible for a rogue LBS to reverse (decode) the encoding and thus invade the privacy of users.

Let us introduce [11] the *Hilbert curve H*, a space-filling transformation of bounded 2-dimensional space, which can be applied to location-based services, as first suggested in [5]. Assuming that a square space is divided into 2^{2N} cells in a $2^N \times 2^N$ grid, a bijective function h of order N maps each cell, i.e., each pair (x, y) where x and y are integers in $0 \cdot \cdot (2^N - 1)$, into an integer in $0 \cdot \cdot (2^{2N} - 1)$. Figure 1(a) shows an example for $N = 3$ (i.e., an 8×8 grid). Values of h for each cell is shown within it; the sequence $0 \cdot \cdot 63$ defines a curve that fills the grid passing through each cell exactly once. By abuse of notation, we will use this function h to refer to the curve H as well. The bottom left cell corresponds to the origin of the X-Y coordinates. We also refer to the map as a 2-dimensional matrix: $h[0, 0] = 0; h[1, 0] = 1$ in Fig. 1(a). Figure 1(b) shows a *transposed* curve with a similar logic but starting with cells $0 \cdot \cdot 3$ numbered anticlockwise. Since $H[i, j]$ is swapped with $H[j, i]$, this is essentially a matrix transpose operation.

In Fig. 1(a), observe the first four cells 0, 1, 2, and 3 (numbered in a clockwise manner): they form the fundamental *U-pattern*. This pattern appears with a 90-degree clockwise rotation in cells $4 \cdot \cdot 7$ and again in cells $8 \cdot \cdot 11$ (both numbered anti-clockwise); and then appears with a 180° rotation in cells $12 \cdot \cdot 15$ (numbered clockwise). It is easier to think of the pattern in cells $12 \cdot \cdot 15$ as a mirror image of that in $0 \cdot \cdot 3$. Taken together, these four U-patterns form a connected curve covering 16 cells: one quadrant. Cells 16 through 31 are identical to the first 16 cells of the transposed curve (Fig. 1(b)), i.e., a transposition of cells $0 \cdot \cdot 15$. This pattern repeats in the next quadrant, i.e., cells 32 through 47. Finally, the pattern in the last quadrant ($48 \cdot \cdot 63$) is the mirror image of the first ($0 \cdot \cdot 15$). In fact, a similar pattern can be observed within the first 16 cells when broken up into four quadrants.

This function h is contiguity-preserving (i.e., adjacent cells i and $(i + 1)$ represent 2-dimensional spaces that are contiguous). However, contiguous points in 2D-space may not appear as adjacent cells (e.g., numerically distant cells 5 and 58 in Fig. 1(a) can represent contiguous spaces).

Such a Hilbert curve is generated by a *Trusted Server* (TS) which decides the curve's parameters. They are: (1) the *order* of the curve N; (2) the point of origin X_0, Y_0; (3) the *orientation* Θ (*normal* or *transposed*[1] as in Fig. 1(a) and

---

[1] In the original paper [5], this second curve was described as *rotated*.

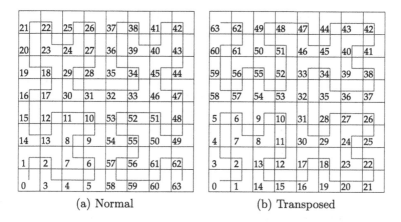

(a) Normal   (b) Transposed

Fig. 1. Normal and transposed Hilbert curves for $N = 3$. The bottom row and leftmost column correspond to row 0 and column 0 of the corresponding matrices.

(b) respectively); and (4) a *scaling factor* Γ that captures the number of meters that each unit cell represents (in the figure, Γ is the distance in meters covered by the entire grid in either the X- or Y-direction divided by 8). Using Γ and the origin, any geographic location (x_0, y_0) in the 2-D space (which could be latitude, longitude), can be converted into a grid cell (x_0^*, y_0^*). Thus, the transformation parameters (unknown to any adversary) are $[X_0, Y_0, \theta, N, \Gamma]$.

The parameter N is chosen in an effort to maintain a low average number of POIs per cell ($\frac{POI}{H}$ ratio); N is increased until that ratio is less than a given threshold.

Based on the generated curve H, the TS creates a table of POIs with Hilbert cell numbers substituted for (x, y) coordinates and sends that table to the server providing the Location Based Service (LBS) to the mobile users. The description of each POI as well as its *category* or *domain* (e.g., restaurant) and *subcategory* (e.g., Vietnamese) are encrypted using an encryption key e. (There may even be sub-sub- and sub-sub-subcategories.) Thus, the LBS obtains a table T of the kind shown in Fig. 2.

Cell	POI description	Category	Sub-category
43	602F568489	A4027D	4715
...	...	...	...
16	9B6C71AA0	399BBA	02AA

Fig. 2. Table T sent from TS to LBS.

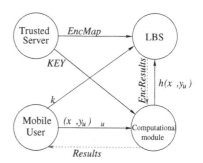

Fig. 3. Information flow from user query.

A mobile user queries the LBS using the Hilbert cell number corresponding to his/her location's two-dimensional coordinates; the LBS finds the numerically closest Hilbert cell number with appropriate POIs and returns them to the user. A computational module must be able to transform the user's geographic location (x_u, y_u) (e.g., latitude, longitude) into a grid cell (x_u^*, y_u^*) and from it into a Hilbert cell number $h(x_u^*, y_u^*)$ using the transformation parameters; and also decrypt the returned POI descriptions using the inverse of e. To perform the above mentioned steps, the mobile user needs a *KEY* from the TS:

$$KEY = \{[X_0, Y_0, \theta, N, \Gamma], \ e^{-1}\}.$$

Figure 3 depicts the overall scheme.

Clearly, if an LBS goes rogue and wishes to invade the privacy of mobile users, it needs to be able to transform the Hilbert cell numbers $h(x_u, y_u)$ into corresponding geographic locations of the cells. The question we ask is the following. *Does it have a method of attack?* An LBS could be in the location mapping business while allowing third-party trusted servers (TS) to hide the true locations of the mobile users in order to attract customers with the promise of enhanced privacy. In any case, an LBS must know the actual geographical locations of the POIs. (After all, it is aware of Google Maps!) So, can it exploit this knowledge? Secondly, can it be involved in collusion with some actual users? Third, can it exploit the weaknesses of typical mobile system software architectures (e.g., Android)?

The paper is structured as follows. In Sect. 2, we review related work. In Sect. 3, we present a sequence of steps an LBS can take, essentially answering the above questions in the affirmative. In Sect. 4, we list the limitations of this approach and outline a counter-strategy that makes location privacy more robust. We end with conclusions and future work in Sect. 5.

2   Related Work

Location privacy for mobile users has been addressed primarily using two approaches: (a) k-anonymity [12] and (b) Spatial encoding. In k-anonymity based approaches, the goal is to send obfuscated region instead of an exact user location and ensure that the obfuscated region contains at least $(k-1)$ other users. This obfuscated region is constructed either by relying on a Trusted Third Party (TTP) with which all users share their exact locations or through a Peer-to-Peer (P2P) approach collaborating directly with $(k-1)$ other users nearby.

We have outlined the spatial encoding based approach already. Techniques like obfuscated locations, k-anonymity, PIR, etc. can be implemented on top of the encoded space to ensure location privacy for mobile users. In [6], the authors store the Hilbert index of POIs generated over the target region in an untrusted server and use PIR-based techniques to serve the user's query. Usage of PIR technique ensures that the untrusted server does not have the complete knowledge of the user's request and related response. Thus, ensuring location privacy to the end user but this approach is computationally very expensive.

Kalnis et al. [4] proposed a k-anonymity-based Hilbert Cloaking (HC) scheme that generates a cloaked (obfuscated) region using a Hilbert Curve. In [7], Lee et al. address the Hilbert curve's drawback while generating a cloaked region i.e., an extended cloaked region is generated (while using Hilbert curves) due to the disconnect in adjacent cells resulting from the *U-pattern*. They propose creating and optimizing a cloaked region that stores adjacent cell information not connected by the *U-pattern*. Ghinita et al. [3] use an HILB-ASR algorithm that implements a Hilbert curve and assigns Hilbert values to users communicating P2P who are further grouped into κ buckets containing κ users, except the last which may contain up to $(2\kappa - 1)$ users. For a user $u \in \kappa$-bucket, his κ-ASR corresponds to the minimum bounding rectangle (MBR) of the users in that respective κ-bucket. To accommodate the mobile user movement and support the flexibility in queries with varying κ, a B^{+}-tree by the order of the Hilbert curve is used. Damiani et al. in [2] propose Hilbert curve-based obfuscation scheme. The map knowledge of the adversary and user's privacy preferences are taken into account while creating the obfuscated region over the target encoded space.

In [10], Niu et al. introduced FGcloak algorithm that generates granular Hilbert curves for the target region based on the high query distribution within the region. Hilbert curve with finer grains (order of the curve) are generated for regions with high query probability i.e., regions with high POI density. Cui et al. in [1], propose Hierarchical Hilbert Curves (HHC)-based spatial k-anonymity algorithm that considers average query density and constructs hierarchical Hilbert index to fill each layer of the target region with a Hilbert curve respectively.

While the above approaches have used Hilbert curves in PIR and cloaking region contexts for location privacy, they have not considered semantics such as categories of the POIs. We believe that ours is the first effort to consider a systematic attack using semantics.

Our approach is loosely based on the insight of Machanavajjhala et al. [8] and others who showed how k-anonymity is compromised by semantics like a lack of diversity.

3   Attack Modeling

Moon et al. [9] had indicated an alternative approach for representing the Hilbert curve by focusing on the rotation aspect of the fundamental U-pattern. We have gone further using that idea and articulated seven canonical forms other than the normal curve [11]. They are obtained through rotations of the normal curve by 90, 180, and 270°, as shown in Fig. 5, along with shifts of the origin to the three other corners; in addition, for each of these, there is a *transposed* curve obtained by matrix transposition. Thus, we get eight canonical forms of the curve.

We first provide a sequence of steps that the LBS can take if it wishes to decode the spatial transformation constructed by the TS. Next, we outline two other strategies it can take: collusion and exploitation of the underlying system weaknesses.

Both the TS and the LBS know about an underlying map of the area since it is public knowledge:

$$Map = \{((x_i, y_i), POI_i) \mid 1 \leq i \leq K\}$$

Map contains the (x_i, y_i) Cartesian coordinate values of all K POIs in the region. Either the TS selects a large subset of the map and performs spatial encoding, or both the TS and LBS know exactly which large set of POIs are being encoded by TS. In either case, the TS sends to the LBS $EncMap$, an encoded map, which represents the Hilbert cell numbers of M POIs in the map ($M \leq K$):

$$EncMap = \{(h(x_i^*, y_i^*), e(POI_i) \mid 1 \leq i \leq M\},$$

where (x_i^*, y_i^*) is the cell corresponding to the geographical coordinates (x_i, y_i).

As mentioned in Sect. 1, the TS sends a KEY to a computational module, allowing it to compute $h()$. The computational module needs to do so in order to transform a user's location into the corresponding Hilbert cell number. (It may also use the KEY to decode the result cell numbers returned by the LBS into geographical locations but that may be unnecessary as the textual descriptions are typically enough.) It also allows decryption (using e^{-1}) of the encrypted POI descriptions returned by the LBS. Based on the above, we list the knowledge levels of each actor in Table 1.

Table 1. Comparison of knowledge levels of entities.

ACTOR	KNOWS	DOES NOT KNOW
MobileUser	k (x_u, y_u) Map	KEY (x_u^*, y_u^*) $h(x_u^*, y_u^*)$ $Map, EncMap$
Trusted server	KEY $Map, EncMap$	k (x_u, y_u) (x_u^*, y_u^*) $h(x_u^*, y_u^*)$
Computational module	KEY (x_u, y_u) (x_u^*, y_u^*) $h(x_u^*, y_u^*)$	k $Map, EncMap$
LBS	k $h(x_u^*, y_u^*)$ $Map, EncMap$	KEY (x_u, y_u) (x_u^*, y_u^*)

The LBS knows both Map and $EncMap$ but cannot map one to the other. It knows the Hilbert cell number of the user location $h(x_u^*, y_u^*)$ but does not know the actual location (x_u, y_u). It is easy to see that the computational module has access to both the KEY and the user's location. Placing it within the TS provides excessive knowledge with the TS; since it cannot be at the LBS, it can only be in the mobile user's device (this is in line with the original architecture [5]). Clearly, the computational module must be protected from the LBS.

3.1 Semantics Based Decoding

Using the Map Knowledge. The following observations guide us in formulating a strategy for the LBS.

- It is very difficult to get a uniform POI/H ratio when POI category, subcategory, etc., are included. Providers of unique or unusual services, e.g., Ethiopian restaurants, are few in number.
- The distribution of subcategories with respect to categories (that are of interest to consumers) cannot be uniform. For example, the number of subcategories of *Pets* cannot rival that of *Restaurants*.
- Without including category, there are some unusually large geographical clusters, e.g., shopping arcades/malls.

Our decoding strategy can be summarized by the following steps to be taken by the LBS with Map and $EncMap$ as inputs.

1. Compute N from the $EncMap$ index available in T.
2. Derive (x^*, y^*) coordinates for a given h-value from $EncMap$ index using a heuristics-based approach.
3. Derive Γ based on observations from step 2.
4. Derive θ based on observations from step 2.

We will now expand on each of these steps.

Step 1: The LBS would guess N, the order of the curve. This can be done by first scanning the table T obtained from the Trusted Server and finding h_{max}, the maximum value of the *Location* column, i.e., the maximum Hilbert cell number that contains a POI; and next, computing the closest even power of 2 that is higher or equal; and finally, since that must be $2N$, obtaining N. In other words, deriving $N = \frac{1}{2} \log_2 n$, where

$$n = min\{m \mid m = 2^{2k} \text{ for some } k \text{ and } m \geq h_{max}\}$$

There are two cases to consider here.

1. $2^{2(N-1)} - 1 < h_{max} < 2^{2N} - 1$
   For a simple example, suppose $N = 3$, meaning the Trusted Server has an 8×8 arrangement of $2^{2 \times 3} = 64$ grid cells, and yet h_{max}, the maximum *Location* value in T, is 40. In this case, it derives $n = 64$; $N = \frac{1}{2} \log_2 64 = 3$ correctly.
2. $h_{max} < 2^{2(N-1)} - 1 < 2^{2N} - 1$
   Suppose the setup is the same but h_{max}, the maximum *Location* value in T, is 14. Note that this happens only in the unlikely case when more than three-fourths of the area under the Trusted Server's map is devoid of any point of

interest. In this case, it derives $n = 16$; $N = \frac{1}{2}\log_2 16 = 2$ incorrectly.

However, a comparison of Fig. 1(a) and (b) shows that the subregion containing the Hilbert grid cells 0 through 15 is disjoint from the remaining three-fourths of the entire grid. Thus, the LBS can proceed to locate actual locations of POIs in this subregion using the following steps. In other words, the ignorance of the LBS about the remainder of the 8×8 grid is not a setback. Later, if it learns of location values greater than 15, it will revise its knowledge of N based on that value and continue without losing the decoded information it has collected.

Step 2: The LBS would then attempt to associate a few h values with actual (x, y) coordinates.

The LBS would sort table T based on category, subcategory, etc., (without decrypting the entries) and use the following heuristics to reverse-map a few (x, y) from their corresponding $h(x^*, y^*)$ values. Note that the LBS has the actual map of the area. Though the TS can provide a strict subset of the POI categories, it is not in its commercial interest to do so; furthermore, as outlined in the next subsection, collusion can uncover them quite easily.

Heuristic 1: Retrieve the category hierarchy CH supported by the server. This is rarely a secret since the location service needs to publicize its coverage of categories, subcategories, etc., in order to entice its subscribers/users.

After sorting the table T by category, sub-category, etc., compare the unique triples (the three counts for sub-, sub-sub-, and sub-sub-subcategories) for each category against those in CH. This should reveal most categories. If some of the counts are not unique, a tree comparison can be performed of the hierarchy tree structure. (This is more time-consuming but it need be done once only when the encoded map is sent.)

There is an assumption here: that each (sub-)category has at least one instance; hence, it will appear in the table T. This is a reasonable assumption since the server has an incentive to publicize only those categories it has entries for. In a medium-sized US city, almost all subcategories do have at least one instance (with a few exceptions: a non-capital city will lack any instance of *Embassies*).

Heuristic 2: If there is only one entry with a particular category, the LBS can uniquely identify it, find its actual location from the map and its Hilbert grid cell number from table T. Indeed, the revelation of each category is unnecessary. It is enough to locate those which have very few instances. For example, it is rare that a city has more than one town hall/civic center/convention center / ... / ski resort/commercial airport.

Heuristic 3: Look for two POIs of a particular category but with very different surroundings. For example, suppose there are exactly two hospitals in the entire region with one surrounded by restaurants and the other in an isolated, sprawling campus.

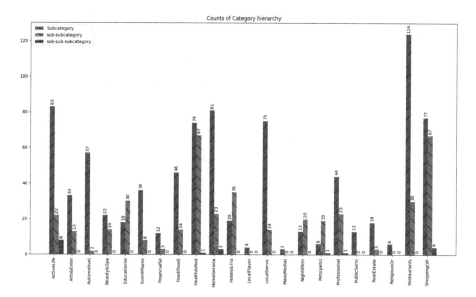

Fig. 4. Gross counts of the category hierarchy.

Heuristic 4: Look for a cluster of POIs with a known diversity, e.g., a set of eight restaurants interleaved with two gas stations in close proximity on an arterial road. In Hilbert space, this cluster of POIs would fall in the same or adjacent cells. In a small city, it is common to find only one instance for most categories: one high school, one mortuary service, one college/university, etc., but a large number of restaurants. Here the unusual multiplicity and clusters of restaurants make them easy to spot.

We applied the above heuristics on the city of Albuquerque, New Mexico, USA (population of ≈560,000). First, we obtained a category hierarchy CH from Yelp [13]. Gross counts are shown in Fig. 4; for example, the category *Pets* has 6 subcategories, 19 subcategories and 1 sub-subcategory. Actually, we have greater detail that we did not use: the subcategory *Pet Stores* has 3 sub-subcategories while *Pet Services* has 16 sub-subcategories, one of which, *Pet Sitting* has one sub-sub-subcategory, *Pet Boarding*. In other words, the structure of the hierarchy tree is not captured in our gross counts; it would have been useful had the count tuples themselves not been unique. But the figure makes clear the fact that each category has unique counts.

The *Hotels and Travel* domain has 19 and 35 subcategories and sub-subcategories respectively. Among those 19, there are two with a single instance each: *Airport* and *Ski Resort*. To disambiguate between those unique encrypted ids, the LBS can refer to the map which shows the airport and the ski resort on the south and north ends of the city respectively. While the airport has a busy freeway, many hotels and restaurants near to it, the ski resort is more secluded being surrounded by just a few restaurants. Thus, by identifying the placement and surrounding POIs, the LBS can distinguish between the airport and the

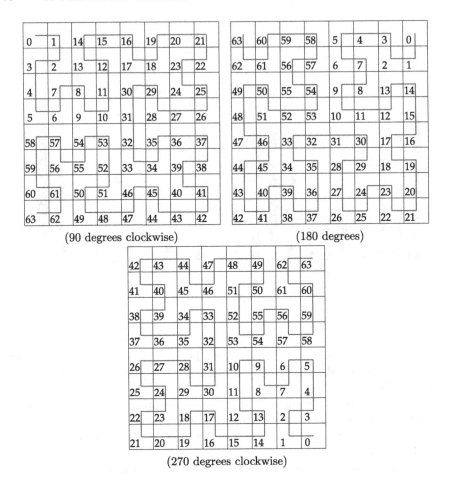

(90 degrees clockwise)   (180 degrees)

(270 degrees clockwise)

Fig. 5. Hilbert curve for N = 3 rotated by 90, 180, and 270° clockwise.

ski resort in the Hilbert space as well. Within the *Hotels and Travel* domain, the *Boat Tour* sub-subcategory also has one instance; the LBS can locate it in Hilbert space as well.

Step 3: With two POIs identified using the above steps, the LBS computes the scaling factor Γ. It generates the Hilbert grid for order N, assumes each grid is x meters by x meters, takes two cells located in the previous step and computes the distance d as a function of x. Knowing that the actual distance is A meters, it computes $\Gamma = \frac{A}{d}$, i.e., each cell represents a Γ meters × Γ meters region. For example, having decoded cells 16 and 43, it calculates d as the length of the line joining the two cells in terms of x (hypotenuse of a right-angled triangle).

Step 4: At this point, the value of θ is not known, i.e., it is not clear whether the normal or the transposed curve is being used; also it could be rotated at 90, 180, or 270° with the origin being in one of the corner cells. The previous step was possible in spite of these unknowns because the distances were not affected. Now, those unknowns will be tackled.

Suppose the POIs identified (using the map knowledge or known distribution of certain sub-category POIs) are in cells 16 and 43. When the curve is constructed using normal orientation as shown in Fig. 1(a), cell 16 is west-southwest of 43. We will now see how the placement of these cells changes with the implementation of transpose and rotations. Further, we will explore how observations pertaining to these variations can be used to discard assumptions of any of rotations or transpose.

- In the transpose of the normal curve (Fig. 1(b)), the cell 16 is not west-southwest of 43 anymore, but rather south-southwest. Owing to this variation, the transpose possibility can be discarded.
- In the 90° rotation case with the origin at $(0, 7)$ (Fig. 5), cell 16 is north of the cell 43.
- In the 180° rotation case with the origin at $(7, 7)$ (Fig. 5), 16 is east of 43.
- In the 270° rotation case with the origin at $(7, 0)$ (Fig. 5), cell 16 is but south-southeast of 43.

From the above observations, the Hilbert curve variations from transpose, rotations, and transpose of rotations can be discarded.

The practical implementation of a system with above steps is feasible in terms of performance because the generation of the curve, though exponential in N (there are 2^{2N} cells) and the heuristics are done offline.

3.2 Collusion

Now, we take a completely different tack and examine the knowledge state listed in Table 1 to find opportunistic collusion strategies for the LBS. The LBS knows $h(x_u^*, y_u^*)$ and needs to know (x_u, y_u). Two actors have that knowledge: the Mobile User and the Computational Module. We examine the first actor here and the second in the next subsection.

How can the collusion with the Mobile User take place? If the LBS colludes with a mobile user or instructs a team of employees to become subscribing users, such a user (or users) can send a query to the LBS while storing a table containing the queries with time-stamped locations. Since each query must have a return address, the LBS can later create a table of actual locations (x_i, y_i) along with $h(x_i^*, y_i^*)$ it received in the query. With such a cooperating mobile user driving around the region while sending queries, the LBS could create a very accurate decoding function.

3.3 Exploiting Underlying System Weakness

The other actor that has everything the LBS needs is the *Computational Module*, which must reside in the user's device (as we have explained above). Now, we are not aware of any truly tamper-proof application software module in mobile phones today. Thus, it is hard to believe that such a module cannot be tampered with. All the tampering that is needed is access to the KEY either after it is stored by this module or when it receives it from the Trusted Server.

The LBS could take advantage of the underlying weakness of the mobile device software system and coax the user to install a privacy-invasive app. For example, the LBS can serve an advertisement to install an invasive app while servicing the mobile user's request. If the mobile user installs this app, then his actual location (x_u, y_u) would be transferred to the LBS with every location query request (that also has $h(x_u^*, y_u^*)$). A sequence of requests like this over time will result in LBS partially or completely decoding the spatial transformation.

4   Limitations of the Strategy and Counter-Measures

In Step 4, with two of the POIs in T located on the map, the LBS has a problem concluding normal versus transposed (value of θ) when those two points are on a diagonal. For example, cells 2 and 40 are in identical positions in Fig. 1(a) and (b). The same is the case for pairs of cells in parallel diagonals such as 16 and 26. In this case, the LBS would have to go back to the heuristics and find another POI that is not co-linear with the pair on the diagonal. Thus, the LBS needs either two non-diagonal points or two points on a diagonal and one point non-co-linear with those two. (Actually, the limitation applies to only one of the diagonals. For example, in Fig. 1(a) and (b), cells 23 and 61 interchange their positions, thus enabling differentiation.

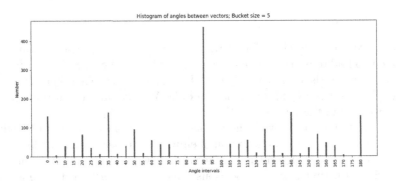

Fig. 6. Histogram of angular separation between similar vectors in normal and transposed curves.

We considered every vector from one hilbert cell to another (from i to j for every i, j) in the normal curve and its corresponding vector in the transposed curve and computed the angle between the two vectors (their magnitudes were always the same). Figure 6 shows a histogram of those counts for $N = 3$ (8×8 grid); only 140 out of 2016 ($= (64 \times 64 - 64)/2$) cell pairs (i.e., 6.9%) were aligned at $0°$, i.e., the normal curve was indistinguishable from the transposed. For the

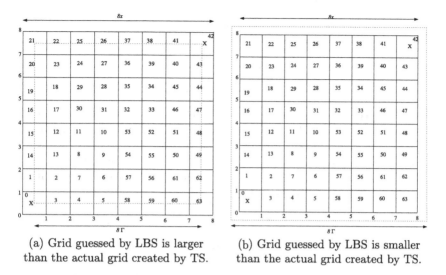

(a) Grid guessed by LBS is larger than the actual grid created by TS.

(b) Grid guessed by LBS is smaller than the actual grid created by TS.

Fig. 7. Initial error: LBS centers X in a cell in an $8x \times 8x$ grid; actual grid is $8\Gamma \times 8\Gamma$.

rest, it becomes possible to tell them apart. For $N = 4$, that ratio drops to 3.9% (= 1280 out of 32,640).

Second, the LBS does not know the exact locations of the centers of the cells. For example, if it locates a known POI with cell 42. It still does not know exactly where within the cell the POI is located. This introduces an error in precision. What is the magnitude of the error? Consider Fig. 7. The maximum error occurs when the POIs of corner cells, e.g., 0 and 42, the origin and top right respectively, are located at the extreme corners. The LBS will lay out its inferred grid (shown with solid lines) positioning those POIs in the centers of those cells. But the Trusted Server's grid (only outer boundary shown with dotted lines) may have positioned those POIs either at their extreme outer corners (Fig. 7(a)) or their extreme inner corners (Fig. 7(b)) or anywhere in between. For those two extremes, it is possible to show that if the size of the LBS grid is x and that of the TS is Γ, then the two cases correspond to

$$8x = 8\Gamma + x \quad \text{and} \quad 8\Gamma = 8x + \Gamma$$

leading to $x = 1.14\Gamma$ and $x = 0.875\Gamma$ respectively. Since the correct values is $x = \Gamma$, there is an error of roughly 14% in the scaling factor. However, this is based only on initial knowledge of these two POIs. As the LBS learns about a few more POIs, it will be able to decrease its error.

4.1 Counter Measures

In order to mitigate the threat posed by the attack strategy outlined above and make the privacy scheme more robust, we propose the following steps.

Step 1: Include in the KEY an offset parameter c, which is a positive integer. Effectively, this defines a new Hilbert function h' obtained from h:

$$h'(x,y) = h(x,y) + c$$

$$KEY = \{[X_0, Y_0, \theta, N, \Gamma], c, e^{-1}\}$$

Since Hilbert values of both user locations and POIs will be transformed, the search process will be unaffected. Of course, $h'()$ values will now exceed $2^{2N} - 1$, but this will be addressed in the next step.

Step 2: Increment N by 1. This will increase the number of cells from 2^{2N} to $2^{2(N+1)} = 4 \times 2^{2N}$, i.e., provide four times the area, thus accommodating the increased range of h' provided that

$$0 < c < 3 \times 2^{2N}.$$

This extra space can be filled with fictitious POIs, leading to a uniform distribution of instances. There will be no more tell-tale single instances of POIs; the imbalance between the number of restaurants and pet items will be eliminated. The attack will become much more difficult for the LBS. Furthermore, the distribution of categories can be equalized by the addition of bogus encrypted categories that do not correspond to any publicized (known to users) category.

Note that the Computational Module will be using h' instead of h to translate the user locations. Consequently, no user will ever be located in the fictitious area. Thus, the search process will not be effected.

Another advantage of this offset is that even if the LBS locates two POIs, say in cells 16 and 43, it remains unsure whether or not this corresponds to the pair 15 and 42, or 14 and 41, etc. Since these pairs have different vector lengths, now it is unsure about Γ. Without the offset, the vector length was invariant across the canonical forms of the curve.

Step 3: Over time, the LBS can find out from the collection of hilbert values of user locations, that much of the hilbert space is never occupied by users and therefore fictitious. Hence, the TS must take steps to send fake user queries containing locations in that fictitious space by making use of some bogus subscriptions.

Last, regarding the collusion between the LBS and the Mobile User, there is a possible counter-measure that the TS could employ: generate a unique Hilbert curve for each individual user. But this means a separate key and encoded map must be stored at both the TS and the LBS for each of the tens of thousands of users. This strategy is challenging for implementation: key management alone would be a matter of concern.

5   Conclusion and Future Work

In this paper, we pose the question, "can spatial transformation-based privacy preservation [5] compromise location privacy?" and answer it in the affirmative by considering the semantics of POIs, collusion, and underlying system weaknesses. However, we then consider limitations of the proposed attack strategies and offer appropriate counter-measures.

For future work, we will implement and test the heuristics-based approach on varied distributions of POIs derived from publicly available maps. Using the practical implementation, we will assess the *KEY* strength for varied distributions of POIs. Further, we would like to quantify the error bounds and how they get relaxed with the increasing POI exposure.

Acknowledgment. We thank our anonymous reviewers for their constructive comments.

References

1. Cui, N., Yang, X., Wang, B.: A novel spatial cloaking scheme using hierarchical Hilbert Curve for location-based services. In: Cui, B., Zhang, N., Xu, J., Lian, X., Liu, D. (eds.) WAIM 2016. LNCS, vol. 9659, pp. 15–27. Springer, Cham (2016). https://doi.org/10.1007/978-3-319-39958-4_2
2. Damiani, M.L., Bertino, E., Silvestri, C.: Protecting location privacy against spatial inferences: the probe approach. In: Proceedings 2nd SIGSPATIAL ACM GIS 2009 International Workshop on Security and Privacy in GIS and LBS, pp. 32–41 (2009)
3. Ghinita, G., Kalnis, P., Skiadopoulos, S.: PRIVE: anonymous location-based queries in distributed mobile systems. In: Proceedings 16th International Conference on World Wide Web, pp. 371–380 (2007)
4. Kalnis, P., Ghinita, G., Mouratidis, K., Papadias, D.: Preventing location-based identity inference in anonymous spatial queries. IEEE Trans. Knowl. Data Eng. **19**(12), 1719–1733 (2007)
5. Khoshgozaran, A., Shahabi, C.: Blind evaluation of nearest neighbor queries using space transformation to preserve location privacy. In: Papadias, D., Zhang, D., Kollios, G. (eds.) SSTD 2007. LNCS, vol. 4605, pp. 239–257. Springer, Heidelberg (2007). https://doi.org/10.1007/978-3-540-73540-3_14
6. Khoshgozaran, A., Shahabi, C.: Private information retrieval techniques for enabling location privacy in location-based services. In: Bettini, C., Jajodia, S., Samarati, P., Wang, X.S. (eds.) Privacy in Location-Based Applications. LNCS, vol. 5599, pp. 59–83. Springer, Heidelberg (2009). https://doi.org/10.1007/978-3-642-03511-1_3
7. Lee, H.J., Hong, S.T., Yoon, M., Um, J.H., Chang, J.W.: A new cloaking algorithm using Hilbert curves for privacy protection. In: Proceedings 3rd ACM SIGSPATIAL International Workshop on Security and Privacy in GIS and LBS, pp. 42–46 (2010)
8. Machanavajjhala, A., Kifer, D., Gehrke, J., Venkitasubramaniam, M.: l-diversity: privacy beyond k-anonymity. ACM Trans. Knowl. Discov. Data **1**(1) (2007)
9. Moon, B., Jagadish, H.V., Faloutsos, C., Saltz, J.H.: Analysis of the clustering properties of the Hilbert space-filling curve. IEEE Trans. Knowl. Data Eng. **13**(1), 124–141 (2001)
10. Niu, B., Li, Q., Zhu, X., Li, H.: A fine-grained spatial cloaking scheme for privacy-aware users in location-based services. In: 2014 23rd International Conference on Computer Communication and Networks (ICCCN), pp. 1–8 (2014)

11. Paturi, A., Mazumdar, S.: Exploring origin and rotation parameters while using Hilbert curves in mobile environments. In: Proceedings International Conference on Mobile Services, Resources, and Users MOBILITY 2018 (2018)
12. Sweeney, L.: k-anonymity: a model for protecting privacy. Int. J. Uncertain. Fuzziness. Knowl.-Based Syst. **10**(5), 557–570 (2002)
13. Yelp, Inc. Category list. Copyright 2004–2018. https://www.yelp.com/developers/documentation/v3/category_list

Towards an Effective Privacy Impact and Risk Assessment Methodology: Risk Assessment

Majed Alshammari$^{(\boxtimes)}$ and Andrew Simpson

Department of Computer Science, University of Oxford,
Wolfson Building, Parks Road, Oxford OX1 3QD, UK
{majed.alshammari,andrew.simpson}@cs.ox.ac.uk

Abstract. It is increasingly recognised that Privacy Impact Assessments (PIAs) play a crucial role in providing privacy protection for data subjects and in supporting risk management for organisations. However, existing PIA processes are typically not accompanied with proper guidelines and/or methodologies that sufficiently support privacy risk assessments and illustrate precisely how the core part of the PIA—a risk assessment—can be conducted. We present an approach for assessing potential privacy risks built upon a privacy risk model that considers legal, organisational, societal and technical aspects. This approach has the potential to underpin a systematic and traceable privacy risk-assessment methodology that can complement PIA processes.

1 Introduction

In order to anticipate and prevent the processing operations that may lead to privacy violations or harms, the adverse impacts of these operations need to be proactively assessed in the early stages of the design process [6]. This has led to the emergence of the concept of a *Privacy Impact Assessment (PIA)*. PIAs tend to focus more on legal and organisational aspects than on social and technical ones [6,7]. As such, it is necessary for PIA processes to be complemented by a privacy risk-assessment methodology that adopts an appropriate privacy risk model that considers organisational, legal, societal and technical aspects [2].

We present a methodical approach for assessing potential privacy risks built upon a privacy risk model that considers legal, organisational, societal and technical aspects. It illustrates the main steps of analysing and assessing the risk of privacy harms that may result from the processing of personal data. The approach has the potential to help underpin a systematic and traceable privacy risk-assessment methodology that can complement PIA processes in a holistic and effective fashion. We argue that this contribution lays the foundation for developing rigorous and systematic PIA methodologies.

2 Background and Motivation

Several countries have developed different PIA processes and/or methodologies [13]. The UK PIA handbook [12], for example, was based on extensive

© Springer Nature Switzerland AG 2018
S. Furnell et al. (Eds.): TrustBus 2018, LNCS 11033, pp. 85–99, 2018.
https://doi.org/10.1007/978-3-319-98385-1_7

reviews of existing PIA methodologies [3,13]. In addition, the Privacy Impact Assessment Framework (PIAF) [14] is a project funded by the European Commission to develop a step-by-step guide to the PIA process. As another example, in [13] a 16-step guide to the PIA process is described.

The core of a PIA is a risk assessment, which involves risk identification and risk mitigation [9]. Although PIAs are expected to follow the same philosophy, existing PIA processes largely fall short in this respect [6,9]. Existing processes cannot be applied easily: they are imprecise, lengthy or improperly structured [9]. They are typically not accompanied with proper guidelines, methodologies or risk models that sufficiently support privacy risk assessments or illustrate precisely how the technical part of the PIA can be conducted [6,9]. For example, the steps of the process described by the UK PIA handbook [12] are generic and individual risks are not well-matched with corresponding controls. Importantly, it cannot be used as a process reference model [9].

Privacy risk assessments need to go beyond traditional security assessments to consider the nature of the risks arising from the processing of personal data, not least because the nature of privacy harms differs from the adverse impacts of security events; such impacts may extend beyond individuals to relatives, friends or wider society [10]. This necessitates adopting a risk model that defines the key risk factors that have impacts on the privacy of data subjects and establishes a conceptual relationship among these factors [6].

Typically, risk-assessment methodologies rely upon well-defined attributes of the key risk factors to determine levels of risk [8]. The specification of these factors, along with their attributes, requires an appropriate model that can be used to identify and analyse risks to the privacy of data subjects that may arise from the processing of personal data. To determine levels of risk, a risk assessment requires an assessment approach that establishes a set of assessment rules that specify the range of values the risk factors can assume [8]. Multiple threat scenarios need to be identified before assessing the severity and likelihood of privacy risks, which, in turn, require an analysis approach that describes how combinations of risk factors are identified and analysed to ensure adequate coverage of the problem space at a consistent level of detail [8]. To define a reasonable subset of all possible threat scenarios, it is useful to consider the nature of the relationships among these factors, the level at which these factors are characterised, and the dependencies between the attributes of these factors.

This gives rise to two questions: *how might one represent the relationships among the key risk factors in a way that is analytically useful for assessment?*; and *how might one use the attributes of the key risk factors identified in the risk model as inputs to determine the levels of risk in risk assessments?*

3   Building on Existing Approaches

3.1   Existing Approaches

With a focus on context-independent privacy-risk assessment approaches that may complement PIA methodologies, a number of privacy risk-management processes, frameworks and methodologies have been proposed. We review, and subsequently build upon, two of these methodologies: [4,6]. We have chosen these as they explicitly define risk models that distinguish the key terms, assessable risk factors and relationships among these factors. With a focus on assessing the levels of privacy risks, we analyse these methodologies in terms of the risk model and the type of assessment approach.

The Methodology for Privacy Risk Management (CNIL)

The CNIL methodology [4] defines a risk model that illustrates feared events, threats, vulnerabilities and risk sources. A privacy risk is composed of one feared event and all the threats that make it possible. For a feared event to occur, one or more risk sources exploit, accidentally or deliberately, one or more vulnerabilities of supporting assets through different threats.[1]

A feared event describes both the adverse event and its potential impacts on subjects. It does not define the feared event by a set of attributes to help support the assessment approach; rather, it provides a set of the main types of feared events that affect the processing operations according to the types of primary assets. These focus on the availability, integrity and confidentiality of the primary assets. In addition, it takes into account the risks arising from the processing of personal data in a broader context by considering the potential impacts on identity, human rights, privacy and civil liberties. It does not define a privacy harm by a set of attributes to help support the assessment of its severity.

The risk level is assessed in terms of severity and likelihood, with levels of risk being based on two key risk factors: feared events are used to assess the severity, which depends on the level of identification of personal data and the prejudicial effect of the potential impacts; threats are used to assess the likelihood, which depends on the level of vulnerabilities of the supporting assets and the level of capabilities of the risk sources.

The prejudicial effect of the potential impacts is assessed on the level of consequences, the irreversibility of these consequences, and the level of difficulty with which these consequences can be overcome. The level of vulnerabilities is assessed on the ease of exploitation of the supporting assets. In particular, it focuses on threat actions that exploit the vulnerabilities of supporting assets rather than the primary assets.

The capabilities of risk sources are assessed based on their skills, time available, motivation, financial resources, etc. However, it does not explicitly consider the value of personal data to risk sources and the background knowledge when assessing their motivation.

The CNIL methodology uses a semi-quantitative approach that uses a fixed scale of levels (negligible, limited, significant, maximum), along with corresponding numbers. The risk levels are located on a risk map with severity and likelihood on its axes, with the aim of ordering and prioritising these risks.

---

[1] The PIA for smart grid and smart metering systems [5] is an example of a PIA that adopts the CNIL methodology to identify, analyse and assess potential privacy risks.

The Privacy Risk Analysis Methodology (PRIAM)

PRIAM [6] concretely defines a risk model that defines key risk factors with well-defined attributes: privacy harms, feared events, privacy weaknesses and risk sources. It also illustrates the relationships among these factors and describes the dependencies between their attributes. A privacy harm results from one or more feared events. Each feared event results from the exploitation of one or more privacy weaknesses by one or more risk sources.

The risk level is assessed in terms of severity and likelihood for each privacy harm. PRIAM estimates the severity of a privacy harm based on its intensity and victims, which are influenced by the 'irreversibility' and 'scale' attributes of the associated feared event respectively. The likelihood of a privacy harm is computed from the likelihood of its corresponding feared events derived from the likelihood of successful exploitation of associated privacy weaknesses, which depends on the capabilities of risk sources and the exploitability of privacy weaknesses. 'Harm trees' describe the many-to-many relationships among the key risk factors, representing possible exploitations as pairs of privacy weaknesses and risk sources.

The victims attribute is assessed according to the category of affected data subjects, whether they are 'individuals and their families', 'specific groups of individuals', or 'society as a whole'. Based on these categories, it is difficult to distinguish between the range of a privacy harm that affects data subjects only and the range of a privacy harm that affects data subjects along with their families. As such, it is useful to distinguish data subjects from their families when assessing the range of a privacy harm. In so doing, an additional level of assessment needs to be defined for comparison. This requires the establishment of an assessment rule that assesses whether the privacy harm affects data subjects only or data subjects together with their relatives, friends or colleagues.

The intensity of a privacy harm is assessed on its consequences, the irreversibility of these consequences, and the difficulty with which these consequences might be overcome. The capabilities of risk sources are assessed on their motivation (based on the value of the privacy breach and the incentives of the risk source) and capacity (based on the resources of the risk source and the exploitability of the relevant privacy weaknesses).

PRIAM uses a qualitative assessment approach involving various scales for assessing the severity of privacy harms; it also uses a semi-quantitative assessment approach that adopts a set of rules for assessing their likelihood.

3.2   The Problem Statement

The risk factors that have impacts on privacy risks and their contribution to the assessment of the overall risks vary between these approaches. This emphasises that these factors need to be defined in the context of data protection, and their contribution to the assessment of the overall risks needs to be defined at an appropriate level of detail. Further, the conceptual relationships between these factors need to be characterised by illustrating the dependencies between the nominal and assessable attributes of each risk factor, and the dependencies between the nominal and assessable attributes of all risk factors. In addition, the assessment rules that specify the range of values the key risk factors can assume need to reflect the assessable attributes of these factors to facilitate their roles in risk assessments and their translation into qualitative terms for multiple stakeholders. Moreover, risk factors need to be represented in a way that is useful for analysis and assessment—with a view to developing a well-defined step-by-step guide can be developed to identify and assess potential privacy risks in a systematic and traceable manner.

3.3 The Contribution

To appropriately identify, assess and analyse the risk of privacy harms, a systematic and traceable privacy risk-assessment methodology—consisting of a well-defined risk model, an assessment approach, an analysis approach and an underlying process—is required. In [2], we defined a privacy risk model that supports the definition of the key risk factors (along with their attributes and conceptual relationships) by refining the risk model of [6]. In addition, we presented an analysis approach that describes how combinations of risk factors can be identified and analysed to ensure adequate coverage of the problem space at a sufficient level of detail. The results of the analysis approach can be used to develop and model threat scenarios that describe how the threat events that may result from the successful exploitation of primary assets' vulnerabilities by a set of threat sources can contribute to or cause privacy harms. In the following, we build upon those foundations by defining an assessment approach that refines the risk assessment approach of [6] in a number of ways.

First, it refines the harm tree approach by adding an additional level that separates threat sources from privacy vulnerabilities to represent the conceptual relationships among the key risk factors in a way that is analytically useful for analysis and assessment (addressing the first question of Sect. 2). Second, it adopts the risk model of [2] that: characterises the risk factors by well-defined attributes (nominal and assessable) to facilitate the identification, analysis and assessment of these factors in a systematic and traceable manner; and describes the dependences between the nominal and assessable attributes of the key risk factors, to refine how each risk factor can be used as an input to estimate the levels of risk (addressing the second question of Sect. 2). Third, it adopts the fixed levels of scale, along with the corresponding values of [4], with refined assessment rules that reflect the assessable attributes of the key risk factor (addressing the second question of Sect. 2).

4   A Risk-Assessment Approach

Our approach consists of four steps. The first step is to represent the conceptual relationships among the key risk factors for each privacy harm from which a reasonable set of all possible threat scenarios can be generated. The second

Table 1. Assessing the overall values from combinations of values, inspired by [4].

Sum of values	Overall values
<5	1. Negligible
=5	2. Limited
=6	3. Significant
>6	4. Maximum

step is to assess the severity of privacy harms. The third step is to assess the likelihood of occurrence. The fourth step is to assess the risk levels of privacy harms in terms of their severity and likelihood. We consider each in turn.

Our approach is built upon the risk model and the analysis approach of [2]. We consider the results of the analysis approach as relevant information that is necessary for determining the values of the attributes of key risk factors. In addition, we adopt the fixed scale of levels and the corresponding values of [4] (1. Negligible; 2. Limited; 3. Significant; and 4. Maximum) as assessment scales with refined and/or newly defined rules for assessing the key risk factors of the risk model of [2]. These scales can be easily translated for multiple stakeholders and allow relative comparisons between values in different scales or even within the same scale. Table 1 illustrates a set of rules for assessing overall values from combinations of values that can be applied to the key risk factors.

4.1 Step 1: The Construction of Harm Trees

In the risk model of [2], a privacy harm results from one or more threat events, each of which results from the successful exploitation of one or more vulnerabilities by one or more threat sources. Thus, it is useful to generate multiple threat scenarios describing how the threat events caused by the most likely threat sources can contribute to or cause a privacy harm.

In [6], a harm tree describes the relationship between a privacy harm (a root node) and all possible feared events (intermediate nodes) that exploit privacy weaknesses (leaf nodes) by the most likely risk sources, which are both represented as pairs of the form (privacy weakness, risk source). We slightly refine the harm tree by adding an additional level to present a privacy harm (a root node) and all possible threat events (intermediate nodes) that exploit the vulnerabilities of primary assets (intermediate nodes) by the most likely threat sources (leaf nodes), as illustrated in Fig. 1. We use 'AND' and 'OR' connectors to combine child nodes and indicate whether all or some child nodes are necessary to enact the parent node. This refinement is to represent all possible exploitations of a vulnerability for each threat event by one or more threat sources. This helps analyse the exploitation of a vulnerability when there is collusion between two or more threat sources (when those threat sources are connected to a privacy vulnerability via 'AND'). In addition, it helps provide focus on the most important vulnerabilities that need to be addressed when a vulnerability is connected to several threat sources or its exploitation may lead to several threat events.

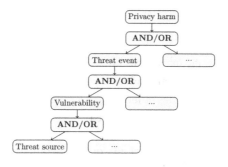

Fig. 1. The structure of the refined harm tree.

Table 2. Intensity of a privacy harm.

Values	The affected data subjects encounter...
1. Negligible	insignificant adverse consequences, which can be reversed without difficulty and last for a short time
2. Limited	slight adverse consequences, which can be reversed with some difficulty and do not last for a long time
3. Significant	serious adverse consequences, which can be reversed with great difficulty and last for a certain length of time
4. Maximum	severe adverse consequences, which cannot be reversed at all and last for a long time

4.2   Step 2: The Assessment of the Severity of a Privacy Harm

The *severity* of a privacy harm essentially depends on the intensity of adverse consequences of a threat event and the range of these consequences suffered by a variety of data subjects.

The *intensity* of a privacy harm represents the level of adverse consequences on the affected data subjects. It is based on the 'adverse consequences' attribute of the privacy harm, which indicates the duration of adverse consequences and their extent of damage. It is influenced by the 'nature', 'category' and 'scope' attributes of the corresponding threat event that reflect the irreversibility of the consequences. The factors that influence irreversibility vary between threat events according to their classification in the risk model of [2]. As such, the 'nature' attribute abstractly represents other specific attributes of the threat events that are classified according to the stages of the lifecycle model of [1]. These attributes, in turn, help assess the extent of damage caused by the adverse consequences and the difficulty with which these consequences can be reversed. Table 2 illustrates the rules for assessing the intensity value of a privacy harm.

The *range* of a privacy harm represents the scope of an adverse impact of a threat event encountered by a variety of subjects. It is based on the 'affected data subjects' attribute and influenced by the 'scope' attribute of the threat event that reflects the domain of the adverse event, assessed, perhaps, in terms of the number and categories of potential subjects whose personal data is impacted.

Table 3. Range of a privacy harm.

Values	Description
1. Negligible	Only specific individuals are affected
2. Limited	Specific individuals and their relatives and/or friends are affected
3. Significant	Specific categories of individuals are affected
4. Maximum	The whole of society is affected

Table 4. Exploitability of a vulnerability.

Values	The exploitation of the primary asset's vulnerability...
1. Negligible	does not appear possible
2. Limited	appears to be difficult
3. Significant	appears to be possible
4. Maximum	appears to be extremely easy

Table 3 illustrates the rules for assessing the value of the range of a privacy harm. These are a refinement of the rules of [6,7] to distinguish between the range of a privacy harm. The severity of a privacy harm is assessed by adding the assessed value of the intensity and the assessed value of the range, then selecting the overall value according to Table 1.

4.3   Step 3: The Assessment of the Likelihood of a Privacy Harm

The *likelihood* of a privacy harm is the highest value of the overall likelihood of occurrence of associated threat events. The overall likelihood of each threat event is a combination of the likelihood of the threat event occurrence and the likelihood of the threat event resulting in adverse impacts.

The *seriousness* represents the level of a vulnerability, which is based on its 'exploitability' and 'severity'. The 'exploitability' attribute indicates the level of exploitation of a primary asset's vulnerability, whereas the 'severity' attribute indicates the relative importance of mitigating a primary asset's vulnerability. Both are influenced by the attributes of the relevant element of context-relevant processing norms of [2]: personal data, data-processing activities, involved actors and processing principles. These include the attributes of personal data: 'category', 'type', 'sensitivity' and 'linkability'. All these attributes are used to estimate the degree to which the vulnerability of the primary asset can be exploited, and to enable the threat source to conduct adverse actions that breach these norms and violate contextual integrity.

Table 4 illustrates the rules for assessing the value of the exploitability of a vulnerability. Table 5 illustrates the rules for assessing the value of the severity of a vulnerability. The seriousness of the vulnerability is estimated by adding the estimated value of the exploitability and the estimated value of the severity, then selecting the overall value according to Table 1.

Table 5. Severity of a vulnerability.

Values	The successful exploitation of the primary asset's vulnerability...
1. Negligible	leads to insignificant impacts
2. Limited	leads to slight impacts
3. Significant	leads to serious impacts
4. Maximum	leads to severe impacts

Table 6. Motivation of a threat source.

Values	The threat source...
1. Negligible	does not have any specific motives based on the value of personal data
2. Limited	has indistinct and unreasonable motives based on the value of personal data
3. Significant	has definite and reasonable motives based on the value of personal data
4. Maximum	has multiple, definite and strong motives based on the value of personal data

The *capability* of a threat source represents the motives, skills, resources or power that make them able to exploit the vulnerabilities of a primary asset. It is mainly estimated based on the values of the 'motivation' and 'ability' as assessable attributes of the threat source, which are determined by the values of 'type', 'resources', 'role' and 'responsibility' as nominal attributes of the source.

The 'motivation' attribute indicates the value of personal data to threat sources that stimulates their motives to exploit vulnerabilities of the primary assets. In general, personal data has value both to data subjects and to the entities that collect and process it. In addition, it has a nuisance value when it is exploited for unfair or malicious purposes. The value of personal data is influenced by the attributes of the personal data as a primary asset: 'category', 'type', 'sensitivity' and 'linkability'. The motive is influenced by the 'type' attribute of the threat source. Table 6 illustrates the rules for assessing the value of the motivation of a threat source.

The 'ability' attribute indicates the level of resources by which a threat source is able to exploit the vulnerabilities of a primary asset. These resources include the skills, background knowledge, privileges, financial and technical resources. These assessable attributes are influenced by the 'type' attribute of the threat source. The 'privileges' is influenced by the roles of the threat source and assigned responsibilities, if any. Further, technical and financial resources are influenced by the 'type' attribute. The 'background knowledge' is influenced by other factors, such as the type of relationship with the data subject. Table 7 illustrates the rules for assessing the value of the ability of a threat source.

The capability of the threat source is estimated by adding the assessed values of motivation and ability, then selecting the overall value according to Table 1. The likelihood of occurrence of a threat event is estimated by adding the assessed values of capability and exploitability of the relevant primary assets' vulnerabilities, then selecting the overall value according to Table 1. The likelihood of the

Table 7. Ability of a threat source.

Values	The threat source...
1. Negligible	does not appear to have specific skills, background knowledge, privileges, financial and technical resources to exploit the vulnerability
2. Limited	has insufficient skills, background knowledge, privileges, financial and technical resources to exploit the vulnerability
3. Significant	has real and significant skills, background knowledge, privileges, financial and technical resources to exploit the vulnerability
4. Maximum	has definite and unlimited skills, background knowledge, privileges, financial and technical resources to exploit the vulnerability

threat event resulting in adverse impacts is estimated by adding the assessed value of capability and the assessed value of the severity of the relevant primary assets' vulnerabilities, then selecting the overall value according to Table 1. The overall likelihood of occurrence of a threat event causing adverse impacts is estimated by adding the assessed value of the likelihood of occurrence of the threat event and the assessed value of the likelihood of the threat event resulting in adverse impacts, then selecting the overall value according to Table 1. The likelihood of occurrence of a privacy harm is the highest value of the overall likelihood of the corresponding threat events.

4.4   Step 4: The Assessment of the Risk Level of a Privacy Harm

The risk level of a privacy harm is assessed as a (likelihood, severity) pair. These pairs are used to determine the order in which the identified risks should be managed according to their severity and likelihood. We adopt the 'risk map' of [4] to locate the assessed risks according to their levels. The likelihood of a privacy risk is plotted on the X-axis; its severity is plotted on the Y-axis.

5   An Illustrative Example

The European Electronic Toll Service (EETS) [11] aims to support interoperability between Electronic Toll Pricing (ETP) systems at a European level to calculate and collect road-usage tolls. The main actors are users (individuals who subscribes to an EETS provider in order to get access to EETS), EETS providers (legal entities that grant access to EETS to road users), and toll chargers (public or private organisations that are responsible for levying tolls for the circulation of vehicles in an EETS domain). A user is required to provide a set of personal data specified by a responsible toll charger, as well as to be informed about the processing of their personal data. Accordingly, the EETS provider provides the user with an On-Board Unit (OBU) to be installed on-board a vehicle to collect, store, and remotely receive and transmit time, distance and location data over time. In this paper, we assess the values of the attributes of the risk factors identified in [2].

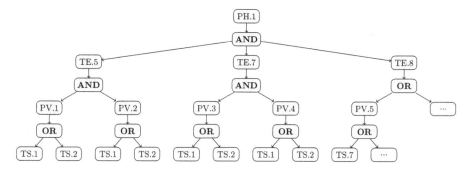

Fig. 2. The structure of the harm tree for the privacy harm PH.1.

5.1 The Construction of Harm Trees

Figure 2 shows the harm tree for the privacy harm PH.1: Increased car insurance premium. It occurs when a EETS provider (TS.1) or a toll charger (TS.2) makes excessive data inference to derive driving patterns (TE.5) for EETS users and shares these driving patterns with car insurance companies (TE.7). An insurance provider (TS.7) makes excessive data inference to re-identify its current or potential customers (TE.8) by linking the derived data to particular drivers to find out their health conditions and vehicle use, or to discover whether a policy holder is where they claim to have been at any point in time. An 'improper data model' (PV.1) and a 'lack of data minimisation' (PV.2) that may be exploited by TS.1 or TS.2 lead to the occurrence of TE.5. An 'improper purpose specification' (PV.3) and a 'lack of logs and audit trails' (PV.6) that may be exploited by TS.1 or TS.2 lead to the occurrence of TE.7. A 'weak anonymisation technique' (PV.5) that is exploited by TS.7 leads to the occurrence of TE.8.

5.2 Severity Assessment

The intensity of PH.1 is based on the extent of damage caused by, the irreversibility of and the duration of, the adverse consequences of associated threat events TE.5, TE.7 and TE.8. TE.5 is categorised as a type of 'identification'. It is characterised as unanticipated by EETS users; it is also characterised as extensive. TE.7 is categorised as a type of 'disclosure'. It is characterised as extensive and accurate. TE.8 is categorised as a type of 'identification'. It is characterised as unanticipated by EETS users; it is also characterised as extensive. The adverse consequences of these threat events are identified as a series of related impacts started by discovering private facts about EETS users, then revealing sensitive information beyond expected boundaries and ended by charging higher rates of insurance premium. They are assessed as slight because calculating insurance premium depends on other factors, including address, occupation, claims history, etc. The duration of these consequences may last for a certain length of time: the period of cover. However, they may last for longer than the period of cover when the disclosed data is used as 'driving history' by insurance providers to calculate car insurance quotes. Once profiles are created, disclosed to insurance providers and sensitive information is inferred, it is technically difficult to reverse these consequences. As such, the intensity of PH.1 is assessed as '2. Limited'.

PH.1 may affect specific EETS users based on their driving patterns. They may also affect specific categories of EETS users based on their health conditions. Together, these may impact insurance premiums. Thus, the range of this privacy harm is assessed as '3. Significant'. The severity of PH.1 is assessed as '2. Limited' by adding the assessed value of the intensity and the assessed value of the range, and selecting the overall value according to Table 1.

5.3   Likelihood Assessment

The likelihood of occurrence of TE.5, TE.7 and TE.8 is assessed on the capability of TS.1, TS.2 and TS.7 and the exploitability of PV.1–PV.5 for each possible exploit.

The motivations of TS.1, TS.2 and TS.7 are based on the values of location-related data to those sources and their motives according to these values. The utility of 'identification and contact data' and 'location data' makes such data highly valuable to EETS providers, toll chargers and insurance providers. It also has a nuisance value when it is exploited by insurance providers. Thus, the motivation of TS.1 and TS.2 are assessed as '3. Significant' and the motivation of TS.7 is assessed as '4. Maximum'.

The ability of those sources is based on their skills, background knowledge, privileges, and technical and financial resources. According to the 'type' attribute of TS.1 and TS.2, they are insiders and institutions. This implies that they have technical skills and detailed background knowledge about conceptual, logical and physical data models, as well as about the processing operations. It also implies that they have legitimate privileges to collect and process location-related data according to their roles and responsibilities. EETS providers and toll charges play the roles of data processors and data controllers respectively. Based on these, they have access rights to both the 'fine-grained location data' and 'identification and contact data'. In addition, they have both technical and financial resources to benefit from the values of the collected data by creating comprehensive and identifiable profiles. As such, the abilities of TS.1 and TS.2 are assessed as '4. Maximum' and '3. Significant' respectively.

According to the 'type' attribute of TS.7, they are outsiders and institutions. Insurance providers are third parties that do not have direct roles with respect to the processing of personal data. Based on this, they do not have access rights to the 'fine-grained location data' and 'identification and contact data'; rather, they can legally process this data when it is anonymised. In addition, they have both technical and financial resources to benefit from the values of the disclosed data by making excessive inference. As such, the ability is assessed as '2. Limited'. The capability of TS.1 is assessed as '4. Maximum'; those of TS.2 and TS.7 are assessed as '3. Significant'.

The seriousness of PV.1–PV.5 is based on the exploitability and severity of each exploit. The ease of the exploitation of PV.1 is influenced by the

Table 8. The seriousness of PV.1, PV.2, PV.3, PV4 and PV.5.

Vulnerability	Exploitability	Severity	Seriousness
PV.1	3. Significant	3. Significant	3. Significant
PV.2	3. Significant	3. Significant	3. Significant
PV.3	3. Significant	3. Significant	3. Significant
PV.4	3. Significant	3. Significant	3. Significant
PV.5	3. Significant	4. Maximum	4. Maximum

Table 9. The overall likelihood of occurrence of TE.5, TE.7, TE.8, TE.4 and TE.5.

Code	Exploit	Threat event	L.O.	L.R.	O.L.
EX.1	TE.5 - PV.1 - TS.1	TE.5	4. Maximum	4. Maximum	4. Maximum
EX.2	TE.5 - PV.1 - TS.2		3. Significant	3. Significant	3. Significant
EX.3	TE.5 - PV.2 - TS.1		4. Maximum	4. Maximum	4. Maximum
EX.4	TE.5 - PV.2 - TS.2		3. Significant	3. Significant	3. Significant
EX.5	TE.7 - PV.3 - TS.1	TE.7	4. Maximum	4. Maximum	4. Maximum
EX.6	TE.7 - PV.3 - TS.2		3. Significant	3. Significant	3. Significant
EX.7	TE.7 - PV.4 - TS.1		4. Maximum	4. Maximum	4. Maximum
EX.8	TE.7 - PV.4 - TS.2		3. Significant	3. Significant	3. Significant
EX.9	TE.8 - PV.5 - TS.7	TE.8	3. Significant	4. Maximum	4. Maximum

L.O.: Likelihood of occurrence. **L.R.:** Likelihood of resulting in adverse impacts.
O.L.: The overall likelihood.

relevant element of context-relevant processing norms. The relevant element of the processing norms is 'attributes', which refers to personal data. In this context, personal data is classified into two types: 'identification and contact data' and 'location data'. Both types are categorised as 'collected data'. These types of data are not sensitive in themselves; rather, they are valuable and can be used to derive sensitive data, such as driving history or patterns, and health conditions. The fine-grained location data can easily be linked with 'identification and contact data' with reasonable effort as they are modelled, collected and processed by an EETS provider and accessed by a toll charger. The vulnerability of 'improper data model' can be easily exploited by EETS providers and toll chargers. Thus, the exploitability of PV.1 is assessed as '3. Significant'.

The severity of PV.1 is influenced by the relevant element of context-relevant processing norms. The relevant element of the processing norms is 'attributes', which refers to personal data. Thus, PV.1 enables TS.1 and TS.2 to breach the processing norms and violate the contextual integrity by making unjustified inference (TE.5) with the aim of deriving driving patterns for EETS users based on their deriving history. This type of aggregation is a threat event that may lead to the privacy harm PH.1. As such, the severity of PV.1 is assessed as '3. Significant'. The seriousness of PV.2, PV.3, PV.4 and PV.5 are similarly assessed based on the corresponding exploitability and severity, as per Table 8.

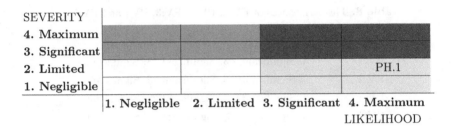

Fig. 3. Risk map in the context of EETS.

The threat event TE.5 may result from the exploitation of PV.1 and PV.2: both vulnerabilities are necessary for the occurrence of TE.5. The vulnerability PV.1 may be exploited by two different threat sources: TS.1 or TS.2. With reference to the harm tree, either one of those sources is sufficient to exploit the vulnerability PV.1. This leads to four possible exploits: EX.1–EX.4. According to the 'AND' connector, two of them are necessary for the occurrence of TE.5. In this case, the highest value of the overall likelihoods of EX.1 and EX.2 is taken: '4. Maximum'. Similarly, the highest value of the overall likelihoods of EX.3 and EX.4 is taken: '4. Maximum'. The overall likelihood of the threat event TE.5 is assessed as '4. Maximum' The overall likelihood of occurrence of all possible exploitations of TE.7 and TE.8 are similarly assessed, as per Table 9. As such, the likelihood of occurrence of PH.1 is assessed as '4. Maximum' by taking the highest value of the overall likelihood of occurrence of TE.5, TE.7 and TE.8.

5.4   Risk Level Assessment

The risk level of PH.1 is assessed as a pair of likelihood and severity: (4. Maximum, 2. Limited). Figure 3 shows that PH.1 corresponds to 'limited risks'.

6   Conclusions

We have presented a privacy risk-assessment approach that expands the PRIAM methodology in a number of ways. It assesses the level of a vulnerability by analysing its exploitability and severity, which are influenced by the characteristics of the main elements of context-relative processing norms. It also assesses the motivation of a threat source by analysing the value of personal data and the motives behind conducting data-processing activities that may lead to privacy harms in the given context. Third, it assesses the irreversibility of a threat event. Finally, it uses fixed levels of scale that for multiple stakeholders.

We will build upon this work in a number of ways. First, we will use additional case studies to further validate the approach and highlight its usefulness and practical impact in various domains. Second, we intend to identify a risk-assessment process to underpin a privacy-risk assessment methodology that can complement PIA processes. We also plan to use such a methodology as a means for managing the assessed privacy risks in a structured manner.

Acknowledgments. The authors would like to thank the reviewers for their constructive comments.

References

1. Alshammari, M., Simpson, A.: Personal data management: an abstract personal data lifecycle model. In: Teniente, E., Weidlich, M. (eds.) BPM 2017. LNBIP, vol. 308, pp. 685–697. Springer, Cham (2018). https://doi.org/10.1007/978-3-319-74030-0_55
2. Alshammari, M., Simpson, A.C.: Towards an effective PIA-based risk analysis: an approach for analysing potential privacy risks (2017). http://www.cs.ox.ac.uk/publications/publication11663-abstract.html
3. Clarke, R.: An evaluation of privacy impact assessment guidance documents. Int. Data Priv. Law **1**(2), 111–120 (2011)
4. Commission Nationale de l'Informatique et des Libertés: Methodology for Privacy Risk Management (How to implement the Data Protection Act) (2012). https://www.cnil.fr/sites/default/files/typo/document/CNIL-ManagingPrivacyRisks-Methodology.pdf
5. European Commission: Data Protection Impact Assessment Template for Smart Grid and Smart Metering systems (2014). http://ec.europa.eu/energy/sites/ener/files/documents/2014_dpia_smart_grids_forces.pdf
6. De, S.J., Le Métayer, D.: PRIAM: a privacy risk analysis methodology. In: Livraga, G., Torra, V., Aldini, A., Martinelli, F., Suri, N. (eds.) DPM/QASA -2016. LNCS, vol. 9963, pp. 221–229. Springer, Cham (2016). https://doi.org/10.1007/978-3-319-47072-6_15
7. De, S.J., Le Métayer, D.: A refinement approach for the reuse of privacy risk analysis results. In: Schweighofer, E., Leitold, H., Mitrakas, A., Rannenberg, K. (eds.) APF 2017. LNCS, vol. 10518, pp. 52–83. Springer, Cham (2017). https://doi.org/10.1007/978-3-319-67280-9_4
8. National Institute of Standards and Technology (NIST): Privacy Impact Assessment (PIA) (2012). https://www.nist.gov/document/nist-tip-pia-consolidatedpdf
9. Oetzel, M.C., Spiekermann, S.: A systematic methodology for privacy impact assessments: a design science approach. Eur. J. Inf. Syst. **23**(2), 126–150 (2014)
10. Solove, D.J.: A taxonomy of privacy. Univ. Pa. Law Rev. **154**(3), 477–564 (2006)
11. The European Commission: The European Electronic Toll Service (EETS): 2011 Guide for the Application of the Directive on the Interoperability of Electronic Road Toll Systems (2011). http://ec.europa.eu/transport/themes/its/road/application_areas/electronic_pricing_and_payment_en
12. UK Information Commissioner's Office (ICO): Privacy Impact Assessment Handbook (2009). www.adls.ac.uk/wp-content/uploads/2011/08/PIA-handbook.pdf
13. Wright, D.: Making privacy impact assessment more effective. Inf. Soc. **29**(5), 307–315 (2013)
14. Wright, D., Wadhwa, K.: A privacy impact assessment framework for data protection and privacy rights (2011). http://www.vub.ac.be/LSTS/pub/Dehert/507.pdf

Proactive Security Measures

PERSUADED: Fighting Social Engineering Attacks with a Serious Game

Dina Aladawy[1], Kristian Beckers[1,3], and Sebastian Pape[2,3(✉)]

[1] Institute of Informatics, Technische Universität München (TUM),
Boltzmannstr. 3, 85748 Garching, Germany
[2] Faculty of Economics and Business Administration, Goethe University Frankfurt,
Theodor-W.-Adorno-Platz 4, 60323 Frankfurt am Main, Germany
sebastian.pape@m-chair.de
[3] Social Engineering Academy (SEA) GmbH,
Eschersheimer Landstrasse 42, 60322 Frankfurt am Main, Germany

Abstract. Social engineering is the clever manipulation of the human element to acquire information assets. While technical security of most critical systems is high, the systems remain vulnerable to attacks from social engineers. The challenge in defeating social engineering is that it is a deceptive process that exploits human beings. Methods employed in social engineering do not differ much from those used to perform traditional fraud. This implies the applicability of defense mechanisms against the latter to the context of social engineering. Taking this problem into consideration, we designed a serious game that trains people against social engineering using defense mechanisms of social psychology. The results of our empirical evaluation of the game indicate that the game is able to raise awareness for social engineering in an entertaining way.

Keywords: Security controls · Social psychology · Gamification

1 Introduction

Chris Hadnagy [9] defines social engineering as "Any act that influences a person to take an action that may or may not be in their best interest". Kevin Mitnick told in an interview the following about the relevance of social engineering: "The hacker is going to look at the weakest link in the security chain, [...] if they see it's your people – if you don't educate your people about social engineering and they're easy targets – then that's where the attacker is going to attack." [6] Mitnick's statement was made over a decade ago and is still of utmost importance today as several current studies confirm [4,15].

In a previous work, we provided a mapping between social psychology and IT-security regarding Social Engineering defence [17]. In particular, we analysed social psychology methods of training against persuasion and mapped them to trainings in IT security. One identified gap is the lack of using *inoculation*, the repeated confrontation of people with a challenging situation in order to trigger

© Springer Nature Switzerland AG 2018
S. Furnell et al. (Eds.): TrustBus 2018, LNCS 11033, pp. 103–118, 2018.
https://doi.org/10.1007/978-3-319-98385-1_8

an appropriate response. Our contribution in this work is filling the identified gap with a serious game called *Persuaded*.

Djaouti et al. [5] define serious games as follows "A serious game or applied game is a game designed for a primary purpose other than pure entertainment.". We choose a serious game, because games recently built a reputation for getting employees of companies involved in security activities in an enjoyable and sustainable way. Williams et al. [20] introduced the protection poker game to prioritise risks in software engineering projects. Shostack [18] from Microsoft presented his Elevation of Privileges card game to practice threat analysis with software engineers. Furthermore, games are used as part of security awareness campaigns [7] and particularly as a part of social engineering threat analysis [1].

Our contribution Persuaded has inoculation incorporated into the core game mechanics to trigger resistance to social engineering attacks through exposing people to realistic attack scenarios. We designed our serious game to achieve the following goals: (a) increasing awareness of social engineering, (b) training resistance to persuasion and (c) addressing the general population. In order to provide the validity of the attack scenarios, we took all of them from scientific publications. The game enables employees to learn about social engineering, while practicing simultaneously. This immediate application of learned knowledge has proven to have lasting effects [8].

The game works as follows. Employees get confronted with a possible social engineering threat and have to select a defense mechanism. This defense mechanism is a pattern of behaviour ensuring a secure outcome. For example, an employee gets a phishing mail and is asked to open its attachment. Afterwards the player selects a countermeasure: "Do not open the email and inform the information security department immediately". The player gets immediate feedback whether the chosen defense is correct. In particular, the offered defenses can be part from a company's security policy. Non surprisingly, Soomro et al. found that development and execution of information security policy had a significant impact on the quality of management of information security [19]. Earlier, Pahnila et al. already concluded that appraisal and facilitating conditions have significant impact on attitude towards complying with the security policy while sanctions and awards do not have a significant effect on the intention to comply [14]. Thus, enabling employees to become familiar with the security policy in a playful way contributes to the holistic security of the company.

The remainder of the paper is organised as follows: We start with an overview of related work (Sect. 2) and a description of our game (Sect. 3). In the next sections we describe the study and its results. We end with a discussion of the results, threats to validity and the conclusion.

2   Related Work

As security is usually a secondary task, computer security training has often been perceived to be an uninteresting enforcement to users and managers. The approach of developing serious games has therefore been adopted to provide knowledge and training in that field.

CyberCIEGE is a role playing video game, where a player acts as an information security decision maker in an enterprise. Players' main responsibilities are to minimize the risk to the enterprise while allowing users to accomplish their goals. Similar to Persuaded, the game offers a simulation of the reality particularly portraying the need to maintain the balance between productivity and security. As decision makers, players get to make choices concerning users (i.e. How extensive will background checks be?), computers (i.e. How will computers be networked?) and physical security (i.e. Who is allowed to enter a zone?) while monitoring the consequences of their choices. When compared to Persuaded, we recognized CyberCIEGE offered several advantages common to those offered by Persuaded. For instance, players are in a defensive mode and they get to make decisions and experience their consequences. CyberCIEGE even incorporates assets and resources in the game, which is a missing element in Persuaded. On the other hand, the game requires longer time to learn and to play [10].

PlayingSafe is a serious game in the domain of social engineering. It consists of multiple choice questions which are wrapped in typical mechanics of a board game. Since questions provided are exclusive to social engineering, the game is very similar to ours. The main difference lies however in the focus in the topic of social engineering. PlayingSafe asks questions in the fields of Phishing, advanced fee fraud, spam and others, being a category that covers less common attacks. Our game on the other hand covers a broader field without offering depth in each topic. Additionally, our game incorporates strategy favouring the entertainment element, in order to enhance the game experience the game provides [12].

SEAG is a serious game designed to raise awareness of social engineering. The game utilizes levels that tackle different cognitive aspects and hence provide an effective learning experience. The first level consists of quiz-like questions to build a knowledge base for the players. The second level is a match game where players have to match social engineering terms with respective pictures. Finally, the players are presented with real life scenarios to analyse pertaining to threat. This simulation of real life application of the learnt lesson should test players ability to detect attacks- an approach very similar to inoculation [13].

3   Game Description

To fill the gap, identified by Schaab et al. [17], we designed a game that does not only provide knowledge, but rather trains people by implementing theories from social psychology on the resistance to persuasion. In this section, we give a brief overview of key design decisions, their rationale and our goals (cf. Fig. 1).

Game Requirements: We refined our goals and report them in the following categorised by key areas of game design.

Ease to Learn: A low level of complexity allows to learn the game more easily, and thus is more attractive to novices in game play.

Ease to Play: To be easily integrated into the players' daily routine, the game should have a minimum of necessary preparations and a short play time. Given online games require less preparation than tabletop games, it should be online.

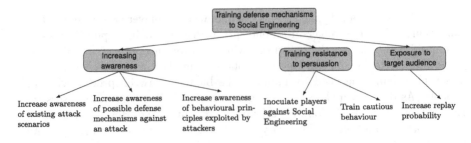

Fig. 1. Definition of goals for the game

Replay Value: The replay value depends to a large amount on the ease to learn and play of the game. In order to maintain the appeal to expert players as well, game mechanics should provide a substantial entertainment element along with long term motivation and challenging the players. As multi-player games depend on the availability of other players, a single player game is preferred.

Player's Role: In order to inoculate players against social engineering, they have to be in the position of an attack receiver.

Textual Content: Since our awareness goals cater for presenting attack/defense scenarios, the game design should support the presentation of textual content.

Game Mechanics: In order to create a single player game with easy rules and low complexity, we decided to aim for a patience and solitaire game approach [11] instead of e.g. involving machine learning approaches [3] which would tend to result in a game with multi-player feeling. Thus, the player may choose between playing cards from his/her hand or draw the next card from the deck. As known from patience games, the deck is shuffled automatically for each game.

Types of cards and card functionalities: Four types of cards were chosen.

1. *Attack* cards include attack scenarios in textual form.
2. *Defense* cards describe a pattern of behaviour that protects the player against an exploitation attempt. A defense card exists for each attack card.
3. *See The Future* cards allow the player to take a peek on the three upper cards in the card deck.
4. *Skip turn* cards allow the player to take the upper card of the deck and put it below the deck.

Mechanics and rules: A turn in Persuaded consists of the following rules:

1. Play an action card or draw a card from the deck.
2. If you draw any card that is NOT an Attack, the turn is over. Put the card to your hand cards.
3. If you draw an Attack card, you *have to* play a Defense card. The correct (wrong) defense gains you 10 (−5) points. The Defense card is only discarded if you had a correct match. Otherwise it's put back in the deck.

4. If you draw an Attack card and don't have *any* Defense card in your hand, you lose one heart (life). If you lost all three hearts the game is over.
5. The game is won if the deck is empty and is lost if the player loses all 3 lives before finishing the deck.

These mechanics have several consequences. Drawing an Attack card *forces* the player to play a Defense card. Thus, even if a player notices he has no matching defense, he has to burn a defense card. This was introduced to further encourage cautiousness when drawing cards from the deck. The player needs to use *See the future* cards to have a peek on the pile and then postpone attacks if he does not have a matching defense by playing a *Skip turn* card. This also forces the player to match upcoming attacks and defenses in hand before drawing form the pile.

Long Term Motivation: As known from patience games, the deck is shuffled automatically for each game. This causes each game to be different from the game(s) before. Thus, the player needs to come up with different moves to win the game and can not simply try until he/she finds the 'optimal solution'. Additionally, the introduced randomness, causes Attack cards to appear before their respective Defense cards in the deck. Therefore – if action cards are not distributed accordingly – this may lead to situations where the player simply has to guess what might be the 'best next move'. The idea behind this rationale is that not only has the player to learn how to make best use of "See the future"- and "Skip turn"-cards, but also needs to have some luck in order to achieve the best possible score. We balanced it in a way, that it is always possible to win, but might not be possible to get the maximum score.

Game Content: In order to provide the knowledge needed to increase players' awareness, scenarios of attacks and their respective defenses were incorporated in the game. We selected eight attack scenarios that represent different social engineering attack types, namely Baiting, Phishing, Tailgating, Mail attachment, physical and virtual Impersonation, Voice of Authority and Popup Windows. The attacks were inspired by a card game for eliciting security requirements [2]. Defense cards, on the other hand, confronted us with challenges, as it is not very intuitive to act against behavioural principles, which is exactly the element exploited by social engineering. We identified explicit defenses encouraged from best practice by security departments in different companies. Initially, defenses were meant to be generic and applicable for several attack scenarios. However, resulting from our selection of proposed scenarios, we noticed, that all had similar generic defenses, i.e. to verify the source or the person. Hence, we decided to incorporate one-to-one matches thereby providing eight specific Defense cards.

Game Interface Design: In confirmation with Don Normann's Design principles [16] for user interface design, we opted for an intuitive user interface that adheres to the needs of novices as well as experts in game play. The proposed design was further tested and adapted according to the feedback we received during the piloting phase.We used different colors for each type of the *cards* (see Fig. 2). For the attack/defense scenarios, we kept the text as short as possible and divided the content in up to three bullet points. Action cards consist of graphics

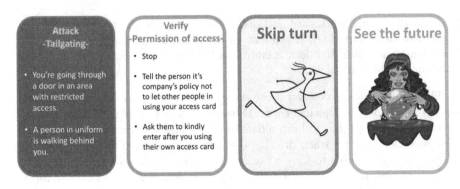

Fig. 2. From left to right: Attack card, Defense card, Skip card, See the future card

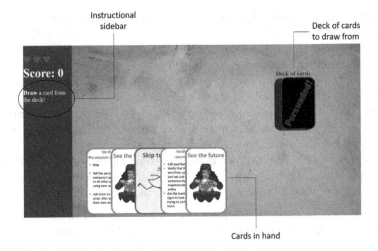

Fig. 3. Initial game setting

that reflect their functionality, attack and defense cards have titles summarizing their content. However, titles of matching pairs are not the same. This design decision was intentionally incorporated, in order to assure that players have to read the cards' contents. The *Game Setting* (see Fig. 3) was designed to be both intuitive and informative.

Cards in Hand: The overlapping display of the current cards in hand simulates the holding of cards in real life (cf. Normann's mapping principle). When a player moves the mouse over a card, this card is emphasized by moving the other cards to the left and right to allow the player a complete view of the card. This enhances the player's experience while maintaining readability of the content.

Scoring: As score and lives function as a reward and punishment system, it is important to make sure, they capture players' attention when they change. Therefore, we decided to reflect modifications of scores and lives using dynamic feedback. In addition to using coloured terms such as "Defended", "Wrong match" and "Persuaded", the decrease or increase of score and lives is at the top left.

We show the game in detail in our Video Tutorial for Persuaded[1]. Furthermore, we stored the data of our experiment and an extensive technical report online[2].

4   Study Design

Prior to conducting the case study, Persuaded has been evaluated through several rounds during the design and the development phase. First of all, the scenarios were tested for suitability of attacks and defenses, in addition to the ease of understanding of the presented content. Following this, the game's functionality and mechanics were tested during a piloting phase. The participants for the pilot tests were very heterogeneous. Play tests and semi-structured interviews were conducted with 3 security experts, a psychology expert, a games engineering student, an informatics student and a philosophy student. Feedback provided in this phase, was largely incorporated in the design and the implementation. The content was reviewed by 2 security experts and 2 informatics students. The scenarios' text was reviewed by a student in Translation Studies.

4.1   Preparation and Collection of Data

The flow of a session with a subject consisted of the following steps:

1. Answer the pre-questionnaire.
2. Watch the game tutorial as many times as you need.
3. Ask questions about the game rules.
4. Play the game.
5. Answer the post-questionnaire.

We employed first and second degree methods for our data collection. Before the session started, subjects were encouraged to provide feedback throughout the session. Many subjects took this into account and offered valuable feedback on the questionnaire, the game and the tutorial. Some subjects even played the game in a think aloud mode, which turned out to be very useful feedback. Furthermore, second degree data was collected during the game play to evaluate to what extent the game adheres to requirements specified in prior sections. We logged all decisions made during the game, making it possible to replicate the entire round. In addition, the time to play as well as the final score and number of lives left was collected. This enabled us to analyse the effects of our random factor on the entire game experience.

---

[1] https://youtu.be/UWhc1e6ngd0.
[2] https://sites.google.com/site/researchpersuaded/.

Pre- and Post Questionnaires. The effect of inoculation can be measured by observing peoples' reactions to stronger persuasive attacks as the ones they were inoculated with. This implied that we have to present players with stronger scenarios of social engineering after the game in order to be able to derive whether it was effective or not. This however, was not enough as an effect measurement as we were not aware, whether people were vulnerable before the game at all or not. Hence, we decided to conduct questionnaires before and after the game was played. The questionnaires presented social engineering scenarios as single choice questions, where players had to choose one of the given behaviours as a reaction to the given situation. The same scenarios with the same reactions were presented both in the pre-and post-questionnaire. This was intentionally done in order to be able to measure effects of the game as change of answers. In addition to the situations presented in the pre-questionnaire, demographic data was collected to draw conclusions for different types of people given our exposure goals. Moreover, data concerning technical background was collected which might be relevant to scenarios such as *Phishing* and *Popup Window* as well as malicious *Mail Attachments*. Lastly, items were used to measure background knowledge of social engineering and to measure the subjective perception of vulnerability in order to have an indicator of optimism bias. Players were also asked to indicate at which point they understood the game to measure the learning curve and the effectiveness of the tutorial and whether they would play this game again or not.

4.2 Data

The equation introduced to evaluate the questionnaires was:

Learning outcome $= \sum$ security-aware behaviour in post-questionnaire $- \sum$ security-aware behaviour in pre-questionnaire.

For quantitatively evaluating the players' decisions throughout the game, we relied on the following data.

Matching of Attacks and Defenses. We used a half automatic analysis process to measure the number of attacks that were correctly defended as well as the number of burned defense cards. This data maps the understandability of the content of the cards. Moreover, as we are not game designers we decided to use them as an indicator of the impact of certain game elements such as the randomness of the cards' order and the variability of Attack and Defense cards.

Usage of Action Cards. We also collected data concerning the number of cards that were foreseen and the number of cards that were unknowingly drawn. This information was not only used to evaluate the game flow, given that Flow cards are key elements of the winning strategy. They were also used as an indicator of players' risk behaviour and alertness during the game play.

Reward and Punishment System. Lastly we collected the score data as well as the number of lives left. This information was employed to test whether our reward and punishment systems are effective or whether they are influenced by the random element in the game.

5   Results

The study was conducted with 21 participants including 9 female and 12 male participants. The age ranged from 19 to 35 years. Given our exposure goals, we sampled subjects with different backgrounds regarding their studies. 16 of the participants indicated they are university students, while 5 are currently pursuing an academic career. We disregard one participant's results. These were invalid due to changes of the content of the questionnaires. In contrast to the variation in age and occupation, our sample is very homogeneous in technical background. It is important to mention that at this point, we only consider technical background in relation to how often the computer is used, which is sufficient for understanding the game content. Answering this question, 95% indicated they use their computers daily while 43% use it daily for job related matters.

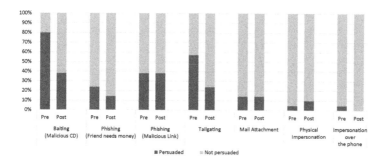

Fig. 4. Number of reactions reflecting falling for the attack in comparison to security aware reactions before and after the game

5.1   Results Relevant to Inoculation

Our game is an implementation of inoculation against social engineering. Its effectiveness as a training method was evaluated using pre- and post-questionnaires in addition to several metrics.

Reactions to Situations. Participants were given social engineering scenarios and asked to choose one reaction, they were most likely to adopt if confronted with such a scenario. The questions proposed three answers with one mapping the security-aware behaviour when encountering a potential threat and the other two options reflecting extreme reactions. The first extreme is a paranoid reaction, whereas the second reflects falling victim for the attack. Results from the pre-questionnaire show that in 5 of the 7 scenarios the majority of the participants would have behaved in a manner that would not endanger them. In the other two scenarios, a high number of subjects would have fallen for the attack.

The results of the post-questionnaire show significant differences. For the *Tailgating* scenario which describes the situation of meeting a strange lady who is locked out of the house building and whether a person should verify her identity before letting her in or not, the number of participants indicating they would behave in a security-aware manner rises from 43% to 76%. Nevertheless, the *Baiting* attack which questions whether free handed CDs from street musicians should be scanned or not, remains the one scenario where the reaction indicating falling for the attack is the one chosen the most. For the *Phishing (Malicious Link)* and *Mail attachment* attack, the numbers do not show significant change. For the remaining scenarios only slight changes are noticeable, once even favouring the rise of number of participants who would fall for the attack as it is the case in the *Physical impersonation* attack. Figure 4 shows an overview of the change in responses triggered by our game. Given inoculation relies on repeatedly confronting individuals with mild persuasive attacks, we also measured the number of times players read an attack card in the game which indicates that each attack is read 1.5 times in average.

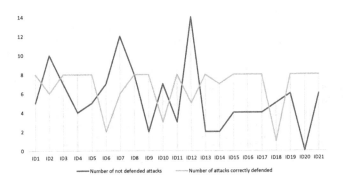

Fig. 5. Defended vs. Not defended attacks for all participants

5.2   Reward/Punishment System

The maximally achievable score is 80 points if the player did not make any wrong match or if the player did a wrong match at the beginning of the game when the score was still 0. Only one player was able to score 80 points and 2 players could score 75 with an average score of 51 points. The majority of players achieved a score of 65 points. Considering the lives maintained in the game, 15 players were able to finish the deck maintaining at least one heart while 6 others lost the game before finishing the deck due to losing their lives (Fig. 5).

5.3   Time to Play

The time needed to play the game ranged from 02:53 min to 16:03 with an average of 08:09 min. We further differentiate the time to play needed to win the game by finishing the cards in deck and the time to play for lost games. The range measured for games that were won through finishing the deck lies between 05:05 and 16:03 min with an average of 8:33 min.

5.4 Matching of Cards

For 15 of the participants, the number of successfully defended attacks is higher or equal to the number of not defended ones. The latter further includes attacks that were drawn without having defense cards in hand. Not defended attacks can be further categorised in mismatched attacks (75% of not defended attacks) and attacks that were drawn without having defense cards in the hand (25% of not defended attacks).

We further distinguish mismatched attacks in those, where the player had the matching defense in hand, as in the player is accountable for the mismatch and those, where the player was forced to play a Defense card. For all participants the number of burned defenses is higher than the number of *truly* mismatched attacks. Moreover, 66% of the participants did not even once mismatch an attack while the matching Defense card is in hand.

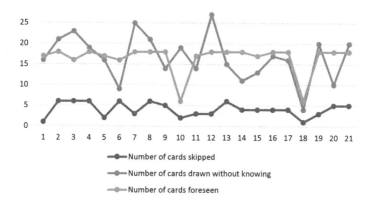

Fig. 6. Overview of skipped cards, cards foreseen and cards drawn blindly

5.5 Action Cards

The key strategy to winning the game is to use *See The Future* cards and then avoid attacks, whose defenses are not in hand, with *Skip* cards. This is why we analysed players' usage of action cards considering players can see a maximum of 18 cards before drawing them and skip a maximum of 6 cards (Fig. 6).

We further analysed players risk behaviour according to when cards are drawn blindly despite having a *See The Future* card. Our results show that a total of 16 players have drawn at least one card without seeing it, having a *See The Future* card in the hand. An average of 2.6 cards were drawn blindly despite having the chance to foresee them. More importantly, however, is the number of cards drawn blindly despite having both a *See The Future* card and a *Skip* card. This card combination would have offered the chance to knowingly avoid drawing that card. This was done by 10 of the participants with an average of 1.6 cards drawn blindly despite having the chance to knowingly avoid them.

5.6   Learning Curve and Replay Value

Finally, subjects were asked to indicate whether they would play this game again. 17 participants (81%) expressed that they would play this game again while the remaining 4 participants claimed they would not. When asked about the understandability of the game mechanics, 14 people (67%) mentioned they understood the game right away (following only the tutorial) while the remaining 7 participants needed some turns to fully understand how the game works.

6   Discussion

Through the conduction of interviews with the players, we could collect feedback that is of value to future work. More importantly, the feedback showed potential threats to the validity of the data collected in the questionnaires.

6.1   Feedback on Pre-Questionnaire:

The pre-questionnaire included social engineering scenarios, where players had to chose a reaction. Particularly, the baiting scenario, where street musicians would intentionally offer malicious CDs, was perceived by two participants to be an "interesting new attack, [they] have never thought of". The tailgating attack was stated to be relevant to one of the participants. Particularly these two attacks were the only ones in the pre-questionnaire, where most participants chose the reaction, that would favour the attackers intentions. We conclude, that these attacks were new to the participants choosing that reaction. This is backed up by the interview comments in addition to the results of the final question in the post-questionnaire where seven participants indicated the *Tailgating* attack was new to them while four indicated the same for the *Baiting* attack. Improvement suggestions were to incorporate an "other" option as a possible reaction to the situations and to collect data on the used operating system, given it implies a certain security level provided by the technology alone.

6.2   Feedback on the Game Mechanics:

We received extensive feedback on our randomness factor of our game.

General Perception: The general perceptions during game play provided feedback that conforms with our design goals. One participant stated, that for them the game simulates the reality. The player further explained, that in real life, it is rather difficult to expect social engineering attacks and always be ready for them, which they found was mapped through the random factor. Furthermore, the player mentioned that usually even the most cautious people might fall victim for social engineering again supporting the vulnerability in the game, where players are not able to defend themselves when drawing attacks before their respective defenses. Another participant provided feedback on the challenge level in the game saying that "one has to think". For this player, the game was also "easy to understand", reflecting the modesty of the trade-off between those two conflicting elements. Finally, the player emphasised the importance of the game being single player for the replay value, saying that he can "play the game another 3 times just right now". This data conforms with the data collected on replay in the post-questionnaire underlining the high potential for replay of the game.

Understanding of the Game Mechanics: We opted for ease of learning, realised by simple mechanics, a detailed tutorial and an intuitive game interface design. Several questions asked during game play, however, indicate otherwise. Misconceptions and uncertainty were particularly common regarding the functionality and usage of action cards. Examples for questions, we received concerning action cards are: *What does a "See the future" card really do?*, *What does a "Skip" card really do?*, *How many cards are skipped by playing a "Skip" card?*, *Will skipped cards be added in the deck?*. We cannot determine, whether these questions were asked due to lack of understanding or rather to confirm prior understanding of the functionality. However this data explains the relatively small numbers of wasted *See The Future* cards and *Skip* cards, which were played without having foreseen what was being skipped. We assume the wrong usage of the action cards happened at the beginning of the game, as four players have indicated, they needed some turns to fully grasp the game mechanics. Five players asked for the number of cards in the deck. We assume, this was asked in order to develop certain strategies rather than to indicated extensive length of the game duration, which is further supported by our measurement of game duration being 09:45 min in average.

Card Content: The serious element of Persuaded lies in the content of the cards. This is why, it is important to monitor whether cards are read in detail or not. Four players indicated after the first couple turns, that they have not been reading the cards' contents, while two others attempted to match the titles of attack and defense cards in the beginning. Still, all six players started reading the content of the cards after a couple of turns. We assume this was motivated by the punishments they received for wrong matches. This data is particularly relevant to data collected on the number of mismatched cards while having the correct defense in hand. Given this only happened to an average of 0.52 cards, we build the assumption that *truly* mismatched cards were rather a result of not reading the cards than a result of the complexity of the content. Still, one player further indicated, that the match between attacks and defenses was not always clear. This was however intentionally incorporated in the design, as we wanted players to reflect about the scenarios and the defenses instead of recognizing the matches from the cards. Furthermore, one player suggested, it would be better to see all the cards before playing the game to create a mental scheme of matching cards. Thereby, players can solely focus on training the strategy during the game and would strengthen the mental scheme by recalling matches between cards.

Randomness in the Game: The randomness of the game was not very welcomed by the participants. Although one player indicated, it provided a simulation of real life, four other players perceived themselves to have no control in the game with two players evaluating the game as unfair. An important aspect influenced by the randomness is replay value. Replay value is usually supported by the probability of the player to excel in the game play. Having a random factor largely limits improvements in the game as players' decisions are only partially relevant for the game results. This was further confirmed by two players, who said they would only play the game again, if they could get better at it.

7   Threats to Validity

We discuss potential threats to the validity according to Wohlin [21].

Construct Validity. Questions in the post-questionnaire are supposed to indicate probable reactions of the participants to given scenarios. There is, however, a possibility that participants remember their answers to the same questions during the pre- questionnaire. However, if players are aware, the game has educational purpose, this might lead to a conscious choice of the correct answers to indicate having understood the content. In addition, several metrics were derived from players' decisions during the game session as explained in the previous section. This data is however subject to effects of concentration and motivation during the game. Moreover the results assume that the functionality of the game and the different cards is understood at the beginning of the game in contrast to the feedback received on the learning curve.

Internal Validity. We measure the learning outcome as the difference between the sum of correctly answered questions in the pre- and post-questionnaire. We cannot determine whether players are inoculated by the scenarios of the game or by the scenarios mentioned in the pre-questionnaire as these also reveal persuasive arguments used by social engineers. This effect of an inoculation at an early point is attempted to be overcome by hiding the subject of the study from participants until the questions of the pre-questionnaire are answered.

External Validity. We conducted the case study with a heterogeneous population regarding their educational background and could identify acceptability of the game even for subjects without prior knowledge in security or social engineering. However, our results regarding the effectiveness and the learning outcome of the game are to be considered taking the random factor of the game and other threats to validity into account.

8   Conclusion

We designed, implemented and evaluated a serious game for training social engineering defense mechanisms, called "Persuaded". Several goals were specified and refined to achieve the serious purpose of the game: *Increase awareness:* of attack scenarios, defense mechanisms and exploited behavioural principles. *Train resistance to persuasion* by inoculation against social engineering and to train cautious behaviour. Finally, to cater for *exposure to the general population* through increasing replay probability and ease of understanding of the social engineering threat. Results of our case study indicate great potential for the application of social psychology defense mechanisms to social engineering. Our serious game offers a tool for monitoring decision making processes and risk-taking behaviour. More importantly, it was successful at raising awareness to new attack scenarios in an entertaining way such that people would enjoy learning about social engineering and how they can defend themselves against it.

Acknowledgements. This research has been partially supported by the Federal Ministry of Education and Research Germany (BMBF) with project grant number 16KIS0240.

References

1. Beckers, K., Pape, S.: A serious game for eliciting social engineering security requirements. In: Proceedings of the 24th IEEE International Conference on Requirements Engineering, RE 2016, pp. 16–25. IEEE Computer Society (2016)
2. Beckers, K., Pape, S., Fries, V.: HATCH: hack and trick capricious humans - a serious game on social engineering. In: Proceedings of British HCI 2016, pp. 1–3. ACM (2016)
3. Bowling, M., Fürnkranz, J., Graepel, T., Musick, R.: Machine learning and games. Mach. Learn. **63**(3), 211–215 (2006)
4. Dimensional Research: The Risk of Social Engineering on Information Security: A Survey of IT Profesionals (2011). http://docplayer.net/11092603-The-risk-of-social-engineering-on-information-security.html
5. Djaouti, D., Alvarez, J., Jessel, J.-P.: Classifying serious games: the G/P/S model. In: Handbook of Research on Improving Learning and Motivation Through Educational Games: Multidisciplinary Approaches, pp. 118–136 (2011)
6. ENISA: Social engineering: exploiting the weakest links. Whitepaper, October 2008. https://www.enisa.europa.eu/publications/archive/social-engineering
7. Gondree, M., Peterson, Z.N.J., Denning, T.: Security through play. IEEE Secur. Priv. **11**(3), 64–67 (2013)
8. Greitzer, F.L., Kuchar, O.A., Huston, K.: Cognitive science implications for enhancing training effectiveness in a serious gaming context. J. Educ. Resour. Comput., **7**(3), (2007)
9. Hadnagy, C.: Social Engineering: The Art of Human Hacking. Wiley, Hoboken (2010)
10. Irvine, C.E., Thompson, M.F., Allen, K.: Cyberciege: gaming for information assurance. IEEE Secur. Priv. **3**(3), 61–64 (2005)
11. Morehead, A.H.: The Complete Book of Solitaire and Patience Games. Read Books Ltd., Redditch (2014)
12. Newbould, M., Furnell, S.: Playing safe: a prototype game for raising awareness of social engineering. In: Australian Information Security Management Conference, p. 4 (2009)
13. Olanrewaju, A.-S.T., Zakaria, N.H.: Social engineering awareness game (SEAG): an empirical evaluation of using game towards improving information security awareness. In: Proceedings of the 5th International Conference on Computing and Informatics, ICOCI 2015 (2015). Accessed 16 Oct 2016

14. Pahnila, S., Siponen, M., Mahmood, A.: Employees' behavior towards IS security policy compliance. In: 40th Annual Hawaii International Conference on System Sciences, HICSS 2007, p. 156b. IEEE (2007)
15. PWC: Information Security Breaches Survey (2016). https://www.pwc.be/en/documents/media-centre/publications/2016/information-security-breaches-survey-2016.pdf
16. Rogers, Y., Sharp, H., Preece, J., Tepper, M.: Interaction design: beyond human-computer interaction. netWorker: Craft Netw. Comput. 11(4), 34 (2007)
17. Schaab, P., Beckers, K., Pape, S.: Social engineering defence mechanisms and counteracting training strategies. Inf. Comput. Secur. 25(2), 206–222 (2017)
18. Shostack, A.: Threat Modeling: Designing for Security, 1st edn. Wiley, Hoboken (2014)
19. Soomro, Z.A., Shah, M.H., Ahmed, J.: Information security management needs more holistic approach: a literature review. Int. J. Inf. Manage. 36(2), 215–225 (2016)
20. Williams, L., Meneely, A., Shipley, G.: Protection Poker: the new software security "game". IEEE Secur. Priv. 8(3), 14–20 (2010)
21. Wohlin, C., et al.: Experimentation in Software Engineering: An Introduction. The Kluwer International Series in Software Engineering. Springer, Boston (2012). https://doi.org/10.1007/978-1-4615-4625-2

Developing and Evaluating a Five Minute Phishing Awareness Video

Melanie Volkamer[1]([envelope]), Karen Renaud[2,3], Benjamin Reinheimer[1],
Philipp Rack[1], Marco Ghiglieri[1], Peter Mayer[1], Alexandra Kunz[1],
and Nina Gerber[1]

[1] Karlsruhe Institute of Technology and Technische Universität Darmstadt,
Darmstadt, Germany
{melanie.volkamer,benjamin.reinheimer,philipp.rack,marco.ghiglieri,
peter.mayer,alexandra.kunz,nina.gerber}@kit.edu
[2] Abertay University, Dundee, Scotland
k.renaud@abertay.ac.uk
[3] University of South Africa, Pretoria, South Africa

Abstract. Confidence tricksters have always defrauded the unwary. The computer era has merely extended their range and made it possible for them to target anyone in the world who has an email address. Nowadays, they send phishing messages that are specially crafted to deceive. Improving user awareness has the potential to reduce their effectiveness. We have previously developed and empirically-validated phishing awareness programmes. Our programmes are specifically designed to neutralize common phish-related misconceptions and teach people how to detect phishes. Many companies and individuals are already using our programmes, but a persistent niggle has been the amount of time required to complete the awareness programme. This paper reports on how we responded by developing and evaluating a condensed phishing awareness video that delivered phishing awareness more efficiently. Having watched our video, participants in our evaluation were able to detect phishing messages significantly more reliably right after watching the video (compared to before watching the video). This ability was also demonstrated after a retention period of eight weeks after first watching the video.

Keywords: Phishing awareness · User study · Retention study

1 Introduction

More than twenty years after its emergence, phishing still succeeds [1,37,43]. Phishing attacks are increasingly sophisticated. It used to be easy to spot phishing messages due to poor language use and incorrect spelling; nowadays phishers are far smarter, sending plausible-looking messages calculated to deceive. They have also migrated from exclusively using email to plying their trade on a range of messaging platforms including messages in social media and messaging apps.

S. Furnell et al. (Eds.): TrustBus 2018, LNCS 11033, pp. 119–134, 2018.
https://doi.org/10.1007/978-3-319-98385-1_9

A very popular trick is to entice the target to follow a link that will install malware or visit a *doppelgänger* website. The latter will persuade victims to divulge sensitive information, such as their access credentials. Automated detection is a powerful defence, but far from 100% effective [3,15]. To narrow the gap left by technical measures, we need to make recipients of online messages aware of how to detect phishing attempts.

Our research group has a long history of developing phishing awareness programmes (including apps, flyers, reading material, presentations for seminars) and have carried out several user studies verifying their effectiveness [5–7,26,28,33,39–41]. Our initial programmes required learners to spend between 20 to 45 min completing the awareness programmes. Evaluations showed that all programmes significantly increased phishing detection rates. However, companies are concerned about the amount of time employees have to commit to these programmes. In response, we developed a video, which made it possible for us to shorten the time people needed to commit, because we could benefit from the visualisation functionality videos offer. The video now lasts only 5 min. The video was developed iteratively, incorporating feedback from people with various backgrounds (such as lay users, video producers, psychologists and security experts). The final video was evaluated by 89 participants who detected phishing messages significantly more often after watching the video. Many were able to demonstrate a retained ability to do this eight weeks later. The video was improved even further based on the feedback provided during the evaluation and the result of the evaluation, i.e. for those attack types participants performed worst, the explanations in the video were improved. Thus, our contribution is twofold: (1) the developed video based on previous research on phishing awareness programmes, and (2) its evaluation both straight after watching the video and during a retention study eight weeks after watching the video. We published the video[1] under the Creative Commons licence CC BY-SA 4.0 to remove all barriers to its use.

2   Development Process

2.1   Identification of the Relevant Content

The content to be covered is the following. The video should make the watcher aware of commonly-used phisher *strategies*. For example, trustworthy-looking messages, with familiar design and language employing psychological tricks to entice victims to click on an embedded link. They should also be aware of the possible *consequences* of clicking on a link. For example, malware could be downloaded onto their device. The web page they visit could look authentic, but actually be owned by a phisher. If credentials are divulged on this *faux* site, they could be used to facilitate identity theft. The video also deliberately addresses common phish-related *misconceptions* identified in the literature [11,12,17,18,20].

---

[1] German Phishing Video: https://www.youtube.com/watch?v=XeslAkZIuwY&t=9s
English Phishing Video: https://www.youtube.com/watch?v=F4y2wzYpIKw.

These include the following: (1) Phishers only send emails. In fact, they also use other mediums such as short text and social networking messages; (2) Phishing always harvests online banking credentials. In fact, phishers can actually fake any arbitrary web site: credentials are what they want; (3) The displayed name of the sender can be trusted to reflect the actual sender. In fact, details are faked very easily. The displayed sender name cannot be relied upon to signal authenticity; (4) Only wealthy people are targeted by phishers. On the contrary, anyone can be targeted, independently of how well known they are, how wealthy or their status in an organisation. (5) Technical security mechanisms are able to catch and block all phish messages. Actually, sophisticated phishers design their messages in such a way that the technical measures do not catch them; (6) The 'S' in HTTPS is an infallible signal of integrity. In reality, many phishers use website certificates to ally fears[2]; and (7) Trustworthy phrases in a website URL are a signal of trustworthiness. In fact, these are merely tricks used by the unscrupulous to trap the unwary. Thus, the video should help people to distinguish between phishing and genuine messages. Similar to our more time-consuming awareness programmes, we focus the learner's attention on the difference between the URL's actual destination and the destination it seems to be. Only by examining the link can people reliably distinguish between phish and genuine messages. The following instructions, explanations, and hints were included in the video:

Instruction-1: Locate the Actual Destination of a Displayed Link

The first step in phish detection is to know how to identify the actual destination the link will send people to. It might be in a tooltip, a status bars or in a special dialogue. They also need to be aware of the nuances behind links. Sometimes the actual destination is concealed behind a button or image or text like 'click here'. The actual destination is often hidden unless the person knows how to look for it. In rare cases the actual URL is displayed in the clear. The displayed tooltip might be faked too, in order to lull people into a false sense of security.

Instruction-2: Identify the So-Called Who-Area of the URL

After people have identified the actual destination URL, they should know how to identify the domain, what we refer to as the *who-area*. In the video, we told people that this is the last two terms that are separated by a dot before the first stand-alone "/" of a URL[3].

We also tell them that phishers deceive people by embedding the genuine company name somewhere in the URL *rather than the who-area*. They could place it either before or after the who-area. They should not rely on the signal conveyed by the use of HTTPS. Examples of phishing URLs are provided:

      https://www.gmail.com.mail-nows.com/login
    https://mail-nows.com/https://www.gmail.com/login.

---

[2] To avoid confusion we used https in all our phishing examples.

[3] The study was carried out in Germany which meant we focused on domains with two terms e.g. amazon.de and we did not consider other conventions followed by countries like the U.K. with three terms, e.g. amazon.co.uk.

Instruction 3: Check Authenticity of the Who-Area

Having located the who-area, the final step is to verify its authenticity, basically by checking it character by character. They are made aware of the fact that phishers often (1) use trustworthy terms (e.g. 'secure-shop.com') in the who-area; (2) stealthily replace characters. For example, they might replace a 'd' with 'cl' or introduce typos such as 'mircosoft'.

2.2 Video Development

We developed a story and a text for the voice-over based on the content being communicated by the messages, together with someone professionally developing awareness videos. We used simple language and non-technical terms (e.g. use of the phrase "who-area" for domain). We labelled screenshots to direct their attention to the location of important information (e.g. the status bar). We asked people of different ages with varying backgrounds and levels of expertise with IT and security to provide feedback to help us to improve and refine the video. The professional video producer developed the video using our text and underlying story. The video was improved, based on feedback from a number of people who were representative of the anticipated participants.

3 Evaluation – Methodology

The evaluation focused on the video's effectiveness in order to reveal significant improvements, in terms of phish detection ability. The following hypotheses were formulated:

H1: Participants, having watched the video, correctly judge the legitimacy of messages more often i.e. identify more phishing messages, and identify legitimate messages more reliably.

H2: Eight weeks after watching the video, participants correctly judge the legitimacy of messages more often i.e. identify more phishing messages, and identify legitimate messages more reliably.

3.1 Study Design

We conducted an online between-subjects study in two sessions. Hypothesis 1 is evaluated with the data from the first session and hypothesis 2 is evaluated with the data from both sessions. The tasks in the first evaluation session were:

1. Judge screenshots of messages. Decide whether each is a phish or legitimate.
2. Watch the video.
3. Judge screenshots of messages. When participants were asked to judge messages, the question was: "*Is this a fraudulent message?*". Possible answers were: '*Yes, it is a fraudulent message*'. '*No, it is not a fraudulent message*'.
4. Provide video feedback (free text answers).

5. Provide demographic information.
6. Grant permission for us to contact them to engage with a retention study. If they consented, we requested their email address and provided them with a random code to ensure an anonymous link between sessions.

During the second session (approximately eight weeks later), consenting participants were invited to participate in the retention study, which required them again to judge screenshots of phish and legitimate messages (i.e. purely step 3 from the first session). We used the SosciSurvey online platform. The study was pre-tested and the feedback from the pre-test addressed and refinements effected. The changes were mainly related to the content of the messages participants were asked to judge. We decided to go for a quiz-like evaluation, with security being the participant's primary task. The alternative would have been a study design in which the participant's primary task is related to a cover story. This would theoretically not prime them to expect and detect phish messages. We had a number of reasons for choosing the former design. While one could argue that the second option would have more external validity, it would have been hard to maintain the deception in a lab study. As soon as participants watched the video they would have known what the study was about. We could have attempted a field study i.e. getting people to watch the video then sending phishing alike messages at some unpredictable time in the future and measure how many click on links or open an attachment. It is challenging to measure the participant's ability to identify phish at a distance though. If they do not click, the message might not have been delivered, or they might not click because they do not have an account with the "source". When they click, it might be because they know of the study setting and want to know what happens if they click. We would not be able to determine whether they actually inspected the URL or not, which is what the video trains them to do correctly. In particular, in a field study, we cannot control whether some receive the email on a smartphone with a more challenging setting than on a laptop. Thus, there are many uncontrollable factors that could confound the findings.

Therefore, we decided to go for a study design in which security is participants' primary task. Note that improved awareness is only the first step towards taking action. In other words, if a user is not able to detect a phish when the primary task is security, it is unlikely that he/she will detect the phish when security is a secondary task. Thus, it is worth using a study design in which security is participants' primary task. In essence, this gives us an upper boundary for video effectiveness: the best we can hope to achieve.

3.2 Material

Messages were designed in such a way that a judgement could only be made based on the actual URL. We had to acknowledge that participants could consider a message as phish because they did not know the sender or did not have an account with the web service provider. Therefore, we asked participants to imagine the following scenario. They were Max Müller, who has an account with all web services used in the study, and who has a colleague named Jonas Schmidt. Furthermore, they were told that it was important for them to decide whether a message was legitimate or not because the fraudulent messages would harm them and ignored genuine messages could lead to negative consequences (we wanted to avoid their simply classifying all messages as phishes, just to be safe). This scenario was displayed when screenshots of messages had to be judged.

We used 16 messages in each task (pre, post, retention). All messages contained plausible content. They were displayed during the evaluation in a randomized order. Some more information about the messages:

- One half contained suspicious links, the other half legitimate links.[4]
- We derived messages from messages received from web services and private contacts. Messages from web service providers were in the original design with original text (only the URL was replaced for the "phishing" messages).
- For all screenshots, the mouse was positioned so that the actual URL was displayed, depending on the software in place either in the tooltip (with Outlook) or in the status bar (with Thunderbird or a web browser). The usage of both types was equally distributed both for phishing messages as well as for legitimate messages. It was technically not possible to only show the URL when participants actually position the mouse on the link on SoSciSurvey.
- We designed phishing messages where *instruction-1* was enough to judge as well as those where *instruction-2* or *instruction-3* was needed (see Table 1)

Table 1. Overview of presented phishing messages (SB = Status Bar; TT = Tooltip)

Web address	Type	Inst.	Sender of message
https://162.179.34.56/login	TT	1+2	Service (DHL)
https://www.secure-documents-online.com/...	SB	1+2	Person (Colleague)
https://control-center.1uncl1.de/...	TT	1+3	Service (1 und 1)
https://www.volksbanknig.de/...	TT	1+3	Service (Volksbank)
https://www.google.com.best-photos.com/..	SB	1+2	Service (Google)
https://www.zehrukol.com/ebay.com/...	TT	1+2	Person (Colleague)
https://www.bahncard.bahm.de/...	SB	1+3	Service (DB)
https://www.cognstar.de/...	SB	1+3	Service (Congstar)

3.3   Recruiting and Ethics

An attempt was made to recruit participants from a wide range of ages. Recruitment also took place via online platforms, social networks, flyers and personal

---

[4] Due to the fact that we used a quiz-like evaluation, we could present half-half although, in a realistic setting, half of people's messages would not usually be phish.

invitations. Participants were not compensated for participating but we encouraged participation by telling them they learn how to avoid falling victim.

The requirements for research involving the human being, defined by the ethics committee of our university[5], were satisfied. This includes the fact that all data was collected independently of the identity of the participants. The email addresses they provided to permit us to contact them for the retention study were stored in a different database in a different order (as compared to their answers in the two sessions). The entries from the first session were linked to the one from the retention by asking participants to provide a random looking but well-defined code—well defined because they were told how to generate it based of names and birthdays from particular relatives. Furthermore, no third party (besides SosciSurvey) has a copy of the data and no third party was involved in the evaluation of the data.

4   Evaluation – Results

There are two groups of people in our sample: Those participating only in the first session (89: 39F/50 M $\bar{x} = 36.1$ years) and those who participated in both sessions (22: 12F/10 M $\bar{x} = 38.09$ years). There were no statistically significant differences between the groups; neither for age nor for gender. The distribution of the degree of education is as follows: from the 89 participants in the first session 50 have a university or university of applied science degree and 21 have an A-level qualification. The corresponding numbers for those 22 who participated in both sessions are: ten and five respectively. For the descriptive statistic see Table 2.

Table 2. Overview of detection rates in % and their standard deviation (SD) for all participants (all), those participating only in session 1 (G1) and those participating in both sessions (G2)

	Pre	Post	Retention
Phish G1	65.5 (SD 28.6)	83.8 (SD 20.5)	
Phish G2	42.6 (SD 29.3)	86.9 (SD 18.3)	81.3 (SD 16.3)
Phish all	59.8 (SD 30.3)	84.55 (SD 20.0)	81.3 (SD 16.3)
Legitimate G1	75.8 (SD 21.2)	87.7 (SD 17.3)	
Legitimate G2	75.0 (SD 21.1)	88.1 (SD 17.9)	83.0 (SD 20.3)
Legitimate all	75.6 (SD 21.1)	87.8 (SD 17.3)	83.0 (SD 20.3)

The performance change in detecting phishing and legitimate messages was measured in terms of correctly detected phish and legitimate messages. The difference in performance before and after watching the video H1 was analysed

---

[5] https://www.intern.tu-darmstadt.de/gremien/ethikkommisson/zustndigkeit/zustndigkeit.en.jsp.

using a Repeated Measures ANOVA for both groups separately: (1) those participating only in session one and (2) those participating in both sessions. Furthermore we analysed the retention performance changes H2 using the Repeated Measures ANOVA considering only the answers from those participating in both sessions. The Mauchly Test indicates that there is a violation of Sphericity and therefore a Greenhouse-Geisser correction was needed for the comparison of pre- and post-performance. There was no violation of Sphericity to compare pre- and retention-performance.

4.1 Phishing Detection

Pre-post for All Participants: We first report the Repeated Measures ANOVA with Greenhouse-Geisser correction for violated sphericity for the detection of phishing messages by all participants: The within-subject factor in time (pre and post performance) is significant with $p < .001$ and a $\eta^2 = .526$, i.e. the performance in detecting phishing messages changes significantly. In combination with the descriptive data (see Table 2), detection of phishing messages increases significantly after watching the video. Thus, H1 can be accepted.

Participants During Retention: A Repeated Measures ANOVA for fraudulent detection reveals a significant effect for the time (pre-, post- and retention-performance) with $p < .001$ and a $\eta^2 = .636$. A post-hoc test with Bonferroni correction shows that there is a significant difference between pre- and post- with $p < .001$ and there is a significant difference for pre- and retention-performance with $p < .001$. Thus, H1 and H2 can be accepted for the group of participants taking part in both sessions.

4.2 Identifying Legitimate Messages

Pre-post for All Participants: We first report the Repeated Measures ANOVA for identification rates. The within-subjects factor in time (pre- and post-performance) is significant with $p < .001$ and a $\eta^2 = .219$, i.e. the performance in detecting legitimate messages changes significantly. In combination with the descriptive data (see Table 2), the identification of legitimate messages improves significantly after watching the video. Thus, H1 can be accepted.

Participants during Retention: A Repeated Measures ANOVA reveals a significant effect for the time (pre-, post- and retention-performance) with $p = .019$ and a $\eta^2 = .173$. A post-hoc test with Bonferroni correction shows that there is a significant difference between pre- and post-performance with $p < .001$. Thus, H1 can be accepted.

4.3 Individual Messages

We also looked at the individual messages and their performance in order to improve the video. The corresponding mean values are depicted in Tables 3 and 4 respectively (note the number for pre and post are for all 89 participants).

Table 3. Detection rate, in %, for individual phishing URLs

Web address	Pre	Post	Ret.
162.179.34.56/login	55.1	93.3	81.8
control-center.1uncl1.de/...	63.6	93.3	90.9
www.google.com.best-photos.com/...	55.1	84.3	81.8
www.zehrukol.com/ebay.com/...	65.2	73.0	54.5
www.secure-documents-online.com/...	47.2	68.5	77.3
www.bahncard.bahm.de/...	66.3	91.0	90.9
www.cognstar.de/...	53.9	80.9	86.4
www.volksbanknig.de/...	73.0	92.1	86.4

Two particular phishing messages stand out where participants performed more poorly, as compared to the other phishing messages:

- Message using the legitimate URL (...docs.google.com/...) as HTML link in the text but "https://www.secure-documents-online.com" as the actual URL in the status bar. The message was identified correctly by 68.5% (lowest result) of participants after watching the video and 77.3% (second lowest result) in the retention session.
- Message using the actual URL "https://www.zehrukol.com/ebay.com/software?id=12123213124" in the text and in the tooltip: 73.0% (second lowest result) identified this message correctly after watching the video and 54.5% (lowest result) during the retention session.

Table 4. Detection rate in % for individual legitimate URLs

Web address	Pre	Post	Ret.
marketresearch.apple.com/...	61.8	84.3	81.8
photos.google.com/...	82.0	88.8	95.5
our university (anonymised)	94.4	97.8	100.0
www.dropbox.com/...	80.9	88.8	81.8
www.gutefrage.net/...	83.1	97.8	81.8
buchung.lufthansa.com/...	88.8	86.5	77.3
www.vodafone.de/...	51.7	71.9	59.1
accout.wire.com/...	62.5	86.5	86.4

Two legitimate messages stand out (the first one was particularly troublesome):

- "https://www.vodafone.de/(...)": 71.9% identified this correctly in the first session, with only 59.1% during the second session.

– "https://buchung.lufthansa.com/servlet/cc?soDBYCTTDVYTEz0.
26wa7uDU.261f7uuF.3df4D.2e.26EaEXEPNRTOOL_LINKEhttp:DVMD...":
The identification rate after watching the video was 86.5% with 77.3% correct
identification during session 2.

4.4 Open Feedback

Positive comments mentioned the simplicity of the video, the clarity of the content and the general comprehensibility. In particular, they liked the fact that the
video was not overloaded with information. Regarding the overall design, participants liked the idea of using this type of animated video for general knowledge
transfer. Feedback for improving the video was: *'More examples of the different
phishing tricks'* and *'Summary at the end of the video'.*

5 Discussion

The five-minute video significantly improved phish and legitimate message detection. In other words, after watching the video, participants were able to detect
phishing URLs without becoming overly cautious.

    The retention part of our study is of special interest since in real life people do
not receive phishing messages on a daily basis due to improvements in technical
measures that filter out these messages. It is unlikely that people will use their
newly-acquired knowledge very often, so they are likely to forget instructions
and hints from the video. Our participants improved significantly in terms of
detecting phishing messages, whereas detection rates for legitimate messages
stabilised. We suggest possible explanations for this observation:

– "www.vodafone.de/(...)": The mean detection rate, after watching the video,
  was 71.9% with 59.1% at retention. The message contained a telephone number and, instead of starting with 'Dear Martin ...', it started with 'Dear +1
  121 34329'[6]. A paragraph in the email stated that Vodafone would always
  address their customers by their name. The issue, in this case, is that Vodafone does send emails to the phone number if the customer has not provided
  their name. We acknowledge that we did not spot this problem ourselves
  during the video refinement.
– "https://buchung.lufthansa.com/s(...)/cc?soDBYCT(...)": The mean detection rate, after watching the video, was 86.5% with 77.3% at retention. The
  problem here might be the length of the URL. The path contains HTTP twice,
  includes a number of dots and the term 'redirect'. This probably elicited sus-
  picion. Again, the email was not altered from the original sent out by the
  company, besides changing the name of the customer.

    The two phishing messages that evaded detection to the greatest extent were
related to hints provided in *instruction-2*. In the first case, participants did

---

[6] The number we used in the message was randomly chosen, but realistic.

not detect the mismatch between the HTML-text-based URL displayed in the message and the actual destination URL displayed in the status bar. In the second case, participants are likely to have considered the path to be relevant in making their judgement. An improved video will have to explain these cases more clearly. The video did a great job with respect to *instruction-3*. While these cases always performed worst in previous evaluations, they performed better after the video.

Most of the feedback regarding improving the video was related to extending it. This is interesting because we tried to keep it as short as possible while retaining efficacy. Two aspects might be worth considering in terms of improving the video: (1) make the fact that only the URL matters even more salient. (2) provide a summary at the end of the video to consolidate and reinforce concepts.

Note that, unlike studies reported by [29], we did not observe any age differences. This might be because security was their primary task. However, if the study had been carried out in the wild, our findings might well have coincided with those reported by [29].

Finally, it was interesting to observe that those participants who had many issues with detecting phishing messages in the pre-quiz were most likely to participate in the retention study. One possible explanation is that they really enjoyed the video and were thankful for their improved awareness. One additional interpretation is that the video, in particular, addressed those who had very little pre-existing awareness of phishing.

5.1 Limitations

Almost half of the original 89 participants gave us their email addresses to contact them for the retention study. Half of these responded to our retention study request. We ended up with a sample of only 22 participants to participate in the retention session. This means that we cannot realistically generalise the results to the whole population. The participant sample, as a whole, is not representative, as most of our participants had an A-level certificate or university degree. Furthermore, due to the fact that we told participants, during recruiting, that they would learn how to protect themselves against online fraud if they took part, we probably attracted participants who were already interested in this topic. Thus, as future work, we should run the study with a different demographic.

Furthermore, participant performance should definitely be considered a "best-case" scenario, because security was their primary task. Their actual detection rates are likely to be poorer in the real world. However, an increased awareness of phishing detection is a necessary first step to resilience. Before watching the video, people were not able to detect phishes despite it being their primary task. This is why awareness programs are important.

We used the same messages in all sessions. It may be argued that one explanation for post-video improvement was that they already knew what to look for. This might be a valid observation, but the chances seem small because legitimate message detection rates actually decreased. Furthermore, it is unlikely that after eight weeks they would still remember all the messages they had seen before, including the correct judgement. It is also worth mentioning that participants were not given feedback about which messages they had judged correctly, and which not.

Due to technical limitations of SosciSurvey, participants did not need to hover over the link deliberately in order to display the actual destination URL. It was automatically provided on the screenshot. It could be argued that we don't know whether people would hover over links because our study did not require this essential first step. On the other hand, being aware of the need to hover must be helpful.

5.2   Video Improvements

Based on the results, we identified a number of issues with the video, which we addressed in order to maximize performance. The new video lasts only 5:09 min and spends more time on examples. Previously, the who-areas were highlighted in green and only sub-domains highlighted in red. Now this highlighting is extended to the path. Moreover, the video now explicitly tells people when a URL is a phishing URL. We now conclude the video with a summary of the lessons learned, including tips and hints.

6   Related Work

A number of user studies were conducted to gain insights into the mental models of message recipients, or to evaluate the effectiveness of anti-phishing measures. For example, a game-based anti-phishing educational approach in was used by [30], [2,4,13,14,16,32,34–36,42,44]. The effectiveness of some of these games has been evaluated in user studies [4,14,16,30,32,34,35,44] with [16] and [32] comparing the effectiveness of a game-based approach with text-based awareness.

Of these, only the proposal in [32] is further evaluated in a retention study a week later [25]. Usually the participants in user studies are adults, but some researchers have started studying phishing education for children [27].

Another approach to anti-phishing education, utilises the so-called *teachable moments*: participants were sent a simulated phishing email with a suspicious-looking link. If they clicked on it, they were directed to a landing page containing phishing-related information. Such an approach, in particular, has been used by Caputo *et al.* [8]. The authors also conducted a retention study of anti-phishing training in a corporate setting after a period of 90 days. The results of the study, however, did not indicate any significant improvement. A similar approach has been used in further research [19,23,24], both of which conducted retention studies after one week, that did show significant improvements in terms of reducing participants' susceptibility to phishing emails. A further study [22] built upon the evaluation in [23,24] and tested the participants' retention via multiple simulated phishing emails sent over the course of 28 days, with the results showing no significant loss of retention by the end of study. A similar approach but with spear phishing messages was studied in [9,38]. The study in [10] further evaluated the effectiveness of an anti-phishing training based on three simulated phishing trials over a two month period, showing significant improvements even after the end of the study.

Other anti-phishing educational approaches include training materials, educational videos and e-learning modules. As such, a study in [45] evaluated an anti-phishing training coupled with motivational videos. Participants in the control group watched cooking videos instead. The study found that the training increased participants' ability to detect phishing emails, but also increased the rate of false positives. The authors did not test the retention effect of the training. A study reported by [31] compared the performance of several anti-phishing educational approaches, including the game-based approach from [32], training materials from [24] and popular anti-phishing materials found on the web. All of these approaches significantly improved participant ability to detect phishing links. Retention was not tested. An anti-phishing e-learning module was developed by [21] but was only evaluated with a small sample of participants, and retention was also not tested.

7   Conclusion

Modern technology allows confidence tricksters to target a large number of people using phishing messages, at minimal cost. It is still desirable for people to know how to detect these messages as technology is far away from detecting 100%. In this paper we report on the development of a video to raise phishing awareness without deterring confirmation of the legitimacy of genuine messages. We used our knowledge and experience from past research to develop a short yet effective phish-awareness video. Our main aim was to cover the most relevant content in a short video to address the companies' needs to raise awareness, but not necessarily to have the luxury of spending between 20 and 45 min to do so. The video was evaluated by 89 participants. Furthermore, a retention study, in which 22 of these 89 participants took part, was conducted after eight weeks. The results of the study show that the ability of the participants to distinguish between phishing and legitimate links increased significantly directly after watching the video and that, even after eight weeks, the participants were significantly better at detecting phishing links than before watching the video.

Acknowledgements. This work was supported by the German Federal Ministry of Education and Research (BMBF) within the Competence Center for Applied Security Technology (KASTEL) and within the Center for Research in Security and Privacy (CRISP). Thanks to Alexander Lehmann for creating the video; for more of his security and privacy related videos see: https://www.youtube.com/user/alexanderlehmann.

References

1. Anti-Phishing Working Group: Phishing Activity Trends Report, 4th Quater 2016 (2016). https://docs.apwg.org/reports/apwg_trends_report_q4_2016.pdf. Accessed 18 May 2017
2. Arachchilage, N.A.G., Cole, M.: Design a mobile game for home computer users to prevent from "phishing attacks". In: i-Society 2011: International Conference on Information Society, pp. 485–489. IEEE, London (2011)
3. Asudeh, O., Wright, M.: Poster: phishing website detection with a multiphase framework to find visual similarity. In: CCS 2016, pp. 1790–1792. ACM (2016)
4. Baslyman, M., Chiasson, S.: "Smells Phishy?": an educational game about online phishing scams. In: eCrime 2016: APWG Symposium on Electronic Crime Research, pp. 1–11. IEEE, Toronto (2016)
5. Canova, G., Volkamer, M., Bergmann, C., Borza, R.: NoPhish: an anti-phishing education app. In: Mauw, S., Jensen, C.D. (eds.) STM 2014. LNCS, vol. 8743, pp. 188–192. Springer, Cham (2014). https://doi.org/10.1007/978-3-319-11851-2_14
6. Canova, G., et al.: Learn to spot phishing URLs with the Android NoPhish App. In: Bishop, M., Miloslavskaya, N., Theocharidou, M. (eds.) WISE 2015. IAICT, vol. 453, pp. 87–100. Springer, Cham (2015). https://doi.org/10.1007/978-3-319-18500-2_8
7. Canova, G., Volkamer, M., Bergmann, C., Reinheimer, B.: NoPhish app evaluation: lab and retention study. Internet Society, USEC (2015)
8. Caputo, D.D., Pfleeger, S.L., Freeman, J.D., Johnson, M.E.: Going spear phishing: exploring embedded training and awareness. IEEE S & P 12(1), 28–38 (2014)
9. Caputo, D.D., Pfleeger, S.L., Freeman, J.D., Johnson, M.E.: Going spear phishing: exploring embedded training and awareness. IEEE Secur. Priv. 12(1), 28–38 (2014). https://doi.org/10.1109/MSP.2013.106
10. Dodge, R., Coronges, K., Rovira, E.: Empirical benefits of training to phishing susceptibility. In: Gritzalis, D., Furnell, S., Theoharidou, M. (eds.) SEC 2012. IAICT, vol. 376, pp. 457–464. Springer, Heidelberg (2012). https://doi.org/10.1007/978-3-642-30436-1_37
11. Dong, X., Clark, J.A., Jacob, J.: Modelling user-phishing interaction. In: Human System Interactions, pp. 627–632. IEEE (2008)
12. Downs, J.S., Holbrook, M.B., Cranor, L.F.: Decision strategies and susceptibility to phishing. In: SOUPS, pp. 79–90. ACM, Pittsburgh (2006)
13. Hale, M., Gamble, R.: Toward increasing awareness of suspicious content through game play. In: SERVICES 2014, pp. 113–120. IEEE (2014)
14. Hale, M.L., Gamble, R.F., Gamble, P.: CyberPhishing: a game-based platform for phishing awareness testing. In: Hawai'i International Conference on System Sciences, pp. 5260–5269. IEEE, Kauai (2015)
15. Han, X., Kheir, N., Balzarotti, D.: PhishEye: live monitoring of sandboxed phishing kits. In: CCS 2016, pp. 1402–1413. ACM (2016)
16. Helser, S.: Fit: Identity theft education: study of text-based versus game-based learning. In: ISTAS 2015, pp. 1–4. IEEE, Dublin (2015)
17. Jagatic, T.N., Johnson, N.A., Jakobsson, M., Menczer, F.: Social phishing. Commun. ACM 50(10), 94–100 (2007)
18. Jakobsson, M., Tsow, A., Shah, A., Blevis, E., Lim, Y.-K.: What instills trust? A qualitative study of phishing. In: Dietrich, S., Dhamija, R. (eds.) FC 2007. LNCS, vol. 4886, pp. 356–361. Springer, Heidelberg (2007). https://doi.org/10.1007/978-3-540-77366-5_32

19. Jansson, K., von Solms, R.: Phishing for phishing awareness. Behav. Inf. Technol. **32**(6), 584–593 (2013)
20. Kauer, M., Pfeiffer, T., Volkamer, M., Theuerling, H., Bruder, R.: It is not about the design – it is about the content! Making warnings more efficient by communicating risks appropriately. In: Sicherheit, vol. 195. GI (2012)
21. Kawakami, M., Yasuda, H., Sasaki, R.: Development of an E-learning content-making system for information security (elsec) and its application to anti-phishing education. International Conference on E-Education. E-Business, E-Management and E-Learning, pp. 7–11. IEEE, Sanya (2010)
22. Kumaraguru, P., et al.: School of Phish: a real-world evaluation of anti-phishing training. In: SOUPS, p. 3. ACM (2009)
23. Kumaraguru, P., et al.: Getting users to pay attention to anti-phishing education: evaluation of retention and transfer. In: APWG: eCrime, pp. 70–81. ACM (2007)
24. Kumaraguru, P., Sheng, S., Acquisti, A., Cranor, L.F., Hong, J.: Lessons from a real world evaluation of anti-phishing training. In: APWG: eCrime, pp. 1–12. IEEE (2008)
25. Kumaraguru, P., Sheng, S., Acquisti, A., Cranor, L.F., Hong, J.: Teaching Johnny not to fall for phish. TOIT **10**(2), 7 (2010)
26. Kunz, A., Volkamer, M., Stockhardt, S., Palberg, S., Lottermann, T., Piegert, E.: NoPhish: evaluation of a web application that teaches people being aware of phishing attacks. Informatik (2016)
27. Lastdrager, E., Gallardo, I.C., Hartel, P.H., Junger, M.: How effective is anti-phishing training for children? In: SOUPS, pp. 229–239 (2017)
28. Neumann, S., Reinheimer, B., Volkamer, M.: Don't be deceived: the message might be fake. In: Lopez, J., Fischer-Hübner, S., Lambrinoudakis, C. (eds.) TrustBus 2017. LNCS, vol. 10442, pp. 199–214. Springer, Cham (2017). https://doi.org/10.1007/978-3-319-64483-7_13
29. Oliveira, D., et al.: Dissecting spear phishing emails for older vs. young adults: on the interplay of weapons of influence and life domains in predicting susceptibility to phishing. In: CHI 2017, pp. 6412–6424. ACM (2017)
30. Scott, M.J., Ghinea, G., Arachchilage, N.A.G.: Assessing the role of conceptual knowledge in an anti-phishing educational game. In: ICALT, p. 218. IEEE (2014)
31. Sheng, S., Holbrook, M., Kumaraguru, P., Cranor, L.F., Downs, J.: Who falls for phish? A demographic analysis of phishing susceptibility and effectiveness of interventions. In: CHI, pp. 373–382. ACM (2010)
32. Sheng, S., et al.: Anti-phishing phil: the design and evaluation of a game that teaches people not to fall for phish. In: SOUPS, pp. 88–99. ACM (2007)
33. Stockhardt, S., et al.: Teaching phishing-security: which way is best? In: Hoepman, J.-H., Katzenbeisser, S. (eds.) SEC 2016. IAICT, vol. 471, pp. 135–149. Springer, Cham (2016). https://doi.org/10.1007/978-3-319-33630-5_10
34. Sun, J.C.Y., Kuo, C.Y., Hou, H.T., Yu-Yan, L.: Exploring learners' sequential behavioral patterns, flow experience, and learning performance in an anti-phishing educational game. J. Educ. Technol. Soc. **20**(1), 45 (2017)
35. Sun, J.C.Y., Yeh, K.P.C.: The effects of attention monitoring with EEG biofeedback on university students' attention and self-efficacy: the case of anti-phishing instructional materials. Comput. Educ. **106**, 73–82 (2017)
36. Tseng, S.S., Chen, K.Y., Lee, T.J., Weng, J.F.: Automatic content generation for anti-phishing education game. In: ICECE, pp. 6390–6394. IEEE (2011)
37. Verizon: Verizon's. http://www.verizonenterprise.com/verizon-insights-lab/dbir/2017/ (2017). Accessed 18 May 2017

38. Volkamer, M., Stockhardt, S., Bartsch, S., Kauer, M.: Adopting the CMU/APWG anti-phishing landing page idea for germany. In: 2013 Third Workshop on Socio-Technical Aspects in Security and Trust (STAST), pp. 46–52. IEEE (2013)
39. Volkamer, M., Renaud, K., Gerber, P.: Spot the phish by checking the pruned URL. Inf. Comput. Secur. **24**, 372–385 (2016)
40. Volkamer, M., Renaud, K., Reinheimer, B.: TORPEDO: TOoltip-poweRed phishing email DetectiOn. In: Hoepman, J.-H., Katzenbeisser, S. (eds.) SEC 2016. IAICT, vol. 471, pp. 161–175. Springer, Cham (2016). https://doi.org/10.1007/978-3-319-33630-5_12
41. Volkamer, M., Renaud, K., Reinheimer, B., Kunz, A.: User experiences of TOR-PEDO: TOoltip-powered phishing email detection. Comput. Secur. **71**, 100–113 (2017)
42. Wen, Z.A., Li, Y., Wade, R., Huang, J., Wang, A.: What.Hack: learn phishing email defence the fun way. In: CHI EA 2017, pp. 234–237. ACM (2017)
43. Wombat Security Technologies: State of the Phish: Effectively Reducing Phishing and Malware Infections (2016). http://pittsburgh.issa.org/ISSA%20Pittsburgh%20Wombat%20Security%20May%206%202016.pdf. Accessed 18 May 2017
44. Yang, C.C., Tseng, S.S., Lee, T.J., Weng, J.F., Chen, K.: Building an anti-phishing game to enhance network security literacy learning. In: ICALT, pp. 121–123 (2012)
45. Zielinska, O.A., Tembe, R., Hong, K.W., Ge, X., Murphy-Hill, E., Mayhorn, C.B.: One phish, two phish, how to avoid the internet phish. Hum. Factors Ergon. Soc. **58**(1), 1466–1470 (2014)

Biometrically Linking Document Leakage to the Individuals Responsible

Abdulrahman Alruban[1,2(✉)], Nathan Clarke[1,3], Fudong Li[1,4],
and Steven Furnell[1,3,5]

[1] Centre for Security, Communications and Network Research, Plymouth
University, Plymouth, UK
{abdulrahman.alruban, n.clarke, fudong.li,
steven.furnell}@plymouth.ac.uk
[2] Computer Sciences and Information Technology College,
Majmaah University, 11952 Al Majma'ah, Saudi Arabia
[3] Security Research Institute, Edith Cowan University,
Perth, Western Australia, Australia
[4] School of Computing, University of Portsmouth, Portsmouth, UK
[5] Centre for Research in Information and Cyber Security,
Nelson Mandela University, Port Elizabeth, South Africa

Abstract. Insider threats are a significant security issue. The last decade has witnessed countless instances of data loss and exposure in which data has become publicly available and easily accessible. Losing or disclosing sensitive data or confidential information may cause substantial financial and reputational damage to a company. Whilst more recent research has specifically focused on the insider misuse problem, it has tended to focus on the information itself – either through its protection or approaches to detect leakage. In contrast, this paper presents a proactive approach to the attribution of misuse via information leakage using biometrics and a locality-sensitive hashing scheme. The hash digest of the object (e.g. a document) is mapped with the given biometric information of the person who interacted with it and generates a digital imprint file that represents the correlation between the two parties. The proposed approach does not directly store or preserve any explicit biometric information nor document copy in a repository. It is only the established correlation (imprint) is kept for the purpose of reconstructing the mapped information once an incident occurred. Comprehensive experiments for the proposed approach have shown that it is highly possible to establish this correlation even when the original version has undergone significant file modification. In many scenarios, such as changing the file format r removing parts of the document, including words and sentences, it was possible to extract and reconstruct the correlated biometric information out of a modified document (e.g. 100 words were deleted) with an average success rate of 89.31%.

Keywords: Digital forensics · Biometrics · Insider misuse · Data leakage

© Springer Nature Switzerland AG 2018
S. Furnell et al. (Eds.): TrustBus 2018, LNCS 11033, pp. 135–149, 2018.
https://doi.org/10.1007/978-3-319-98385-1_10

1 Introduction

It is deeply worrying for organisations when data exposure originates from an autho-rised individual (e.g. an employee or contractor) who misuses their legitimate access, and the potential for adverse impacts, in this case, is typically higher than that of access by outsiders [1–3]. Insiders are more likely to bypass security controls while outsiders, who typically have limited knowledge of internal infrastructure in a given case, pose a significantly smaller threat. Identifying such criminals, especially if the digital forensics process leads to the presentation of findings in legal proceedings, is a challenging and crucial task. Therefore, one of the aims of the digital forensics process is to produce and test a hypothesis about who did what, where, when and how in relation to an incident under investigation.

Existing methods and tools used by investigators to conduct examinations of digital crime significantly help in collecting, analysing and presenting digital evidence. Essential to this process is investigators establishing a link between the notable/stolen digital object and to the identity of the individual who used it; as opposed to merely using an electronic record or a log that indicates the user interacted with the object in question (evidence). This is a challenging task because it is currently difficult for digital forensic investigators to prove, to the appropriate standard in a court of law, that a specific human used a digital object (e.g. a document or image) at a particular time. An underlying assumption is that the identified computer account—as an example, of which the misuse occurred belongs to the individual who perpetrated the attack. However, with generally poor password use (e.g. shared or stolen accounts) and specific malicious intent, this is unlikely to be true. Thus, correlating such a link is key to identifying the individual(s) responsible.

This paper presents an approach that transparently acquires biometric signals from individuals as they naturally interact with the system, and tries to correlate their bio-metric information with the objects that they interact with, such as documents, email messages and photographs. In this manner, the biometric information of the last individual to access a digital object will be linked to it. Subsequent misuse of such information, through disclosure, for example, would enable an organisation to process the digital object, recover the biometric identifiers and identify the last employee who accessed it.

The remainder of the paper is organised as follows: Sect. 2 highlights the related work in the area of action logs and watermarking. Section 3 introduces the proposed approach, including the core process. Section 4 presents the experimental analysis and evaluates the robustness of the proposed method. Section 5 discusses the findings and possible directions for future work, and Sect. 6 provides concluding remarks.

2 Related Work

The current solution for detecting insider misuse involves a layering of security countermeasures that includes comprehensive logging of servers (including authenti-cation requests) so that logs can be correlated to understand who was using what machine at what time, resulting in specific actions on the network [4–8]. Assuming encryption is in place, proxy-based network decryption and storage of network traffic is required to identify the misuse (possibly over prolonged periods of time). If third-party encryption is used, it can be challenging to decrypt and perform a deep inspection of the captured traffic [9–11].

A limited number of studies have tried to leverage soft biometric signals to detect malicious insiders' activities [12, 13]. Both studies proposed systems that employ the use of human bio-signals such as electroencephalography and electrocardiogram to detect insiders' malicious activities. For detection, they measure the difference in bio-signals deviations between normal and malicious activity phases. Although both systems deployed their approaches in real-life scenarios and achieved high detection accuracy, the experimental setup relies on users wearing a headset that continuously monitors bio-signals and a finger sensor to capture them. However, it is both unrealistic and non-user-friendly to wear these sensors in real life continuously.

Other researchers have employed steganography and watermarking techniques to embed specific data that could point to the action generator [14–17]. While the nature of conventional watermarking or steganography processes is not to modify the digital object in a manner that is noticeable, it does nonetheless modify the document. There may be situations where this modification is not desirable, for instance when preserving the integrity of the object is crucial.

Therefore, the proposed approach in this study seeks to provide a mapping technique between the digital object and biometric identifiers, storing the mapped information alongside document identifiers in a centralised storage repository. When the mapped (imprinted) objects are recovered or analysed, the information stored in the repository is used to recover the biometric information, which is subsequently used to identify the user. The key advantage of this approach is that the underlying digital object is not modified in any way, in contrast to the aforementioned watermarking studies. Also, no explicit biometric information is stored as only the correlation that points to locations within the imprinted object are preserved.

3   The Proposed Approach

The proposed approach takes advantage of Locality Sensitive Hashing (LSH) schemes to generate a less sensitive representation to modification of the document (text). In general, LSH algorithms are mainly used for dimensionality reduction by mapping high dimensional input space into lower dimensional space. A key difference between LSH based algorithms compared to cryptographic schemes is that the former is less sensitive to small changes on the mapped input space. In contrast to hash-based cryptographic schemes, which are designed for ensuring data integrity by maximising its sensitivity to the input space. Both methods map the input stream into a fixed output called digest (hash values). This study leverages LSH property of maximising the probability of a collision for similar inputs. This achieved by directly mapping the biometric feature vector representation of an individual with the computed LSH digest of a given document, this generates a digital—what is called 'imprint' file. The resulted imprint file represents locations within the computed LSH hash value, each of which corresponds to a respective portion of the digital biometric feature vector. The user's biometric

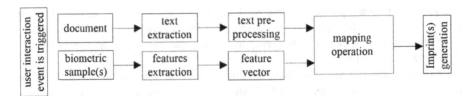

Fig. 1. Biometric information-document correlation generation pipeline.

samples from which the feature vector is computed (e.g. facial features, iris, keystroke analysis or behavioural profiling) are transparently and continuously captured – using suitable sensors – while the person is interacting with the computer. Finally, these generated imprints are stored in a centralised, secure database for later analysis when required. Figure 1 illustrates the process of generating those imprint files which establish the correlation between the acquired biometric information of the corresponding person and the triggered document. Data leakage in the form of a document (whether posted on a public website or captured by the network) can be then analysed by processing the imprint file with the given 'leaked' document, which was already imprinted at some point before it was leaked, to reconstruct the mapped biometric feature vector. Once the sample is extracted, it can be processed by a biometric system in order to determine the last user who interacted with the object.

To illustrate how mapping the biometric feature vector with LSH digest works, assume that the following feature vector needs to be mapped with the given LSH digest as shown in Fig. 2.

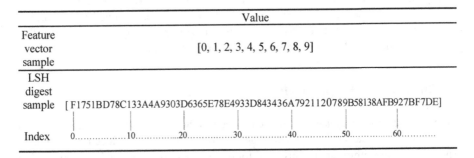

Fig. 2. Examples of a feature vector and TLSH digest sample

In this example, each value (digit) of the feature vector exists in more than one location within the hash digest. The sample digest in this figure was computed using TLSH scheme which outputs 70 hexadecimal characters long (35 bytes). TLSH is a type of LSH schemes developed by TrendMicro [18]. In mapping, "0" is located in two locations; 18 and 47. In the same manner, the mapping process finds all matching locations for the remaining values of the given feature vector as shown in Fig. 3.

By combining those mapped locations (one location from each row), this forms a single imprint. Hence, the total unique imprints that can be generated from the mapped indexes are two as highlighted in light green in Fig. 3. Therefore, using any of these

F.V.	Matched index location within TLSH digest								
0	18	47							
1	1	4	10	44	45	54			
2	43	46	61						
3	11	12	17	19	22	31	32	36	38	55
4	14	29	35	37					
5	3	24	52						
6	21	23	39						
7	2	7	26	41	48	62	65		
8	8	27	34	49	56				
9	16	30	42	50	60				
	1st | 2nd								
	imprints								

Fig. 3. Feature vector—LSH digest mapping matrix (Color figure online)

imprints, it is possible to reconstruct the original (mapped) feature vector from the document by reversing the mapping process. The next subsection describes the correlation generation pipeline including the mapping process step.

3.1 Correlation Generation Pipeline

The generation process of the imprint file which associates individual's biometric signal with a document of interest involves six main steps starting with acquiring document's text and ending with generating the target imprint file.

Extracting Document Text

The document text is extracted from the file, and the text itself is processed, not the document file type. This approach makes it possible to imprint any document type so that its text can be extracted. For example, PDF, DOCX, TXT, HTML or even email messages can all be analysed, and their content can be parsed. Furthermore, the extraction process eliminates any text formatting; therefore, the subsequent steps of the imprinting process rely purely on the text.

Pre-processing the Extracted Text

In this phase, all extra spaces between words, lines, paragraphs and pages that exist in the text are removed and replaced with a single space. This ensures that the computed LSH digest is based only on the plain text, which means that if the document is maliciously manipulated later, for instance by adding extra spaces or page breaks, it will have low or even no effect on the computed hash value.

Computing the LSH Value of the Text

The LSH value can be computed by using one of the known open-source algorithms, including Ssdeep, Sdhash, Nilsimsa or TLSH [18–21]. It is well established that TLSH is more robust than the other schemes regarding the digest entropy, collision likelihood, as well as against manipulation attacks (e.g. removing, swapping, and inserting words) [22]. Therefore, the TLSH algorithm was chosen for use in this study to compute the

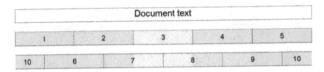

Fig. 4. Slicing document's text into 10-overlapped-folds.

hash digest of the extracted text. Also, two approaches can be used to compute the hash digest of the document as follows:

(a) Only a single hash digest is computed for the whole document, this makes the imprinting process much faster and stores fewer data in the database as only one digest is used to generate the correlation with the biometric signal.

(b) Hashing the text using a different resolution to produce multiple digests per document, for example, per page, half page, and a paragraph or using k-overlapped-folds of the examined document as illustrated in Fig. 4. It presents how document text is sliced into 10-overlapped-folds each of which is processed separately and its LSH value is computed.

In this study, methods (a) and (b) are both examined and evaluated against different possible attack vectors as detailed in Sect. 4.

Also, another LSH hash digest is computed (using, for instance, Nilsimsa) and stored in a centralised database to be used later to locate the associated imprint file when a questioned document is queried. Besides, the biometric signal is hashed using Secure Hash Algorithm (SHA) digest and stored as well. SHA is used for checking the integrity of extracted biometric signal. The reason for using another LSH algorithm is to avoid storing the same LSH digest which was used for generating the imprint. This ensures that having only the imprint in the database without the correlated document makes it impossible to reconstruct the related biometric information.

Mapping Feature Vector with Hash Digest Value
The feature vector and the LSH hash value of the text are mapped to its equivalent location in the text LSH hash value to retrieve the possible locations where they match as described previously in this section.

Generating the Imprints
By retrieving the locations of each character of the feature vector with the object, it becomes possible to generate the imprints based on the obtained list of indexes, which means that multi-imprints of the whole feature vector can be generated by combining those positions.

3.2 Recovery Algorithm

The recovery algorithm to extract and reconstruct the imprinted biometric information out of a questioned document in the case of information leakage–shares the same steps 1–3 of the imprinting process that listed above. This followed by the following steps:

(a) The questioned document hash digest is computed (e.g. Nilsimsa) as input to the next step.

(b) The related-stored imprint file is retrieved by querying the centralised database–using the computed hash digest–where previously generated fingerprints and imprints for all documents are stored.

(c) The retrieved imprint file is mapped with the computed LSH value of the document in question, and the correlated biometric signal is reconstructed out of those mapped locations.

(d) To validate the integrity of the reconstructed biometric signal, its SHA digest is compared against the stored digest generated when the imprint was created.

After explaining how the imprinting and retrieving techniques of the proposed approach work, the next section investigates the feasibility of imprinting biometric information with documents and later recovering them (even after the text is modified).

4 Experimental Analysis

The fundamental research question concerning the imprinting of the biometric signature is how robust the approach is, given subsequent modification of the document – arguably the key attack vector against this approach. An insider who intends to leak a confidential document could maliciously manipulate its content in order to destroy any tracks to avoid being traced. Therefore, to examine the feasibility and effectiveness of the proposed approach, real leaked documents from WikiLeaks were chosen for experimental purposes. WikiLeaks is an international non-profit organisation that publishes secret information, news leaks and classified media provided by anonymous sources [23]. In 2009, it released more than six thousand reports commissioned by the United States Congress. These reports are classified as confidential documents and are now publicly available and accessible online in the form of text files [24]. Table 1 provides statistical information about the used dataset. Leaking repositories such as WikiLeaks and The Intercept typically perform some kind of modifications to the leaked documents. For instance, they watermark uploaded documents and files with extra information such as document ID, date, website address or logo [25].

A number of experiments were designed and conducted to evaluate the proposed approach in such scenarios that consider malicious intent with regard to any possible modification could be performed on the document. The first experiment maps the biometric feature vector with the computed text TLSH digest and retrieves it. The goal is to compute the possible number of imprints that can be generated from the mapping process. In addition, a total of twenty-one attacks were developed. This includes, file, formatting and text-based manipulation methods. These attacks critically examine the

Table 1. Corpus statistics

File size distribution (KB)	#of docs	Doc content	Min	Max	Average
1–99	4,920	Chars.	1,288	874,548	47,345
100–199	853	Words	233	155,614	8,873
200+	227	Lines	38	16,160	981
Total	6,000	Pages	1	622	34

effectiveness of possible modification attacks on the imprinted documents and inspect how such attacks could affect the retrieval performance of the mapped biometric information. These developed attacks are classified into three main categories: file-type conversion, formatting change and content manipulations, as listed in Table 2.

Table 2. Possible document manipulation methods

File-type conversion	Formatting change	Content manipulation
1. PDF to.docx	9. Font resizing	14. Deleting words
2. PDF to.txt	10. Font type changing	15. Deleting sentences
3. PDF to Image	11. Colour changing	16. Deleting lines
4. Docx to PDF	12. Text highlighting	17. Swapping words
5. Docx to txt	13. Line and para spaces	18. Swapping sentences
6. Txt to PDF		19. Swapping lines
7. Txt to.docx		20. Substituting synonyms
8. Txt to Image		21. Inserting new words

The used biometric feature vectors, in the imprinting process, represent real facial features. Fisherfaces feature extraction algorithm is used to compute these vectors for the captured users' faces images [26]. The dimensions of the generated feature vector when using Fisherfaces algorithm is small compared to deep learning approaches as the length of the vector is a prime factor when performing imprinting process. The resulted vector is 4-dimensions with the length of 60 digits. The chosen vector includes frequency of all digits (0, 1, 2, 3, 4, 5, 6, 7, 8, 9) as well as '-' sign, this to ensure that this study covers all possible numbers within the mapping process.

In all manipulation methods above, the original document TLSH value is computed before it is modified, and the resulting digest is then imprinted with the biometric information. After that, the manipulation methods are applied to the imprinted documents. Finally, the TLSH value of the modified version is computed again and compared to the original one. As long as the original text has not changed, the full mapped biometric feature vector should be successfully retrieved by reversing the imprinting process. However, this is not always the case, since a leaked document is highly likely to have been manipulated or modified. Consequently, the computed hash value is directly affected, to what degree is depending upon the scale of modification. Fortunately, TLSH is less sensitive to small changes than cryptographic hashing algorithms, such as SHA, since a small modification in the input drastically changes the output computed digest. This is the so-called avalanche effect.

In contrast, all similar digest schemes have the property that a small change to the file being hashed results in small change to the hash [18]. For example, Fig. 5 shows two samples of computed document hash digests using SHA256 and TLSH. Each presents two values: one for the original document and one for the modified version of the same document. It is clearly shown that the digest of the modified document computed bySHA256 is entirely different to the originals. While the TLSH digest is only slightly affected, the red characters are those changed while the others remain the same with exact locations. Therefore, the TLSH can be used in our approach to give a less sensitive representation for the whole document.

6efa3f05f084127249ebe7e0b37ffdda41db9ceacfbb65c04cd7de6a
SHA256 digest of the original document
49ca48a970f02c40cf85667d1708416ccca84de06d65467856aa3ef1
SHA256 the digest of the modified document

77F1866D9E10AF925F4228F3475961F8C0DAB4751388000565A1B8571D67C7E1F5A6FE1BE78C133A4A9303D6
365E7CE8933D843437A7D21120789B58238AFB927BF7DE
TLSH digest of the original document

4DF1856D4E106F925F4224F7476961F8C0DBB0751388001565A178571D67C7E0F1AAFF1BE78C133A0A9303D6
365E68E5A33D843437A7911520789B58238AFB927BF7EE
TLSH digest of the modified document

Fig. 5. Samples of computed document hash digests using SHA256 and TLSH (Color figure online)

Figure 6 shows the averaged distribution of the number of imprints generated per document for the examined 6,000 documents in the dataset. The histogram indicates that most of the imprinted documents generated more than three imprints. The number of the obtainable imprints mainly depends on the generated TLSH digest entropy and digits frequency. The rate of the entropy and frequency differ from one document to another as this is natural property of hash schemes. Although multiple imprints per document were generated as the figure illustrates, in fact, only one imprint is needed to successfully reconstruct the biometric information. Indeed, having multiple imprints for a given document significantly increases the probability of recovering the mapped information even after the document is exposed to manipulation.

The experimental results of the developed method indicate that the proposed approach is resistant and robust against both file-type conversion and formatting change attacks with an accuracy of 100%. Since the nature of these modification methods does not change the actual text or content which is fed into the LSH algorithm, therefore, the mapped biometric signal is fully retrievable even when the text format or file-type is changed, including converting the document into an image file type. However, in such a case, Optical Character Recognition (OCR) technologies could be used to analyse and convert the image content (printed text) into machine-encoded text.

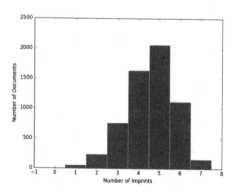

Fig. 6. Distribution of the generated imprints per document.

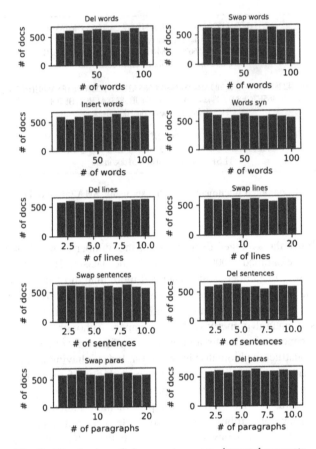

Fig. 7. Distribution of change rate among dataset documents.

In this study, test documents were converted into images (JPEG) to simulate such an attack, and a Tesseract-OCR engine was used to read all those images and recognise and extract the embedded text [27]. As long as the OCR was able to recognise the correct text, which it did, the integrity of the text can be preserved compared to its original version.

For the content manipulation attacks, random settings were configured for the rate of modification, as Fig. 7 illustrates, ranging from 1 to 100 for word-type attacks and 1 to 20 for line and paragraph attacks. As this rate increases, the number of changes rises as well. For instance, in the case of the word-deleting attack, a number of random words between (1, 100) are deleted from each document in the dataset. Also, this applies to all other attacks that fit in the same category.

Table 3 presents the results of retrieving the mapped feature vector under the content manipulation attack methods. In addition, TLSH uses a distance score of '0', which indicates that the files are identical (or nearly identical), while scores above that represent a greater distance between the examined documents. A higher score should represent that there are more differences between the documents [18].

From the data in Table 3, it can be seen that given the capability of recovering biometric identifiers under significant levels of modification—such as deleting 100 words—it is still possible to regenerate the established correlation between the biometric information and the imprinted document with a success rate of (89.31%). In addition, Fig. 8 illustrates how the accuracy changes along with a defined number of deleted words. Two levels of hashing resolutions were applied on the examined documents, one hash digest per document and multi-hash digest using 10-overlapped-folds per document. The overall accuracy is improved when multi-hash digests are generated. In general, a document is counted as correctly identified (feature vector is retrieved) if at least one imprint is perfectly extracted from the imprinted feature vector even when the computed hash digest is not identical to the one from which the original correlation where established.

Furthermore, paragraph attacks (swap and delete methods) have scored low rates, with 47.55% and 46.11% respectively. Indeed, removing a number of paragraphs from the document significantly affects the computed hash digest to a greater degree than other types of modification, such as deleting words or sentences. This can be improved by changing the hashing resolution (i.e. using k-folds). For instance, instead of hashing the whole document and generating a single hash digest, multiple digests are computed for the document, for example per page, half page or paragraph, and correlating the biometric information with the resulted hashes. Figure 9 shows the averaged accuracy and F1-score for the deleted paragraphs attack using 10-overlapped-folds. The overall accuracy is higher than the single hash digest per document approach as it scored 93%. In contrast, the achieved F-score is not high as it computed for all the generated imprints, while only one valid retrieved imprint of a given document is needed to reconstruct the mapped biometric information. Moreover, chances for recovering the correlated biometric signals vary based on the type and scale of attack vector. However,

Table 3. Content manipulation attack methods experimental results.

No	Attack type	Rate (number)	#of retrieved F.V.	Score (%)	TLSH diff (original/modified)[a]		
					Min.	Max.	Avg.
1	Del words	1–100	5,359	89.31	0	217	8
2	Swap words	1–100	5,464	91.06	0	82	7
3	Insert words	1–100	5,304	88.40	1	471	33
4	Words syn.	1–100	5,751	95.85	1	465	30
5	Del lines	1–10	2,708	45.13	7	466	43
6	Swap lines	1–10	2,637	43.95	7	874	71
7	Swap sentences	1–10	5,929	98.81	0	30	3
8	Swap paras	1–10	2,853	47.55	5	125	26
9	Del paras	1–10	2,767	46.11	5	149	26
10	Del sentences	1–10	4,915	82.00	1	788	15
11	Multi attacks[b]	1–10	3,828	64.00	1	456	31

[a] TLSH diff is distance score between two digests (texts).
[b] A number of attack methods are randomly chosen.

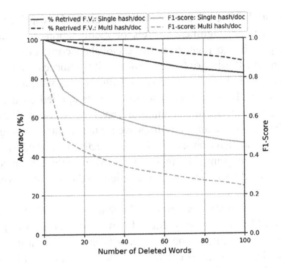

Fig. 8. Averaged accuracy and F1-score for the deleted words attack.

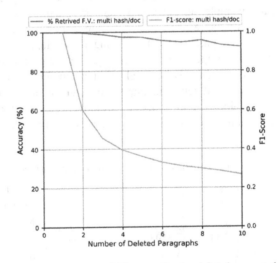

Fig. 9. Averaged accuracy and F1-score for the deleted paragraphs attack.

in many leakage cases, the leaked document might not be exposed to a severe modification. Hence, reconstructing the biometric sample is highly likely to be possible and, as a result, the source of leakage can be identified.

5 Discussion

The most obvious finding to emerge from this study is that the underlying digital objects, documents in this case, are not modified in any form. In addition, the proposed approach also disassociates any biometric information from the digital object itself, thereby minimising any attacks on the biometric data. Which means that the biometric single is not stored by any means in a database, only its correlation to the imprinted object (document/text in this case) is preserved in the imprint file. Thus, it becomes useless without having the imprinted document in presence for the recovery process, since the imprint file that correlates the object with the related biometric signal only contains those locations within the document where the signal can be extracted from. Besides, it allows for larger volumes of information to be imprinted, making it more suitable for digital objects when greater levels of information need to be correlated (i.e. multimodal biometric samples). It does, however, introduce the need for a centralised repository which will grow as users interact with objects and thus requires configuration and management.

Although the above investigation has critically examined the proposed approach against possible malicious attacks and showed robustness and strength, a number of challenges exist and require further research. These include the ability to automate the process of capturing the biometric signal and detecting user interaction with the object instantly, along with establishing the correlation with the interacted object. This requires the development of a smart and active agent that continually captures an individual's biometric information (using a camera in the case of facial information) and performs the imprinting process. Furthermore, the proposed approach raises important privacy concerns for those individuals who are monitored by the system. In which processing, transmitting and storing the biometric samples into a centralised database require a high level of confidentiality and sufficient resources. This obviously needs to be investigated in depth in the future work. More broadly, research is also needed to determine the ability to utilise a broader range of digital objects. Differing objects have varying degrees of stability due to their structure. For example, executable files and their underlying data structure can change considerably given small alterations to a file, in contrast to text. Therefore, the proposed approach needs to be examined for such file-types to fully measure its usefulness and robustness. Also, further study needs to be carried out regarding the ability to utilise soft biometric features such as the gender, age and even race of individuals to increase the discriminative ability and provide more reliable information to the investigator.

6 Conclusion

This paper has introduced a proactive approach to aiding an incident investigator to establish and examine a case of insider misuse, particularly with respect to information leakage, and could increase the likelihood of the evidence being admissible in a court of law. This study has shown that it is possible to successfully recover biometric information even under significant modification attacks. Rather than requiring the complete digital object, it is possible to recover the necessary information with even a modified version of the questioned document.

Acknowledgements. This research was undertaken with the support of the Majmaah University, Majmaah city, Saudi Arabia.

References

1. Titcomb, J.: WikiLeaks releases thousands of hacked Macron campaign emails (2017). http://www.telegraph.co.uk/news/2017/07/31/wikileaks-releases-thousands-hacked-macron-campaign-emails/. Accessed 07 Sept 2017
2. WikiLeaks publishes 'biggest ever leak of secret CIA documents' (2017). https://www.theguardian.com/media/2017/mar/07/wikileaks-publishes-biggest-ever-leak-of-secret-cia-documents-hacking-surveillance. Accessed 09 Sept 2017
3. Moshinsky, B.: LEAKED DOCUMENT: Bank of England has 'significant concern' over post-Brexit approval for Deutsche Bank's UK branch (2017). http://uk.businessinsider.com/bank-of-england-document-deutsche-bank-post-brexit-uk-2017-8. Accessed 07 Sept 2017
4. Rahayu Selamat, S., Sahib, S., Hafeizah, N., Yusof, R., Faizal Abdollah, M.: A forensic traceability index in digital forensic investigation. J. Inf. Secur. **4**(1), 19–32 (2013)
5. Homem, I., Dosis, S., Popov, O.: LEIA: the live evidence information aggregator: towards efficient cyber-law enforcement. In: World Congress on Internet Security (WorldCIS-2013), pp. 156–161 (2013)
6. Magklaras, G., Furnell, S., Papadaki, M.: LUARM – an audit engine for insider misuse detection. Int. J. Digit. Crime Forensics **3**(3), 37–49 (2011)
7. Homem, I., Dosis, S., Popov, O.: The network factor in proactive digital evidence acquisition. Int. J. Intell. Comput. Res. **6**(1), 517–526 (2015)
8. Quick, D., Choo, K.-K.R.: Forensic collection of cloud storage data: does the act of collection result in changes to the data or its metadata? Digit. Investig. **10**(3), 266–277 (2013)
9. Pilli, E.S., Joshi, R.C., Niyogi, R.: Network forensic frameworks: survey and research challenges. Digit. Invest. **7**(1–2), 14–27 (2010)
10. Khan, S., Gani, A., Wahab, A.W.A., Shiraz, M., Ahmad, I.: Network forensics: review, taxonomy, and open challenges. J. Netw. Comput. Appl. **66**, 214–235 (2016)
11. Birk, D., Wegener, C.: Technical issues of forensic investigations in cloud computing environments. In: 2011 Sixth IEEE International Workshop on Systematic Approaches to Digital Forensic Engineering, pp. 1–10 (2011)
12. Hashem, Y., Takabi, H., GhasemiGol, M., Dantu, R.: Towards insider threat detection using psychophysiological signals. In: Proceedings of the 7th ACM CCS International Workshop on Managing Insider Security Threats - MIST 2015, vol. 6, no. 1, pp. 71–74 (2015)
13. Almehmadi, A., El-Khatib, K.: On the possibility of insider threat detection using physiological signal monitoring. In: Proceedings of the 7th International Conference on Security of Information and Networks - SIN 2014, pp. 223–230 (2014)
14. Bouslimi, D., Coatrieux, G.: A crypto-watermarking system for ensuring reliability control and traceability of medical images. Sig. Process. Image Commun. **47**, 160–169 (2016)
15. Chaabane, F., Charfeddine, M., Ben Amar, C.: A survey on digital tracing traitors schemes. In: 2013 9th International Conference on Information Assurance and Security (IAS), pp. 85–90 (2013)
16. Macq, B., Alface, P.R., Montanola, M.: Applicability of watermarking for intellectual property rights protection in a 3D printing scenario. In: Proceedings of the 20th International Conference on 3D Web Technology - Web3D 2015, pp. 89–95 (2015)
17. Alruban, A., Clarke, N., Li, F., Furnell, S.: Insider misuse attribution using biometrics. In: Proceedings of the 12th International Conference on Availability, Reliability and Security - ARES 2017, pp. 1–7 (2017)
18. Oliver, J., Cheng, C., Chen, Y.: TLSH – a locality sensitive hash. In: 2013 Fourth Cybercrime and Trustworthy Computing Workshop, pp. 7–13, November 2013

19. Kornblum, J.: Identifying almost identical files using context triggered piecewise hashing. Digit. Investig. **3**(SUPPL), 91–97 (2006)
20. Roussev, V.: Data fingerprinting with similarity digests. In: Chow, K.-P., Shenoi, S. (eds.) DigitalForensics 2010. IAICT, vol. 337, pp. 207–226. Springer, Heidelberg (2010). https://doi.org/10.1007/978-3-642-15506-2_15
21. Damiani, E., di Vimercati, S.D.C., Paraboschi, S., Samarati, P.: An open digest-based technique for spam detection. In: Proceedings of 2004 International Workshop Security in Parallel and Distributed Systems, vol. 1, no. 1, pp. 559–564 (2004)
22. Oliver, J., Forman, S., Cheng, C.: Using randomization to attack similarity digests. In: Batten, L., Li, G., Niu, W., Warren, M. (eds.) ATIS 2014. CCIS, vol. 490, pp. 199–210. Springer, Heidelberg (2014). https://doi.org/10.1007/978-3-662-45670-5_19
23. WikiLeaks. https://wikileaks.org. Accessed 05 Sept 2017
24. A billion in secret Congressional reports (2009). https://wikileaks.org/wiki/Change_you_can_download:_a_billion_in_secret_Congressional_reports. Accessed 04 Sept 2017
25. The Intercept. https://theintercept.com/. Accessed 05 Sept 2017
26. Belhumeur, P.N., Hespanha, J.P., Kriegman, D.J.: Eigenfaces vs. fisherfaces: recognition using class specific linear projection. IEEE Trans. Pattern Anal. Mach. Intell. **19**(7), 711–720 (1997)
27. Smith, R.: An overview of the tesseract OCR engine. In: Ninth International Conference on Document Analysis and Recognition (ICDAR 2007), vol. 2, pp. 629–633 (2007)

A Decision-Making Approach for Improving Organizations' Cloud Forensic Readiness

Stavros Simou[1]([⊠]), Ioannis Troumpis[1], Christos Kalloniatis[1],
Dimitris Kavroudakis[2], and Stefanos Gritzalis[3]

[1] Privacy Engineering and Social Informatics (PrivaSI) Laboratory,
Department of Cultural Technology and Communication,
University of the Aegean, University Hill, 81100 Mytilene, Greece
{ssimou, chkallon}@aegean.gr, envm6150001@env.aegean.gr
[2] Department of Geography, University of the Aegean,
University Hill, 81100 Mytilene, Greece
dimitrisk@aegean.gr
[3] Information and Communication Systems Security Laboratory,
Department of Information and Communications Systems Engineering,
University of the Aegean, 83200 Samos, Greece
sgritz@aegean.gr

Abstract. Cloud forensic investigation involves a number of different people and requires a lot of effort to resolve an incident. In order for an organization to have better chances to succeed in the investigation, it needs to be well-prepared. Hence, the organization needs to develop cloud forensic readiness. This paper introduces a decision-making approach to calculate the forensic readiness and the compliance level of an organization, and in parallel to classify the unimplemented tasks in a cloud service. The specific approach is based on a decision-based algorithm, the organization's forensic compliance and a number of decision-making criteria.

Keywords: Cloud forensic readiness · Decision-based algorithm
Cloud forensic constraints · Cloud forensics

1 Introduction

Cloud computing has managed to gain popularity among consumers, due to its ability to provide on-demand services with minimal cost from anywhere in the world. The extensive use of cloud computing has attracted many users aiming to gain control on private information and commit malicious actions [1]. Incidents occurring in cloud environments such as stealing confidential information, trafficking illegal material, draining system's resources, etc. are even more demanding, in terms of complexity and expertise needed, and difficult to resolve in comparison to traditional digital environments. Cloud forensic investigation has to deal with evidence that reside everywhere in the world in distributed and virtualized environments [2]. This makes the investigation complex since different jurisdictions are involved in multi-tenancy environments and ambiguous transparency [3–6].

© Springer Nature Switzerland AG 2018
S. Furnell et al. (Eds.): TrustBus 2018, LNCS 11033, pp. 150–164, 2018.
https://doi.org/10.1007/978-3-319-98385-1_11

The past years extensive research has been conducted regarding digital forensic investigation (DFI) in cloud environments. Several researchers have proposed various frameworks, models and solutions. A detailed review concerning the cloud forensic investigation area can be found in Simou et al. [7]. The main goal of these propositions is to make cloud a safer and secure place, where an incident can be solved in a forensically sound manner and a cloud service can achieve and maintain forensicability. In this paper, the term forensicability describes a service that can be forensic-enabled. To succeed in this difficult part, it is necessary to understand the investigation process in relation to the cloud services provided by the Cloud Service Providers (CSPs).

The increasing number of cyber-crime incidents in cloud environments has raised concern for data privacy and security issues. According to a RightScale 2018 report [8], security is still the top challenge for the 77% of the respondents, while 29% see it as a significant challenge. The same report found that 96% of the respondents (small, medium business and enterprises) are using cloud services. Due to data security issues and cloud incidents, organizations need to evaluate their forensic readiness. Forensic readiness describes how well-prepared an organization is to perform a forensic investigation, in case of an incident.

Tan [9] is one of the first researchers who defined the term forensic readiness as, the organization's achievement to maximize the ability of acquiring digital evidence, while minimizing the cost of any digital forensic investigation. Rowlingson et al. [10] moves a step forward by introducing a number of steps that an organization should take, to implement a forensic readiness. ISO 27043:2015 [11] defines readiness as the process that deals with pre-incident investigation, i.e. of being prepared for a digital investigation before an incident has occurred. There are various definitions for cloud forensic readiness by numerous researchers [12–14]. For this paper purposes, cloud forensic readiness is defined as: *"The organization's preparations to minimize the impact of an incident in a cloud forensic investigation, while identifying and acquiring the maximum amount of digital evidence."*

Simou et al. [15], introduced a framework regarding cloud forensic-enabled services, which identifies an organization's forensic readiness in relation to cloud services and calculates if a service is forensic-enabled. However, it is expected that several organizations will not be able to achieve full forensic readiness. In that case, a metric should be introduced to illustrate how close an organization is to become fully forensic ready. Furthermore, another metric is needed to help an organization decide which steps it needs to take, to maximize its forensic readiness, given its resources.

The main purpose of this paper is to provide a reliable methodology to calculate the cloud forensic readiness of an organization and to quantify the priority that the unimplemented tasks should have. The measure of these variables concerns the tasks that are not implemented to be considered as forensic-enabled. The proposed methodology can either be used by organizations with huge impact in the cloud business market, such as Google and Amazon, or smaller in-house cloud service providers.

Our contribution is the introduction of an algorithm that calculates the cloud forensic readiness of an organization by identifying the importance of all the tasks in a cloud service, and classifying the unimplemented tasks in order to prioritize them accordingly. The classification and prioritization is used to decide the order in which the tasks should be implemented.

This paper is organized as follows. Section 2 presents a cloud investigation process as derived from [16] and matches a set of forensic constraints (high-level requirements) to every step of the cloud investigation process in order to understand which constraints should be included in the implementation of a given cloud-service for the latter to be considered as forensic enable. In Sect. 3, a novel approach is described using a decision-making algorithm that calculates the cloud forensic readiness of a service considering a set of predefined decision-making criteria. Section 4, validates the approach, using a real case study. Finally, Sect. 5 provides conclusions and raises discussions for future work.

2 Cloud Forensic-Enabled Framework and Investigation Process

2.1 Cloud Investigation Process

To provide proper and efficient investigation in cloud environments, organizations need to be prepared and act in accordance with forensic standards and principals. One of the most important task an organization needs to be informed is about the level of its cloud forensic readiness. Once its forensic readiness is identified, the organization is aware about its systems' vulnerabilities against the forensic process that would be triggered by a security incident and can act accordingly. Malicious actors use cloud services and infrastructures to explore systems' vulnerabilities and gain control over consumers' data. When an incident occurs, a team is formed to investigate the specific incident. The investigation team could be employees assigned by the organization, Law Enforcement Agents (LEA), or external contractors. All members of the team are responsible to resolve the incident in a forensically sound manner, using guidelines, methods and procedures that meet specific forensic investigation standards.

Simou et al. [16] proposed a generic cloud forensic investigation process, based on a comparison framework and the literature review conducted in [7]. The process consisted of five sequential steps: Incident Confirmation, Incident Identification, Collection-Acquisition, Examination-Analysis, and Presentation, together with three more parallel activities/steps that are running concurrently: Preservation of evidence, Documentation, and Training and Planning. Figure 1 illustrates the forensic investigation process in cloud environments.

Based on the investigation process presented above, we adapt our previously published framework [15], regarding cloud forensic-enabled services and present the role of the forensic constraints, identified in that work, in relation to the investigation process. The seven forensic constraints identified in that work are: internal disciplinary procedures, accountability, transparency, legal matters, access rights, isolation, and traceability. For each forensic constraint a feature diagram was introduced for expressing the basic tasks that need to be realized in order for every forensic constraint to be addressed. All tasks in a forensic constraint must be implemented in order for it to meet the forensic standards. Thus, each feature diagram has only a single valid configuration and no alternatives can be introduced when applying it on every cloud service. All the aforementioned cloud forensic constraints should be applied on a cloud service in order to be forensic-enabled.

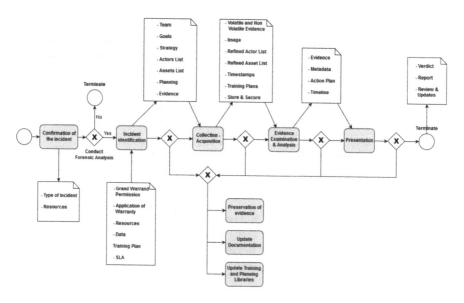

Fig. 1. Process for cloud forensic investigation [16]

2.2   Forensic Constraints in the Investigation Process

In order to identify the seven forensic constraints a detailed study [7] was conducted to identify cloud methodologies, challenges, and solutions and gave us the opportunity to introduce a new category based on the forensic constraints, the forensic requirements. Forensic constraints are requirements related to the forensicability of a service and specify the quality attributes of the service. For each forensic constraint, a feature diagram is created for expressing the basic tasks that need to be realized. Feature modelling assists engineers in modelling the properties of concepts and their interdependencies and organizing them into a coherent model referred to as a feature model [17].

The role of the seven forensic constraints is of vital importance, since the tasks of the constraints fit into specific stages of the investigation process and are used to assist the investigation team. A categorization of the constraints and their tasks in relation to the stages of the cloud forensic investigation process is presented in Table 1. The proposed seven forensic constraints interfere/influence the cloud forensic investigation by contributing to all stages of the investigation process.

Table 1. Forensic constraints' contribution to cloud investigation process

Constraint	Task	Fulfilment
Internal disciplinary procedures	Implement discipline rules	Incident identification – collection and acquisition
	Enable access rights	Preservation of evidence – collection and acquisition
	Enforce legal contracts	Incident identification – collection and acquisition
Accountability	Ensure agreements	Incident identification – evidence examination & analysis – documentation
	Provide assurance	Evidence examination & analysis – documentation
	Monitor actions	Incident identification – evidence examination & analysis – documentation
	Provide attributability	Confirmation of the incident – evidence examination & analysis – documentation
Transparency	Ensure visibility	Evidence examination & analysis – documentation
	Provide procedures and policies of treating data	Evidence examination & analysis – documentation
	Provide notification on policy violation	Evidence examination & analysis – documentation
Legal matters	Define SLAs	Incident identification – presentation
	Ensure jurisdiction	Incident identification – presentation
	Maintain trained personnel	Preservation of evidence – update training & planning libraries – presentation
Access rights	Ensure registration and validation control	Preservation of evidence – evidence examination & analysis
	Enable authentication and authorization control	Preservation of evidence – evidence examination & analysis
	Enable access control	Preservation of evidence – evidence examination & analysis
Isolation	Ensure users do not have access to each other	Collection and acquisition
	Prevent contamination of other users	Collection and acquisition
	Provide confidentiality	Collection and acquisition
Traceability	Monitor users activities	Confirmation of the incident – evidence examination & analysis
	Monitor data logs	Confirmation of the incident – evidence examination & analysis
	Store and secure logs	Evidence examination & analysis
	Link users to data	Evidence examination & analysis

3   Decision Making Approach

All cloud services provided to the users by a CSP should be forensic-enabled for increasing both the security and the trustworthiness of the service. The main purpose of the forensic requirements' contribution to the investigation process is to identify the degree of the cloud forensic readiness of a specific cloud service regarding a forensic investigation. This is necessary for the software analysts of an organisation to understand the forensic readiness and forensic vulnerabilities of their system. In order to calculate that, and in parallel to classify the unimplemented tasks in a cloud service, a decision-making approach is introduced. The specific approach is based on a decision-based algorithm, the organization's forensic compliance and a number of decision-making criteria. In the following section, a detailed description concerning the approach is presented.

3.1   The Decision-Making Algorithm

The first phase of the approach is to identify the importance of all the tasks in a cloud service, classify, and prioritize them accordingly. The algorithm introduces four different steps for calculating specific values that are considered highly important for an organization's forensic readiness. The fifth step of the algorithm concerns the implementation of the selected task and the re-application of the process to identify the next one. The complexity of the algorithm is O(n), and given that the number of tasks is small, should be considered trivial. The algorithm is illustrated as follows.

Step 1. Calculate the Forensic Compliance of each investigation step of the cloud
service in question and the Total Compliance Level of the service.

```
For i 1 to Number of Investigation Stages
   For j 1 to Number of Tasks in Investigation_Step_i
      If Task_j is implemented then
         task_sum = task_sum + 1
      End If
   End For
   CIS_i = task_sum / (Number of Tasks in Investigation_Step_i)
   TCL = TCL + CIS_i
End For
TCL = TCL + / Number of Investigation Steps
```

Step 2. Calculate the effort of each unimplemented task.

```
For i 1 to Number of Unimplemented Tasks
   For j 1 to Number of Variables
      x_j = 0
      For k 1 to Number of Stakeholders
         x_j = x_j + v_k
      End For
      e_i = e_i + x_j / Number of Stakeholders
   End For
   e_i = e_i / Number of Variables
End For
```

Step 3. Calculate the necessity of each unimplemented task.

```
For i 1 to Number of Unimplemented Tasks
   For j 1 to Number of Investigation Steps i is in
      step_impact = (1 + FT_j) / TFT_j
      step_completion = (1-CIS_j)
      step_score = step_impact * step_completion
   End For
   n_i = n_i + step_score
End For
```

Step 4. Calculate the priority of each unimplemented task.

```
For i 1 to Number of Unimplemented Tasks
   p_i = n_i / e_i
End For
```

Step 5. Implement the task with the highest p score and recalculate.

Specifically, in the first step, the compliance of each investigation step is calculated as the fraction of the satisfied tasks to the total number of tasks in each step. The total compliance level is calculated as the average value of the compliance level of each investigation step. Afterwards, necessity is calculated as the contribution of the task in question in each investigation step it participates in, inversely weighed by the completion of the investigation step. Then, the score of each effort variable is calculated as the average score the stakeholders give, and the effort is calculated as the mean value of the effort variables' scores. Finally, the priority score for each task is calculated as the fraction of necessity divided over the effort, and the stakeholders should choose to implement the task with the highest priority.

3.2   Forensic Compliance

To calculate the forensic readiness of a cloud service, and specifically to maintain its forensicability the provider should maintain the level of compliance in relation to the investigation process. First, the total number of supporting tasks (TNT) in relation to the investigation steps need to be specified. It is required to quantify the number of forensic tasks that contribute to the fulfilment of every investigation step. Given that a forensic task can participate in more than one investigation stage, the total number of forensic tasks in the investigation process is forty-five (45), as shown in Table 1. These tasks contribute to the investigation steps and Table 2 presents the quantification per investigation step.

Table 2. The supporting tasks in the investigation steps

Investigation step	Total number of supporting tasks
Confirmation of the incident	3
Incident identification	6
Collection and acquisition	6
Evidence examination & analysis	14
Presentation	3
Preservation of evidence	5
Documentation	7
Update training & planning libraries	1

Since the total number of supporting tasks is known, the second priority of an organization is to calculate the number of cloud service's forensic tasks (FT) that are already implemented, by applying the feature diagrams of each forensic constraint to cloud service's activity diagram [15]. In that way, the organization will be aware about the missing tasks of any cloud service and will be able to calculate the compliance of the investigation stage (CIS) and the total compliance level (TCL). Both type of formulas are shown in Eqs. (1) and (2).

$$CIS_i = \frac{FT_i}{TNT_i} \tag{1}$$

$$TCL = \frac{1}{nIS} \sum_{i=1}^{nIS} CIS_i \tag{2}$$

CIS is defined as the fraction of the number of forensic tasks (FT) in a cloud service divided by the total number of supporting tasks (TNT) and represents the completeness of an activity's forensicability. TCL is the sum of all the CISs divided by the number of investigation stages (nIS). TCLs possible values are $0 \leq TCL \leq 1$, where 0 means that the service does not satisfy any forensic task, and 1 that the service is forensic-enabled. Any value less than 1, means that the service is not forensic-enabled.

To define the level of compliance of a cloud service, even though it is not considered forensic-enabled, can still be very useful, since software developers can get valuable information about the investigation readiness of the services. For example, imagine a cloud service where its total compliance level is 60%. If the organization is willing to raise service's TCL to 100%, this could be succeeded, since the organization's engineers can focus on the desired investigation stages according to the unsatisfied tasks.

However, although calculating the compliance is a useful metric in identifying which tasks must be implemented, it cannot be used as a guide to decide which and in what order the remaining tasks should be implemented. Adding to that, an organization may be willing to increase its forensicability, but due to various factors (cost, complexity etc.), be unable to fully implement all the tasks required. A prioritization of the implementation of the unsatisfied tasks should be introduced, to help stakeholders and IT, decide which tasks should be implemented first. Each task may have different criteria, such as the complexity of the solution, the financial cost, or the participation of the task in a forensic investigation. In the following section an approach is presented in which the priority that should be given to each unimplemented task is quantified, by calculating necessity and effort required to implement it.

3.3   Decision Making Criteria

For the decision-making process we consider a set of indicative criteria that can assist in prioritizing the investigation steps that include unimplemented tasks in order for the stakeholders to consider which tasks should be implemented first based on the necessity and effort required. Of course, the algorithm presented can adopt additional or different variables based on stakeholder needs. In the current section the definition of the variable used are presented along with the respective equations used for their calculation.

Effort is defined as the total work done to achieve something. In our case, effort is the work an organization must produce and maintain in order to implement a solution that satisfies a specific task. A few variables need to be defined in order to understand and quantify the notion of effort. Complexity, cost, and standardization and openness are the variables that are needed. **Complexity** is defined as how hard it is to implement and maintain a specific solution in a cloud environment. This applies both to technical solutions, such as the installation of specific software/hardware, and non-technical, such as legal agreements or employee training. **Cost** is both the initial and continuous monetary cost of the implementation of a specific solution. **Standardization and Openness** is whether there are industry standards regarding the implementation of a task and whether there exist multiple and/or relatively available solutions.

In order to quantify effort, the following method is used. First, each stakeholder assigns a score (an integer between 1 and 10) to each variable, where a high score means more effort required to implement the task. It is not necessary for each stakeholder to provide a score for each variable, if his expertise is not enough. For instance, an organization's Head of IT is not expected to have an informed opinion on legal matters, so it would be pointless to ask him to score the corresponding variables. Afterwards, the average of the scores is calculated as the final score of the variable. Finally, effort is defined as the average value of the above variables. Equations (3) and (4) calculates the **effort**:

$$x = \frac{1}{s} \sum_{j=1}^{s} v_j \tag{3}$$

$$e_i = \frac{1}{n} \sum_{k=1}^{n} x_{ik} \tag{4}$$

where s is the number of stakeholders that scored the particular variable, v is the value that each stakeholder assigns to the variable x, n is the number of effort variables (in our study 3), and x is the final value of each variable. A stakeholders' score is defined as $v \in \{1, 10\}$ and therefore $1 \leq e, x \leq 10$. x is the average value of the scores that each stakeholder gave for the specific variable. It is expected that well-informed stakeholders should assign similar scores, and in that case the mean will represent consensus. Similarly, e is the average value of the variables. There is no reason to individually weigh each variables' importance, since it varies based on the organization's capabilities and priorities. So, the stakeholders will assign a numerical value for each variable that reflects their individual goals and needs. For example, a mega-corporation will view complexity and cost as of less importance than a small cloud-based start-up and will assign scores accordingly. Assigning specific weights to each variable will assume that a variable is objectively more or less important than the others, which is false.

Necessity is defined as the state or the fact of being required or necessary. In this paper, it is defined as the organization's need to implement a specific task to make a cloud service forensic-enabled. According to our previous definition, a cloud service is either forensic-enabled or not, but it would be naive to assume that all tasks that are not yet implemented share the same importance. Our approach suggests that a specific task can be considered more important given its participation in multiple Investigation Steps and the low completion of said steps. The latter assumes that, the more an Investigation Step is completed, the greater the chance is that the forensic investigation will yield actionable results. Furthermore, if an Investigation Step is not supported by any task, it is very likely that the forensic investigation will fail. Therefore, it is preferable for a service to have tasks that support all Investigation Steps, but do not fully satisfy them, from having Investigation Steps that are fully supported and others that are not supported at all. This method assumes that all steps will yield similarly important results for the investigation process, with more specific assignments of weights to follow, after extensive incident review.

Necessity is calculated with the following method. First, the partial necessity of each investigation is calculated, i.e. how important the implementation of the task is for a specific investigation step, by multiplying the expected completion of the step if the task is implemented and the reverse of the current completion of the step. Finally, the partial necessities of each step are summed to calculate the total necessity of the task. Given that, necessity is calculated thusly, as shown in Eq. (5):

$$n_i = \sum_{k=1}^{K} \frac{1 + FT_k}{TNT_k} (1 - CIS_k) \tag{5}$$

where K is the set of Investigation Steps that the task k is in. This formula can be broken down to two coefficients: (a) $\frac{1+FT_k}{TNT_k}$, calculates the expected completion of the investigation step if the task i is implemented, and (b) $(1 - CIS_k)$, calculates the current completion of investigation step k. This means that (a) is the value of implementing i, and will have a bigger impact the less tasks there are in k. (b) will have a smaller value the larger CIS's value is. This means that for each Investigation Step, the score is higher if that step has less tasks and few of them are implemented. Finally, the score for each Investigation Step is summed, to portray the importance of participating in multiple steps. This means that the methodology is biased towards tasks that participate in multiple steps, which is desirable.

Finally, **Priority** is defined as the relative priority the implementation of a task should be given by an organization. Neither effort, nor necessity, are on their own suitable metrics to help an organization decide which task should they implement next. Necessity is a metric of a task's importance, ignoring the amount of resources required to implement it. Effort is a metric of the work and resources required to complete a task but cannot differentiate between tasks of varying importance. A combination of both is required. Therefore, priority is calculated as illustrated in Eq. (6):

$$P_i = \frac{n_i}{e_i} \tag{6}$$

Priority is defined as the fraction of the necessity of the task divided by the effort required to implement it. Based on this, priority will have maximal score when the task in question has high necessity and low effort scores, and minimal with low necessity and high effort scores.

Priority's score is relative, i.e. it is not representative of absolute states. This means that the scores assigned to each task should only be considered in the context of the specific analysis. Furthermore, by implementing a task, the necessity, and, by definition, the priority, scores of the remaining tasks will change, so this methodology should be redone. An organization should strive to implement the tasks with the highest priority scores first.

4   Case Study and Validation

In order to assess the compliance level of a cloud service, a real case study has been used. The case study concerns the University of the Aegean and it has been introduced in a previous paper [15], where two cloud services (Virtual Machine and Nextcloud storage) were chosen to be implemented as forensic-enabled. Both services concern private clouds. The Virtual Machine service is Infrastructure as a Service (IaaS), while the Nextcloud service is Software as a Service (SaaS). While it might be easier to conduct a forensic investigation on private cloud environments, all deployment models (public, private, etc.) have to satisfy the same forensic constraints. Therefore, forensicablity of the cloud service does not take under consideration the deployment model. An extended validation of this case study is used, so as to identify the level of compliance of the two services with the investigation process.

Table 3. The implemented tasks in cloud services

Investigation step	Number of forensic tasks in the VM cloud service (FTs)	Number of forensic tasks in the NextCloud service (FTs)	Total number of supporting tasks (TNTs)
Confirmation of the incident	3	3	3
Incident identification	2	2	6
Collection and acquisition	3	3	6
Evidence examination & analysis	12	11	14
Presentation	1	1	3
Preservation of evidence	3	3	5
Documentation	5	4	7
Update training & planning libraries	0	0	1

Based on the organizational analysis and the cloud forensic requirements analysis [15], both cloud services were found not to be forensic-enabled, since they do not satisfy all seven forensic constraints. Regarding the Virtual Machine (VM) service, three forensic constraints that are not satisfied were identified, involving seven tasks that are not fulfilled. Regarding the Nextcloud service, four unsatisfied forensic constraints were identified, involving eight tasks. Table 3 is produced, by applying the seven forensic constraints to the cloud services' activity diagrams. The Table presents the number of tasks that are already implemented by the University of the Aegean.

Based on Table 3 and the Eq. (2), the total level of compliance of the two cloud services is presented in Table 4.

Table 4. The compliance level of cloud services

Investigation step	Level of compliance VM cloud service (%)	Level of compliance next cloud service (%)
Confirmation of the incident	100	100
Incident identification	33.3	33.3
Collection and acquisition	50	50
Evidence examination & analysis	85.7	78.6
Presentation	33.3	33.3
Preservation of evidence	60	60
Documentation	71.4	57.1
Update training & planning libraries	0	0
Total compliance level TCL	**54.2**	**51.5**

Based on this we can calculate the necessity score of each unimplemented task using Eq. (5), as seen on Table 5.

Table 5. The necessity score of each unimplemented task

Task	Necessity	
	VM cloud service	NextCloud service
Implement discipline rules	0.67	0.67
Enable access rights	0.65	0.65
Enforce legal contracts	0.67	0.67
Ensure agreements	0.71	0.82
Provide assurance	0.38	0.49
Provide notifications on policy violations	–	0.49
Define SLAs	0.77	0.77
Maintain trained personnel	1.76	1.76

As seen here above, there are some tasks that have much higher necessity than average. This is because the tasks in question take part in multiple investigation steps with few tasks and small CIS. For example, *"Maintain trained personnel"*, takes part in three investigation steps, and is the only task that satisfies one of them ("Update training & planning libraries"). This suggests that it is imperative to implement it. On the contrary, "*Provide assurance*" has smaller than average necessity. This is because it takes part in two steps (Documentation and Evidence Examination) both of which have a high CIS and a lot of tasks.

Then, the security team along with the stakeholders assigned values to the effort variable after considering the resources and priorities of the organisation, which enables the calculation of the final "*effort score*" for each task, using Eqs. (3) and (4), resulting in Table 6.

Table 6. The effort score of each unimplemented task

Task	Effort							
	VM cloud service				NextCloud service			
	Cost	Complexity	Standardization	Effort	Cost	Complexity	Standardization	Effort
Implement discipline rules	1	1	1	**1**	1	1	1	**1**
Enable access rights	2.5	2	1.5	**2**	2.5	2	1.5	**2**
Enforce legal contracts	1	2	1	**1.33**	1	2	1	**1.33**
Ensure agreements	1	2.5	6.5	**3.33**	1	2.5	6.5	**3.33**
Provide assurance	5	5	4	**4.66**	5	5	4	**4.66**
Provide notifications on policy violations	–	–	–	–	4	4	3	**3.66**
Define SLAs	1	1	1	**1**	1	1	1	**1**
Maintain trained personnel	5.33	7.77	3	**5.33**	5.33	7.77	3	**5.33**

Since, in our case, most unimplemented tasks concern legal issues, such as writing and enforcing agreements, the cost and complexity to implement them is low, since the University has a legal department. However, the "Ensure agreements" task, got a high standardisation score, since there is no global consensus on how to implement it. Similarly, due to the logistic difficulties "Maintain trained personnel", got a relatively high cost and complexity score. Finally, the priority of each task can be calculated using Eq. (6), as seen on Table 7.

According to our methodology, in both cases, the University should prioritize the implementation of the "Define SLAs" task, which has the highest priority value of 0.77. It is interesting to observe that though "Maintain trained personnel" has a much higher necessity than the rest of the tasks, it still receives a fairly low priority score of 0.33, given its very high effort score. This means that although it is considered quite important for the organization to implement it, its resources are initially better spent on implementing other, easier tasks.

Table 7. The priority score of each unimplemented task

Task	Priority					
	VM cloud service			NextCloud service		
	Necessity	Effort	Priority	Necessity	Effort	Priority
Implement discipline rules	0.67	1	**0.67**	0.67	1	**0.67**
Enable access rights	0.65	2	**0.32**	0.65	2	**0.32**
Enforce legal contracts	0.67	1.33	**0.5**	0.67	1.33	**0.5**
Ensure agreements	0.71	3.33	**0.21**	0.82	3.33	**0.24**
Provide assurance	0.38	4.66	**0.08**	0.49	4.66	**0.10**
Provide notifications on policy violations	–	–	–	0.49	3.66	**0.13**
Define SLAs	0.77	1	**0.77**	0.77	1	**0.77**
Maintain trained personnel	1.76	5.33	**0.33**	1.76	5.33	**0.33**

5 Conclusion

The forensic readiness of an organization is of vital importance since it defines the organization's level of preparation in case of an incident. In this paper, an approach is introduced that calculates the cloud forensic readiness of an organization using an efficient algorithm. It presents a decision-making approach that calculates the level of compliance and some other values to classify the unimplemented tasks of a cloud service. The methodology is based on a decision-making algorithm that identifies the importance of all the tasks in a cloud service, so as to classify and prioritize them accordingly. The prioritization of the unimplemented tasks contains useful information for the stakeholders and software engineers since they can take a decision on which tasks they will implement based on specific criteria and methodology. The methodology was then used in a real case study to validate and assess its accuracy.

In the future, our intention is to better study the effort required to implement a specific task, by performing an empirical analysis with academic and industrial stakeholders and studying the problems associated with the currently offered solutions to each task, to assign specific values, in tandem with the values assigned by stakeholders. This will normalise the lack of experience or expertise of the scoring stakeholders regarding a specific solution. Furthermore, the necessity calculation can be improved by analysing incidents to identify the steps which are more crucial to an investigation.

References

1. Martini, B., Choo, K.K.R.: Distributed filesystem forensics: XtreemFS as a case study. Digit. Invest. **11**, 295–313 (2014)
2. Pătraşcu, A., Patriciu, V.V.: Beyond digital forensics. A cloud computing perspective over incident response and reporting. In: 2013 IEEE 8th International Symposium on Applied Computational Intelligence and Informatics (SACI), pp. 455–460. IEEE, Timisoara (2013)

3. Thethi, N., Keane, A.: Digital forensics investigations in the cloud. In: 2014 IEEE International Conference on Advance Computing (IACC), pp. 1475–1480. IEEE, Gurgaon (2014)

4. Orton, I., Alva, A., Endicott-Popovsky, B.: Legal process and requirements for cloud forensic investigations. In: Ruan, K. (ed.) Cybercrime and Cloud Forensics: Applications for Investigation Processes, pp. 186–229. IGI Global, Hershey (2013)

5. Ruan, K., Carthy, J., Kechadi, T., Crosbie, M.: Cloud forensics. In: Peterson, G., Shenoi, S. (eds.) DigitalForensics 2011. IAICT, vol. 361, pp. 35–46. Springer, Heidelberg (2011). https://doi.org/10.1007/978-3-642-24212-0_3

6. Freet, D., Agrawal, R., John, S., Walker, J.J.: Cloud forensics challenges from a service model standpoint: IaaS, PaaS and SaaS. In: Proceedings of the 7th International Conference on Management of Computational and Collective intElligence in Digital EcoSystems (MEDES 2015), pp. 148–155. ACM, Caraguatatuba (2015)

7. Simou, S., Kalloniatis, C., Gritzalis, S., Mouratidis, H.: A survey on cloud forensics challenges and solutions. Secur. Commun. Netw. 9(18), 6285–6314 (2016)

8. RightScale, State of the Cloud Report 2018: Data to Navigate your Multi-Cloud Strategy. https://www.rightscale.com/lp/state-of-the-cloud. Accessed Mar 2018

9. Tan, J.: Forensic Readiness. Stake, Cambridge (2001)

10. Rowlingson, R.: A ten step process for forensic readiness. Int. J. Digit. Evid. 2(3), 1–28 (2004)

11. ISO/IEC 27043:2015: Information technology – Security techniques – Incident investigation principles and processes. https://www.iso.org/standard/44407.html. Accessed Mar 2018

12. Alenezi, A., Hussein, R.K., Walters, R.J., Wills, G.B.: A framework for cloud forensic readiness in organizations. In: 2017 5th IEEE International Conference on Mobile Cloud Computing, Services, and Engineering (MobileCloud), pp. 199–204. IEEE, San Francisco (2017)

13. De Marco, L., Kechadi, M.-T., Ferrucci, F.: Cloud forensic readiness: foundations. In: Gladyshev, P., Marrington, A., Baggili, I. (eds.) ICDF2C 2013. LNICST, vol. 132, pp. 237–244. Springer, Cham (2014). https://doi.org/10.1007/978-3-319-14289-0_16

14. Kebande, V., Ntsamo, H.S., Venter, H.S.: Towards a prototype for achieving digital forensic readiness in the cloud using a distributed NMB solution. In: Rodosek, G., Koch, R. (eds.) 15th European Conference on Cyber Warfare and Security (ECCWS 2016), pp. 369–378. Academic Conferences International Limited, Munich (2016)

15. Simou, S., Kalloniatis, C., Gritzalis, S., Katos, V.: A framework for designing cloud forensic-enabled services (CFeS). Requirements Eng. (2018). https://doi.org/10.1007/s00766-018-0289-y

16. Simou, S., Kalloniatis, C., Mouratidis, H., Gritzalis, S.: Towards a model-based framework for forensic-enabled cloud information systems. In: Katsikas, S., Lambrinoudakis, C., Furnell, S. (eds.) TrustBus 2016. LNCS, vol. 9830, pp. 35–47. Springer, Cham (2016). https://doi.org/10.1007/978-3-319-44341-6_3

17. Czarnecki, K., Eisenecker, U.W.: Generative Programming: Methods, Tools, and Applications, 1st edn. Addison-Wesley, Boston (2000)

Cyber Physical Systems

Towards Blockchain-Based Identity and Access Management for Internet of Things in Enterprises

Martin Nuss[1](✉), Alexander Puchta[1](✉), and Michael Kunz[2](✉)

[1] University of Regensburg, Universitätsstraße 1, 93053 Regensburg, Germany
martin.nuss@student.ur.de, alexander.puchta@ur.de
[2] Nexis Gmbh, Franz-Meyer-Straße 1, 93053 Regensburg, Germany
michael.kunz@nexis-secure.com

Abstract. With the Internet of Things (IoT) evolving more and more, companies active within this area face new challenges for their Identity and Access Management (IAM). Namely, general security, resource constraint devices, interoperability, and scalability cannot be addressed anymore with traditional measures. Blockchain technology, however, may act as an enabler to overcome those challenges. In this paper, general application areas for blockchain in IAM are described based on recent research work. On this basis, it is discussed how blockchain can address IAM challenges presented by IoT. Finally, a corporate scenario utilizing blockchain-based IAM for IoT is outlined to assess the applicability in practice. The paper shows that private blockchains can be leveraged to design tamper-proof IAM functionality while maintaining scalability regarding the number of clients and transactions. This could be useful for enterprises to prevent single-point-of-failures as well as to enable transparent and secure auditing & monitoring of security-relevant events.

Keywords: Identity and Access Management · Access Control
Blockchain · Internet of Things

1 Introduction

Identity and Access Management (IAM) has become a highly relevant task for enterprises and organizations in recent years [20]. One major change enterprise IAM must deal with is the concept of Internet of Things (IoT). Haller et al. [12] define the term IoT as the integration of physical objects into information networks. By this means, smart devices can interact with services via the internet and participate actively in business processes [12].

When speaking of IoT, the concept of identity does not only encompass user identities but also extends to IoT devices and services [5]. Secure machine to machine (M2M) communication requires reliable mechanisms to establish trust and access control between IoT devices, data and network resources [1]. The communicating IoT devices must be uniquely identifiable to enable authenticity

© Springer Nature Switzerland AG 2018
S. Furnell et al. (Eds.): TrustBus 2018, LNCS 11033, pp. 167–181, 2018.
https://doi.org/10.1007/978-3-319-98385-1_12

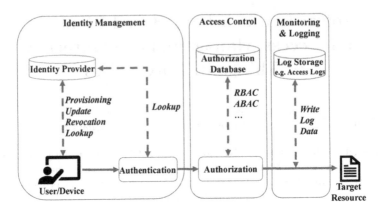

Fig. 1. Overview of IAM functionalities

and to prevent security breaches [3]. In order to achieve this, IAM provides the following three main components. Zhu et al. [33] state that identity provisioning, update, revocation and lookup pose a core set of **Identity Management** operations. The identities of all communicating entities must be secured to prevent identity theft. Data and networks used by IoT devices must be protected by **Access Control** mechanisms to prevent unauthorized access to enterprise resources and confidential IoT data [3]. Finally, IAM incorporates **Monitoring & Logging** functionalities to be able to store and trace critical information in a secure and auditable manner [20]. Figure 1 summarizes these three main functions of IAM.

Various enterprises consider blockchain technology to address IAM challenges in an IoT environment [15]. A blockchain is a distributed database of verifiable records containing transactions which are shared among participating parties. Each transaction is verified through consensus. The records within a blockchain are linked by cryptographic hashes. Each block contains the hash value of the previous block [7]. For a more detailed description please confer Chap. 4. Even though several works propose blockchain technology for access control (e.g. [19, 22]), research has put little emphasis on whether and how blockchain can be applied to the more fundamental concept of IAM in enterprises. The question whether the blockchain technology can deal with the mentioned IAM challenges as a whole in context of enterprise IoT has not been entirely addressed in research yet. In this paper, the following research questions will be examined:

1. Which challenges faces IAM within an enterprise IoT environment?
2. Can blockchain technology be used as an enabler for IAM within enterprise IoT and the corresponding challenges?
3. What is a realistic use case for blockchain-based IAM and enterprise IoT?

Our underlying research methodology is shown in Fig. 2 and is based on the principles of [13]. In order to achieve the research goals defined above, we firstly analyze the relevant body of knowledge for IoT and blockchain technology in

Sects. 2 and 4.1. We afterwards derive challenges which modern IAM has to face within an enterprise IoT context (1) in Sect. 3. Thus, we are able to define constraints and requirements for the integration of blockchain approaches later on. Within (2), blockchain-based approaches for enterprise IAM will be presented in Sect. 4. Furthermore, we show how each component of IAM named above can be supported by blockchain technology. We analyze each component under the aspect of the previously defined challenges. In Sect. 5, we use the results to create a theoretical use case based on our IAM knowledge and the existing literature (3). It intends to show the applicability of our approach. Finally, within Sect. 6, advantages and challenges of blockchain usage will be discussed (4).

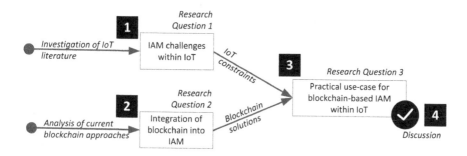

Fig. 2. Methodology

2 Related Work

The topic of IAM, IoT and arising challenges has already been addressed in various research works in recent time.

Adireddy and Gottapu [1] find that IoT devices tend to be unsuitable for intensive operations or large storage due to a lack of computational resource. Zhu et al. [33] state that the large number of different entities which communicate in IoT networks require a robust and extensible structure to enable secure Identity Management. According to Roman et al. [25], a common framework of secure protocols are required to enable governance and interoperability between users and a variety of different devices. Finally, all entities and their identities must be managed in a scalable way in terms of changing space and network requirements over time.

Trnka and Cerny [30] propose an IAM framework which enables device cooperation. The authors leverage a centralized identity store which keeps records of all connected devices with their unique identifiers. The centralized identity store uses role based access control (RBAC) [27] to manage device access. Device accounts and role assignments are created by an administrator. Devices use tokens for authentication. For confidential communication, devices exchange their tokens and compare them to the tokens stored at the central identity store [30].

Salman et al. [26] suggest the use of a gateway layer and a controller layer between the central store and IoT devices to deal with device heterogeneity. Virtual IPv6 addresses are used as device identifiers. The controller layer provides a public key certificate to each gateway within the network. To authenticate, things use their unique IPv6 identifier together with a nonce that is encrypted with the respective gateway's public key [26].

Gusmeroli et al. [11] propose capability based access control (CapBAC) because it provides deeper granularity as well as easy support for right delegation. Capabilities are objects which are issued by entitled subjects to another subject the capability is granted to. Capabilities must be transmitted to all subjects in the network. To illustrate the decision process, let's assume a situation where an employee Alice requests access temperature data of an engine system employed in an assembly line. The responsible administrator Bob issues a capability to Alice which contains the ID of the resource, the IDs of the both parties, the granted rights, a validity period and Bob's signature. Alice saves the capability to her capability list. She can now encapsulate the capability into a service request (e.g. an HTTP GET request) and send it to the access decision service [11].

The majority of the described IAM frameworks addresses the issue that IoT devices tend to be resource constraint by holding only a small share of data and logic on the devices. While Salman et al. [26] address the device heterogeneity problem with an additional controller layer, the other frameworks do not explicitly explain how devices with differing hardware and software can be authenticated or authorized. All IAM frameworks for IoT described in this Section commonly leverage central trusted entities to perform IAM operations. Centralization generally implies reliance on a single-point-of-failure. This means that any vulnerability could enable compromisation of a large stake of a system and its data. A centralized approach does not support end-to-end security. Users need a trust relationship because data security and privacy cannot be reviewed transparently. Ouaddah et al. [21] further state that centralized IAM may become too expensive in large networks in the long term.

3   IAM Challenges in Context of IoT

IoT implies several constraints for enterprise IAM. A number of recently published research indicates the different requirements. After analyzing the content, we were able to derive the following generalized challenges based on the body of literature as well as on our practical experience in IAM. However, note that our goal is not to present an exhaustive list but rather discovering the most important challenges of IAM in the IoT context:

- Physical design constraints (e.g. mobile devices with low power)
- Need for comprehensive and secure IAM mechanisms
- Variability of identities (e.g. interoperability of heterogeneous devices)
- Network scalability

IoT devices (e.g. an RFID tag on clothes) often do not have a high computational capacity and are low powered. Therefore different constraints based on their **physical design** arise. Such devices are not able to execute highly demanding cryptographic operations. This must be especially considered when it comes to authentication and access control within an enterprise IAM. Additionally, IoT devices need to be replaced more often because of their design constraints. Thus, compared to traditional scenarios, the IAM lifecycle has to be executed far more often when IoT applications are involved [1].

This leads directly to the second challenge, the **need for comprehensive and secure IAM mechanisms**. As identities within an IoT context are very large in number it has to be ensured that each device has a managed identity within a supervised IAM platform, information about the identity of all other devices, and the possibility to verify them. Then and only then one can provide a comprehensive view on all identities within an enterprise IoT as well as a secure way for collaboration [33].

One of the further challenges restricting this is the **variability of identities**. Within traditional IAM, identities were mainly humans (e.g. employees or customers). However, within IoT most of the identities will be of non-human origin. They are highly heterogeneous as they have different attributes which need to be managed correctly. An employee holds, for example, attributes regarding his department while an IoT device is assigned an attribute *software version* tracking the current status of its software. To ensure **interoperability**, the IAM environment must be able to manage those attributes, data sources, and policies from different sources [25].

Finally there must be a **scalable mechanism** to manage device identities, authentication, and authorization to enable trusted interactions between devices [25]. An IAM platform has to ensure full operability regardless the number of managed identities and the accompanying requirements for storage and network consumption. However, current approaches are not able to fulfill this as the number of identities within a network is far beyond present numbers [33].

4   Blockchain-Based IAM in an Enterprise Context

Having outlined major challenges for IAM when it comes to regulating IoT, in this Chapter we take a closer look at the blockchain technology (Sect. 4.1) and how it can potentially be applied to address these obstacles (Sect. 4.2).

4.1   Blockchain Technology: Beyond Cryptocurrencies

Blockchain technology was first introduced as enabling technology for the Bitcoin cryptocurrency. Bitcoin implements a blockchain network, i.e. a decentralized set of nodes which all hold a valid copy of the blockchain. The network must establish consensus on the chronology of transactions to establish an authoritative, final transaction log on all nodes [6]. In so-called public blockchains such as Bitcoin, access to the network is not restricted. Thus, anybody can join and participate.

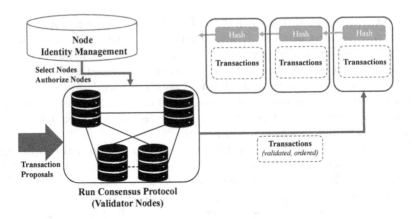

Fig. 3. Simplified validation process for a private blockchain

To prevent public blockchains from being vulnerable to sibyl attacks [8], computationally difficult consensus mechanisms such as proof of work (PoW) in Bitcoin are applied. However, temporary collisions can emerge in public blockchains due to network delays which require the application of conflict resolution rules [31].

In private blockchain networks, participants are known and whitelisted. Such a system is also referred to as private or permissioned blockchain. The nodes which establish a private blockchain must be initially authorized by a trusted authority [29]. This process can be referred to as **node identity management** [31]. Up to now, several blockchain frameworks have been developed for different purposes and with different design and functional properties. The Hyperledger project is one well-known example which aims at the establishment of an open standard for blockchain-based enterprise business transactions. From a security point of view, the Hyperledger architecture intends node authentication via a certificate authority which distributes enrollment certificates to the nodes. Transactions are encrypted using a symmetric key per blockchain which all peers in the network hold. For future versions, more fine-grained encryption for transactions is planned [4].

Due to node identity management, private blockchains can rely on computationally inexpensive, voting-based consensus mechanisms, thus enabling processing of tens of thousands of transactions per second. One class of consensus mechanisms for private blockchains which is currently employed is based on the **Byzantine Fault-Tolerant (BFT) Protocol** [16]. BFT consensus mechanisms offer **consensus finality** which means that all correctly working nodes will process blocks within their copy of blockchain in the same way (e.g. by applying the same rules and policies). This condition prevents the emergence of collisions [31]. The fault assumption underlying BFT consensus requires that among n validating nodes, the number of nodes behaving arbitrarily does not exceed 33% [4]. Figure 3 illustrates a simplified transaction validation process in a private blockchain. An entity which wants to submit data to the blockchain encapsulates the request into a transaction and proposes it to the validating nodes. The validating nodes enforce a given set of contract rules by the replicated execution of **smart contracts**. Smart contracts are self-executing scripts which can enforce the properties of an arbitrary digital contract. A smart contract can be triggered by issuing a transaction to its unique address on the blockchain [6]. The consensus protocol ensures that the transactions applied on each node do not diverge. By means of state-machine replication [28], consistent replication of a smart contract in a decentralized network can be realized [31]. In case of Hyperledger Fabric a BFT-based consensus mechanism is applied [4]. To prevent diverging states between the nodes, smart contracts need to be deterministic. In case of Hyperledger Fabric, smart contracts can be installed to each node in a blockchain network by issuing a so-called deploy transaction. Figure 3 further indicates that node identity management is required to initially select validating nodes. Dynamically changing sets of validating nodes are planned for future versions of Hyperledger Fabric. Non-Validating Nodes are supported which receive transactions and forward them to the validating nodes [4].

Vukolic [31] states that a BFT network always maintains its correct state and consensus finality despite arbitrarily long asynchrony. According to Fischer et al. [9], faulty nodes can lead to a state in which consensus is never reached when a network is entirely asynchronous. Integrity of the blockchain would still be maintained in this scenario. However, the system would be prevented from making further consensus decisions. Thus, availability of the service might be affected.

In the following section, recently published frameworks and approaches which apply the blockchain technology to IAM within an IoT environment will be discussed under consideration of the challenges described in Sect. 3.

4.2 Blockchain-Based Enterprise IAM for IoT

Recent research literature outlines promising approaches and ideas regarding the use of blockchain technology to enhance the security of specific IAM functions for application in an IoT scenario. Even though the ideas presented in the following are to some extent designed for public blockchain use-cases, we find that the adaption to the organizational context could be beneficial regarding the challenges discussed in Sect. 3. Evaluation of advantages and disadvantages and description of a practical enterprise use-case will take place later on.

Identity Management. Zhu et al. [33] propose a blockchain-based identity framework for IoT (BIFIT) for smart home environments. The framework enables the management of IoT devices by their respective device owner. Owner identities are held on a blockchain and managed by transactions. Owners randomly create the key pairs used to generate identifiers and credentials from the same seed used for their own identity. Device identities further contain the owner's signature as an attribute. This approach can be applied to all kind of IoT devices, thus ensuring **interoperability**. The digital identities of owners are created by issuing a transaction to a blockchain which contains an identifier hash value, key pairs, the identity signature, and a storage pointer. The owner identity is stored in the blockchain in a **tamper-proof** way and can be used for validation. Update or revocation transactions can be performed to revoke or update an owner's identity. Lookup transactions for information retrieval can be used to enable reliable authentication. IoT devices only need to store the block header of the identity chain to authenticate other devices. By this means, resource usage is limited to enhance **suitability for resource-constraint devices**. The authors predict a growth rate of blockchain which is far lower than the rate of the Bitcoin network because transactions can only be issued by owners and not by all nodes. This supports **scalability in terms of network and storage consumption** [33].

Access Control. Maesa et al. [17] leverage blockchain to store representations of access rights to a specific resource in a **tamper-proof** way and to manage those rights via blockchain transactions. Access rules are employed by attribute based access control (ABAC) [14] policies. Policies consist of conditions defining a set of allowed values for attributes and specify the actions which subjects are entitled to perform on the addressed resource. Attributes can be related to the subject demanding access, the resource, or the environment. Policies are initially defined by the resource's owner who issues a policy creation transaction to the blockchain. Resource owners can update and revoke policies by issuing update or revocation transactions to the blockchain respectively. Resource owners can change their policies over time. All changes such as policy updates and right transfers are timestamped and logged to the blockchain in a traceable way. Resource owners can issue right transfer transactions which are linked to a particular subject. When receiving a subject's request for access to a resource, a policy enforcement point authenticates the subject by its id and a challenge and queries the blockchain for transactions holding relevant policy data. It then builds a standard XACML policy [10] which is transferred to a policy decision point where it is evaluated against the subject's attributes. Maesa et al. state that putting policy evaluation and execution in a smart contract will be subject to their future research work [17]. The IoT context is not directly addressed in the work of Maesa et al. However, the framework only requires subjects to hold an ID and to sign a challenge which may contribute to **portability to resource-constraint devices**.

Shafagh et al. [29] leverage the blockchain technology to manage ownerships and sharings of data streams provided by IoT devices. Owners can share data streams by issuing a new transaction to the blockchain which holds the identifier of the data stream and the service's public key. The potential impact of a node acting maliciously is limited because each node only holds a small encrypted piece of a data stream. A user who wants to revoke access rights to a data stream changes the encryption key and shares it with all authorized services except the one to be revoked. Additionally, the owner issues a new transaction which replaces previous permissions. This also facilitates monitoring of access management activity. The blockchain does not hold these chunks but only their hash pointer to the previous chunk. It contains a hash pointer of each chunk to ensure **tamper-proof storage**, i.e. integrity. The authors propose a decentralized and encrypted storage layer to further ensure confidentiality of the stored stream data. Besides **security** this also supports **scalability in terms of storage consumption** because only a hash pointer needs to be appended to the immutable blockchain [29].

Storage and Monitoring. Polyzos & Fotiou [23] emphasize that the tamper-proof storage property is beneficious for the development of robust monitoring mechanisms. Users cannot deny having approved a transaction because the authenticity of blockchain is verified by a network of nodes. An attacker would have to forge a digital signature and gain control over a larger share of nodes in the network to alter information held within a blockchain [29]. Thus, only valid transactions can be kept within a blockchain which ensures **non-repudiation** of the logged information [23].

Azaria et al. [2] demonstrate that a blockchain which incorporates smart contracts can provide powerful backup and monitoring functionality. Due to the decentralized nature of storage, a complete log of the issued transactions will remain in the blockchain, no matter whether a user leaves or rejoins the network over an arbitrary period of time. Access to the respective log only requires the download of the latest version of the blockchain. The blockchain log is maintained as long as there are nodes in the network [2].

Maesa et al. [17] state that the persistent, immutable storage of data in a blockchain requires the definition of a protocol which minimizes the amount of data necessary per transaction to enable **scalability in terms of storage space requirements** in the entire network. An easy solution would be the storage of a record containing a link to the data stored in an external database together with a cryptographic hash of the data to store. This approach would still hold the data in a tamper-proof way while needing significantly less storage. However, external storage would not achieve the benefits of decentralized storage in the blockchain in terms of other protection goals such as availability. Thus, Maesa et al. [17] propose an approach where the entire information is stored in the blockchain in an encoded format which aims at rewriting data fields to a representation with constant size. The easiest example would be rewriting the operators AND, OR to the numerical representations 0, 1. To achieve a mapping of attribute names and values in representations of a length of e.g. 1 byte, publicly available conventions must be maintained [17]. This approach might also be applicable to all kinds of structured data which is of interest for monitoring, e.g. access logs to a resource involving a timestamp, a user id, and a target resource. By this means, more scalable blockchain-based monitoring approaches in terms of storage space requirements could be achieved [17].

At this point, we outlined an abstract view of how the blockchain can be applied to the different IAM functions. Figure 4 illustrates a simplified model of the potential interaction of the different IAM functions and the blockchain. It is based on the blockchain implementation proposed by the research work presented in this section. It shows at which position of a generic IAM process adapting the blockchain can be applied usefully and provides an example per IAM operation. Figure 4 illustrates that blockchain technology can be applied

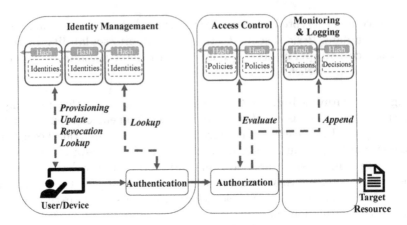

Fig. 4. Blockchain and the IAM functions

to all three basic IAM operations, namely identity management, access control, and monitoring. In the following Section, a use case will focus on the potential applicability of blockchain to IAM in the enterprise domain.

5   Application Scenario for an Enterprise IAM

In this Chapter, a comprehensive use case for the application of the blockchain technology to IAM and enterprise IoT will be described. It addresses the challenges described in Sect. 3 and applies some of the ideas presented in Sect. 4. As the scope of enterprise IAM is usually restricted to corporate systems and users, a private blockchain is assumed in the following. Figure 5 illustrates the use case including all three main components of modern enterprise IAM mentioned within Sect. 1. Each color highlights a specific component.

Let's assume a manufacturing company where employees leverage the support of smart devices. The devices automatically trigger actions based on the analysis of sensor data provided by the machines working in an assembly line. Entitled employees or devices should be able to access sensor data which is aggregated in a sensor data storage as illustrated in Fig. 5. A private blockchain is applied to support all relevant IAM functions as noted above. Thus, each employee and each smart device needs an identity containing different kind of master data such as personal information and references to a department, team, location, etc. The hash of the identity is used as a unique identifier. The **identity management** process which is illustrated by green arrows in Fig. 5 is initiated by entering the identity information of a new employee or device into the system. The encrypted identity information is stored in a central *identity store*. Besides that, a key pair is created and together with the hash of the identity encapsulated into a blockchain transaction which is signed with the private key. In the case of device identities, the firmware and configuration running on the device can be hashed and stored on the blockchain to make potential unauthorized changes

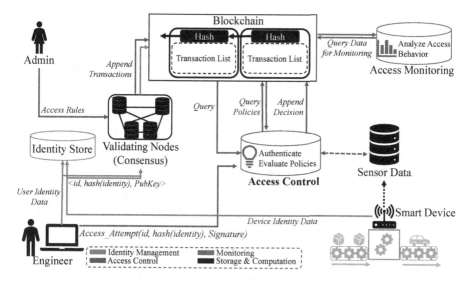

Fig. 5. Potential blockchain-based enterprise IoT scenario (Color figure online)

to the device traceable. Devices will be rejected from access when unauthorized alterations of the firmware or configuration are recognized (as e.g. proposed by [15].

After issuing the transaction, each node in the private blockchain network runs a *consensus protocol*, validates the transaction, and *appends* it to the blockchain. It should be noted that this is a simplified example and does not utilize a specific protocol. Update and revocation transactions are triggered when identity updates or the deletion of an identity by the employee or an authorized administrator take place. If now, for example, a device initiates communication e.g. via smartphone of an employee to deliver sensor data, the employee can (A) identify the device securely by validating its signature using the public key stored in the blockchain. (B) The employee can ensure that the device was not manipulated by comparing the hash value stored in the blockchain with the hash value of the actual data delivered with the request.

To protect critical resources from unauthorized access, suitable access control needs to be applied. In Fig. 5, **access control** operations and entities are illustrated by the blue-colored arrows and entities. Our access control scheme is based on the commonly used ABAC defined by Hu et al. [14]. The scenario starts with an administrator who creates new access control policies and issues them as transactions to the blockchain (*access rules*). For example, employees and devices could hold an attribute *"emergency operations"*. A policy could then enforce that all users or devices which hold this specific attribute are able to access temperature sensor data of engines. However, additional attributes are necessary to read or write more critical information such as prototype blueprints which can be sent to the construction plant.

In the scenario illustrated in Fig. 5 the access control component receives the access request of a user containing the user's attributes (*access_attempt*) and queries the relevant policies from the blockchain (*query policies*). It then assesses the policy rules against the attributes and makes a decision (*authenticate and evaluate policies, append decision*). In a next step, access decision logic could be implemented directly on the blockchain using smart contracts.

Under the aspect of **monitoring** (in color red) all nodes appended to the blockchain can be monitored as the blockchain itself can be regarded as a log storage. Any user action gets appended to the blockchain including the identity's unique identifier as well as additional information regarding its action. This could be the respective entitlement that was evaluated or any further attributes available (e.g. IP address or timestamp). Malicious activities can then be detected by comparing the identity's behavior with the historic usage pattern which remains within the blockchain and can be retrieved by traversing the blockchain and searching for all logs with the identity's unique identifier (*query data for monitoring*). An advantage compared to traditional logging mechanisms is the decentralized data storage within the blockchain. A malicious attacker cannot easily manipulate the log collection (e.g. by deleting logs after an attack) by targeting only one log server. Because the logs are stored on many different devices via blockchain technology an attacker would need to maintain control over a specific amount of devices (based on BFT this would be more than 33% as discussed in Sect. 4.1).

6   Discussion

As described in Sect. 1, the secure and reliable implementation of IAM functions is a precondition to maintain enterprise security. Beyond comprehensive security, IoT requires IAM to deal with additional challenges such as device constraints, heterogeneity, and scalability. However, traditional centralized approaches imply a single-point-of-failure which poses the threat of compromise or failure of highly security-relevant IAM functions such as identity provisioning, permission assignment, access control, or monitoring of user or device behavior in case of e.g. unauthorized data tampering.

All operations which are performed by issuing transactions are immutably logged to the blockchain, thus enabling a transparent, tamper-proof log of all security-relevant operations. However, Sect. 4.1 shows that **public blockchains** lack scalability in terms of large numbers of clients and transactions due to very low transaction processing rates. This reasons the usage of computationally intensive consensus mechanisms. Beyond that, Sect. 4.1 has shown that **private blockchains** offer proper scalability in terms of large numbers of clients and transactions. This makes private blockchains more suitable for common enterprise application scenarios than public blockchains.

The results of the frameworks within Sect. 4.2 further indicate that scalability in terms of space requirements can be managed. The same applies for device interoperability and suitability for resource constraint devices. However, it is worth noting that the latter two challenges depend on the concrete implementation and cannot be solved by the mere deployment of a blockchain. Nonetheless, the research work in Sect. 4.2 addresses those challenges successfully as the design of their frameworks for instance does not require the storage of the entire blockchain on devices, or takes measures to keep blockchain growth on a moderate level.

Private blockchains imply several limitations which may affect potential IAM applications for IoT in enterprises. As stated in Sect. 4.1, the implementation of a private blockchain currently requires a trusted entity at least for initial node identity management. This could as well constitute a single-point-of-failure if a centralized entity is elected for this task. However, according to Rodrigues et al. [24], dynamic reconfiguration of system memberships in BFT-based systems are generally possible after initial election. While private blockchains provide significantly better scalability in terms of large numbers of clients, BFT protocols which are currently employed in several private blockchain architectures are generally considered as not scalable towards increasing numbers of nodes due to a large network latency [18]. This is due to the large number of network interactions required between nodes. However, according to Vukolic [32], node scalability has not been tested intensively yet beyond a network size of 20 nodes. From a security point of view, a too small set of nodes could relativize the increase in security as it might become easier for an attacker to reach the critical number of compromised nodes. As this is a theoretical consideration, further research could examine whether the number of nodes has a practical implication on a system's vulnerability against Sybil attacks which might, for instance, be performed by malicious insiders with sufficient permissions. Even though private blockchains surpass public blockchains in terms of performance and scalability, further research will benchmark whether the performance of private implementations meets the requirements of time-critical use-cases.

7 Conclusion

The rise of IoT poses new challenges for IAM in enterprises. The purpose of this paper is to assess how blockchain-based IAM can deal with theses obstacles, and to demonstrate this in a practical use-case. IoT implies an increased demand for secure and comprehensive IAM operations, interoperability between heterogeneous devices and support for resource constraint devices as well as scalability in terms of network and storage consumption. Private blockchains can contribute several important properties for the enterprise context such as secure tamper-proof storage of IAM data without reliance on a single-point-of-failure. Beyond that, private blockchains provide much better scalability towards large numbers of clients and transactions than public blockchains. Our research indicates that scalability in terms of space requirements, interoperability, and support for resource constraint devices in IAM scenarios are manageable. However, private blockchains might still require a central trusted entity for (initial) node identity management and lack scalability regarding larger networks of nodes. The use case presented in Sect. 5 demonstrates that blockchain can pose a reliable data storage for all major IAM operations and can form the basis for the design of comprehensive IAM architecture in common enterprise IoT scenarios.

Acknowledgment. This research was supported by the Federal Ministry of Education and Research, Germany, as part of the BMBF DINGfest project (https://dingfest.ur.de).

References

1. Adireddy, A., Gottapu, U., Aravamudhan, A.P.: Usercentric federation of access to Internet-of-Things(IoT) devices: a valet key for IoT devices. In: 2016 International Conference on Circuits, Controls, Communications and Computing (I4C), pp. 1–7, October 2016. https://doi.org/10.1109/CIMCA.2016.8053280
2. Azaria, A., Ekblaw, A., Vieira, T., Lippman, A.: Medrec: Using blockchain for medical data access and permission management. In: International Conference on Open and Big Data (OBD), pp. 25–30. IEEE (2016)
3. Babar, S., Mahalle, P., Stango, A., Prasad, N., Prasad, R.: Proposed security model and threat taxonomy for the Internet of Things (IoT). In: Recent Trends in Network Security and Applications, pp. 420–429 (2010)
4. Cachin, C.: Architecture of the hyperledger blockchain fabric. In: Workshop on Distributed Cryptocurrencies and Consensus Ledgers (2016)
5. Chen, J., Liu, Y., Chai, Y.: An identity management framework for internet of things. In: 2015 IEEE 12th International Conference on e-Business Engineering (ICEBE), pp. 360–364. IEEE (2015)
6. Christidis, K., Devetsikiotis, M.: Blockchains and smart contracts for the internet of things. IEEE Access **4**, 2292–2303 (2016)
7. Crosby, M., Pattanayak, P., Verma, S., Kalyanaraman, V.: Blockchain technology: beyond bitcoin. Appl. Innov. **2**, 6–10 (2016)
8. Douceur, J.R.: The Sybil attack. In: Druschel, P., Kaashoek, F., Rowstron, A. (eds.) IPTPS 2002. LNCS, vol. 2429, pp. 251–260. Springer, Heidelberg (2002). https://doi.org/10.1007/3-540-45748-8_24
9. Fischer, M.J., Lynch, N.A., Paterson, M.S.: Impossibility of distributed consensus with one faulty process. J. ACM (JACM) **32**(2), 374–382 (1985)
10. Godik, S., Moses, T.: OASIS extensible access control markup language (XACML). OASIS Committee Secification cs-xacml-specification-1.0 (2002)
11. Gusmeroli, S., Piccione, S., Rotondi, D.: IoT access control issues: a capability based approach. In: 2012 Sixth International Conference on Innovative Mobile and Internet Services in Ubiquitous Computing (IMIS), pp. 787–792. IEEE (2012)
12. Haller, S., Karnouskos, S., Schroth, C.: The internet of things in an enterprise context. In: Domingue, J., Fensel, D., Traverso, P. (eds.) FIS 2008. LNCS, vol. 5468, pp. 14–28. Springer, Heidelberg (2009). https://doi.org/10.1007/978-3-642-00985-3_2
13. Hevner, A.R., March, S.T., Park, J., Ram, S.: Design science in information systems research. MIS Q. **28**(1), 75–105 (2004)
14. Hu, V.C., et al.: Guide to attribute based access control (ABAC) definition and considerations. NIST Special Publication 800–162 (2014)

15. Kshetri, N.: Can blockchain strengthen the internet of things? IT Prof. **19**(4), 68–72 (2017)
16. Lamport, L., Shostak, R., Pease, M.: The byzantine generals problem. ACM Trans. Program. Lang. Syst. (TOPLAS) **4**(3), 382–401 (1982)
17. Di Francesco Maesa, D., Mori, P., Ricci, L.: Blockchain based access control. In: Chen, L.Y., Reiser, H.P. (eds.) DAIS 2017. LNCS, vol. 10320, pp. 206–220. Springer, Cham (2017). https://doi.org/10.1007/978-3-319-59665-5_15
18. Mickens, J.: The saddest moment. Login Usenix Mag. **39**(3), 52–54 (2014)
19. Moinet, A., Darties, B., Baril, J.L.: Blockchain based trust & authentication for decentralized sensor networks. arXiv preprint arXiv:1706.01730 (2017)
20. Osmanoglu, E.: Identity and Access Management: Business Performance Through Connected Intelligence. Newnes, Waltham (2013)
21. Ouaddah, A., Mousannif, H., Elkalam, A.A., Ouahman, A.A.: Access control in the internet of things: big challenges and new opportunities. Comput. Netw. **112**, 237–262 (2017)
22. Outchakoucht, A., Hamza, E.S., Leroy, J.P.: Dynamic access control policy based on blockchain and machine learning for the internet of things. Int. J. Adv. Comput. Sci. Appl. **8**(7), 417–424 (2017)
23. Polyzos, G.C., Fotiou, N.: Blockchain-assisted information distribution for the internet of things. In: 2017 IEEE International Conference on Information Reuse and Integration (IRI), pp. 75–78. IEEE (2017)
24. Rodrigues, R., Liskov, B., Chen, K., Liskov, M., Schultz, D.: Automatic reconfiguration for large-scale reliable storage systems. IEEE Trans. Dependable Secure Comput. **9**(2), 145–158 (2012)
25. Roman, R., Zhou, J., Lopez, J.: On the features and challenges of security and privacy in distributed internet of things. Comput. Netw. **57**(10), 2266–2279 (2013)
26. Salman, O., Abdallah, S., Elhajj, I.H., Chehab, A., Kayssi, A.: Identity-based authentication scheme for the internet of things. In: 2016 IEEE Symposium on Computers and Communication (ISCC), pp. 1109–1111. IEEE (2016)
27. Sandhu, R.S., Coyne, E.J., Feinstein, H.L., Youman, C.E.: Role-based access control models. Computer **29**(2), 38–47 (1996)
28. Schneider, F.B.: Implementing fault-tolerant services using the state machine approach: a tutorial. ACM Comput. Surv. (CSUR) **22**(4), 299–319 (1990)
29. Shafagh, H., Hithnawi, A., Duquennoy, S.: Towards blockchain-based auditable storage and sharing of IoT data. arXiv preprint arXiv:1705.08230 (2017)
30. Trnka, M., Cerny, T.: Identity management of devices in internet of things environment. In: 2016 6th International Conference on IT Convergence and Security (ICITCS), pp. 1–4. IEEE (2016)
31. Vukolić, M.: The quest for scalable blockchain fabric: proof-of-work vs. BFT replication. In: Camenisch, J., Kesdoğan, D. (eds.) iNetSec 2015. LNCS, vol. 9591, pp. 112–125. Springer, Cham (2016). https://doi.org/10.1007/978-3-319-39028-4_9
32. Vukolić, M.: Rethinking permissioned blockchains. In: Proceedings of the ACM Workshop on Blockchain, Cryptocurrencies and Contracts, pp. 3–7. ACM (2017)
33. Zhu, X., Badr, Y., Pacheco, J., Hariri, S.: Autonomic identity framework for the internet of things. In: 2017 International Conference on Cloud and Autonomic Computing (ICCAC), pp. 69–79. IEEE (2017)

Access Control Requirements for Physical Spaces Protected by Virtual Perimeters

Brian Greaves, Marijke Coetzee$^{(\boxtimes)}$, and Wai Sze Leung

University of Johannesburg, Auckland Park 2006, South Africa
{bgreaves,marijkec,wsleung}@uj.ac.za

Abstract. Intelligent computing capabilities are gradually being entrenched into physical spaces, thereby clouding the boundaries between physical and cyber spaces. To date, physically-enabled cyber-attacks have not fully been addressed in cyber space, due to a limitation on available technology. When a sensitive spreadsheet is printed, it leaves the protection of the logical space, and is only protected by security mechanisms of the physical space in which it is located. To provide better protection, a virtual perimeter can be formed around such a document, using location and topology-aware technologies. Making security mechanisms more location and topology-aware requires the investigation of a range of security relevant characteristics and their possible representations. To date, not much research has been done to address the protection of assets within a virtual perimeter. This research makes a contribution by evaluating a number of current access control approaches that address the physical and cyber world together, and then proposes a set of access control requirements for physical spaces that are protected by virtual perimeters.

Keywords: Access control · Virtual perimeter · Topology · Location
Depth sensing

1 Introduction

Recent research indicates that consumer electronics are becoming increasingly more location and context-aware [1]. There are many novel applications using augmented reality, and cyber physical systems that have a need for location precision. In this regard, 3D imaging systems are a focus of recent research and development [1]. By enabling applications to be more location and context-aware, 3D imaging can become a pervasive part of daily life. Due to its properties, 3D imaging has much potential to enhance the security of both physical and logical objects.

Very often, applications are used in indoor environments where popular outdoor positioning technologies such as Global Positioning System (GPS) are not effective [2]. In addition, indoor environments could be open areas or spaces not physically separated by walls and doors. For example, in a laboratory, one can use equipment in one space when you are in its proximity, but may not approach restricted equipment in the corner of the room if you do not have the right clearance. If the restricted equipment is moved to another space in the room, it should stay restricted. Valuable assets thus need to be protected as their topology changes. This can be achieved by considering both a

© Springer Nature Switzerland AG 2018
S. Furnell et al. (Eds.): TrustBus 2018, LNCS 11033, pp. 182–197, 2018.
https://doi.org/10.1007/978-3-319-98385-1_13

physical and a cyber space that addresses structural relationships such as containment, proximity, and reachability [3]. The identification, authentication and access control of both physical and cyber subjects and objects should thus be defined in combination with positioning and proximity. In such cases, it may not be required to know the exact coordinates for entities, but rather to have an understanding of their proximity within a certain space and associated privileges within that space.

Making security mechanisms more location and topology-aware requires the investigation of a range of security relevant characteristics and their possible representations. For example, the physical layout of a room with a physical boundary, or a space in a room defined by a virtual perimeter, and their containment relationships within other rooms or spaces; the proximity of spaces; and the reachability from space to space needs to be defined. Even though location based access control [4] has been an active field of research, it has not been addressed when physical and logical spaces converge [5]. When physical and logical spaces converge, so do the boundaries where access control should be enforced. Limiting access to both physical and cyber objects located in a physical space [6] gives rise to the concept of virtual perimeters that should protect assets similarly to how physical boundaries provide protection.

To date, not much research has been done to address the protection of assets within a virtual perimeter. This research makes a contribution by proposing a set of access control requirements for physical spaces that are protected by virtual perimeters.

Next, a motivating example is provided to give an understanding of the problem to be addressed. Thereafter in Sect. 3, physical, logical and cyber-physical access convergence is described. As location and proximity are important considerations location-based techniques are described. In Sect. 4, five relevant access control models are evaluated to gain an understanding of the state of a modern physical and logical domain for access control. Section 5 presents a set of requirements and finally, Sect. 6 concludes the research and presents considerations for future work.

2   Motivating Example

In this example, the physical space considered is an office building with rooms such as offices, meeting rooms and a printer room. The topology of the physical space gives rise to proximity and reachability relationships. Proximity means that entities are co-located. For example, when offices are shared by a number of employees, they are co-located within those offices. If an employee is granted access to an office when he presents his access token, this indicates reachability. Some offices may be restricted to specific employees due to the sensitive nature of work done there.

In cyber space, the topology represents cyber assets and their relationships. Company laptops issued to all employees may be seen as both physical and cyber entities. For example, Alice's laptop is a physical device that delimits the cyber space containing the cyber documents she is working on. Any topological changes in the physical space can enable the execution of actions in the cyber space. When Alice arrives at work with her laptop, it automatically connects to the wireless network for which she has been authorized. Different threats can arise when changes take place in the physical or cyber space. *Cyber* threats such as ransomware attacks and *cyber-*

enabled physical threats when the smoke detector is compromised by a virus are addressed by well-known countermeasures.

In contrast, *physically-enabled cyber* threats arising from changes that occur in the physical space to cause harm to either physical or cyber assets have not been sufficiently addressed by current research. For example, Alice is a finance officer working in a large shared office space with four others. Her office is restricted to those with access. At times employees from other departments may enter the office to discuss financial matters. If a clerk has a meeting with one of the finance officers, he should not be able to see any sensitive information on Alice's or her co-workers' laptop screens by accident, or by intentionally snooping. A maliciously inclined employee may move around in the office in order to view sensitive information and take pictures of any documents that are on desks. Ideally, the camera on his smart device should be disabled while he is located in the finance office. If Alice prints a document in the printing room, others should not be able to read it while it is printing.

Due to the fact that a malicious employee passes a physical boundary, it is very difficult to ensure that he does not pose a threat. The convergence of physical and logical access control should be enforced to protect cyber assets from changes in physical topology. In order to provide protection against such threats it is important to monitor the physical topology of the physical space. To provide protection against such threats the following research question is identified:

Q1 – how can a virtual perimeter be used to monitor a physical space to provide better protection to both cyber and physical assets?

Related work considering physical and logical access control convergence is described next.

3   Related Work

Access control is a security service responsible for limiting access to resources and services for legitimate users of a system [7]. Access control falls into one of two broad domains, namely physical or logical.

Physical access control is defined as the ability to permit or deny access to a physical location or space based on an entity's physical identity and permissions [8]. A physical space is a real-world location with physical boundaries such as walls that prevent entry other than through a portal such as a door. Physical access control is enforced with guards or locks and keys to physically prevent access to a physical space wherein valuables are stored. As guards can be bribed, and tokens stolen, access control has evolved to replace purely physical systems such as locks and keys with computing devices to enforce biometric authentication or context measurement [9].

Logical access control permits or denies access to logical assets such as files or services based on a set of rules or permissions that allow subjects to perform a fixed set of actions on objects [10]. In finer-grained control [9] aspects such as attributes, context roles or trust are used before deciding whether to permit or deny access. Subjects and objects can be in any physical location as logical entities operate on behalf of the human user.

The convergence of logical and physical access control implies the presence of aspects of the physical and logical domains within a single given domain [11]. The term "convergence" denotes effective cooperation [12]. The focus shifts inward from physical perimeter defense to consider protection of objects at specific locations inside the bounds of the perimeter. Due to the fact that location and proximity provide an important foundation to access control for physical spaces, location techniques and services are described next.

3.1   Location Techniques and Services

Location-based access control systems have driven developments in location-based techniques and services. For this research, it is important that a person should be detected and his position established and tracked as he moves around. The location of a person or device is defined relative to the space and time of others in its environment [13]. Position data is information about location at a specific place and time, within a specific context. The level of accuracy required for position information is determined by how it is to be used. For example, if a system reported that a person is close to restricted equipment, when they are actually busy operating the equipment it would not be acceptable. Location determines if a user is standing in front of a device, and how many times the user has entered a space.

Indoor Positioning Systems (IPSs) compute the position of people or objects inside physical spaces such as buildings in four different manners using [14] *dead-reckoning*, where position of a person is obtained with sensors such as accelerometers and magnetometers; *direct sensing*, that employs infrared, ultrasound, Bluetooth beacons or barcodes; *triangulation* by using Radio Frequency Identification (RFID), infrared or ultrasound; and *pattern recognition* where sensors produce data by means of computer vision or fingerprinting. Systems based on Wi-Fi-fingerprints are not accurate as the there is an error of up to 2 m in a room when positioning people [15].

Recent research points to the fact that vision-based technologies can be used as a more unconventional way to determine the position of users [16]. Camera systems are not very expensive and fairly simple to use. Optical indoor positioning [17] can find the position of users in a scene with 3D models, images, coded markers or projected patterns. By considering global coordinates at the same time stamp, the distance between two objects such as skeletons can be derived in order to discern between different users. The position of each user can however not be determined. One of the deficiencies is that it is complex to identify people in a scenario and therefore additional techniques such as real-time face detection, color, or pattern codes are needed.

4   State-of-the-Art Review of Physical/Logical Access Control Convergence

To understand the manner in which current research addresses the convergence between physical and logical access control, a number of approaches are reviewed and compared against each other with the aim to identify similarities and research gaps. To understand the manner in which current research addresses the convergence between physical and logical access control, a systematic mapping research approach [18] is adopted. The approach formulates a research question (given by $Q1$ in Sect. 2) to use as criteria to identify relevant literature. An evaluation then identifies outstanding research challenges, leading to access control requirements. Recent approaches addressing location-based access control in a physical domain to support either physical or logical access control are selected. The environments vary between smart buildings, rooms and spaces where services are provided based on proximity. The five approaches are *AFBIM* (Authorisation framework using Building Information Models) [18], *TAAC* (Topology-aware access control for smart spaces) [20], *SCLAC* (Soft-computing based location-aware access control for smart buildings) [21], *SEAC* (Sensor enhanced access control) [6], SC (Spatial connector: Mapping access control models for pervasive computing and cloud environments) [22]. Since the focus of this research is on indoor environments, access control systems using Wi-Fi positioning are excluded due to their limited degree of accuracy. It is important to note that these five approaches are by no means exhaustive, but rather a selection of appropriate models that match research question $Q1$, to the best of the authors' knowledge.

4.1   *AFBIM* (Authorisation Framework Using Building Information Models)

This research suggests that assets in smart buildings can remotely be controlled by using networks [19]. Their approach is that physical and logical security operations need to converge to ensure protection at both levels. The convergence of access control is supported by making use of Building Information Models (BIM) [23] as a spatial data model in three key stages of access control namely policy specification, policy administration and decision making. The resultant access control framework addresses both logical and physical resources in one model. This work is the first of its kind where BIMs, as spatial data models, are used for access control. The BIM spatial data model uses Industry Foundation Classes (IFC), an official International Standard ISO/IS 16739 [24] to denote logical representations for physical locations or zones. For example, zones, property sets, adjacency of spaces, portals connecting spaces, and size of spaces can be defined. Such spatial models can hold logical relationships between building elements, such as zones and spaces, which are not normally present in GIS applications. Spatial reasoning addresses e.g. the location of access doors to a space, the reachability analysis between zones, or accessing all temperature sensors in a given space. BIM-XACML was proposed as a new policy language extension to XACML [25] that supports and access control policy using BIMs that can enforce access control restrictions based on object relationships and spatial relationships. For example, a room is shown as <IfcSpace id = "Elab231">. It is assumed that subsystems for closed-circuit television monitoring, lighting control, temperature sensors, smoke sensors, and physical access control to building spaces is available. The model favors lower sensor density by tracking user location using a token-based access approach.

4.2   TAAC (Topology-Aware Access Control for Smart Spaces)

The TAAC model [20] makes use of a Building Information Model (BIM) to represent all topological and contextual information, but then extends it to the BIM-Sec model, focusing on physical access control. A logical representation of the physical building is provided that shows security-relevant contextual characteristics, such as where assets are placed and how security controls should be enacted. The physical spaces are shown e.g. as a building contains rooms, and two rooms are connected through a door. The topology of a cyber space captures e.g. the network and all digital devices within the building and relationships such as a file stored in a device and device connectivity via the network. By representing the status of files as open or not, it can be detected whether agents that are co-located in the physical space of the device in which the file is stored, can see it thereby breaching its confidentiality. The work highlights the fact that spaces such as rooms are limited by walls. Spaces may contain elements such as furniture which are in a specific location in the room. This approach shows that by considering the topology of the cyber and physical space a better view of the attack surface could be seen, leading to the definition of more robust access control policies. Such policies are improved by considering containment and connectivity relationships.

Role-based access control (RBAC) policies support agents with a set of roles which provides access to physical areas and assets, alternatively, attribute-based access control (ABAC) can be applied [26].

4.3   SCLAC (Soft-Computing Based Location-Aware Access Control for Smart Buildings)

SCLAC [21] proposes a distributed location-aware access control mechanism for smart buildings. The problems experienced with traditional location-based services such as GPS for indoor environments are addressed by using the magnetometers found in most modern smartphones, together with a magnetic field map of the building showing where service providers are located. An external hardware infrastructure is not needed such as access points. Each constrained device does not have to process the location data of the whole building space, but only needs to estimate their current location. A limitation is that the solution is highly dependent on data provided by the magnetic sensors of smart phones.

An access control engine is embedded into smart objects that can make access control decisions by considering both the location of a user their access credentials. The location of a user is estimated using a novel indoor localization system based on magnetic field data that is generated by the user's personal phone. The location-aware access control mechanism is thus completely decentralized as no third party is needed to make access control decisions. Firstly, 2D maps of magnetic field measurements of a building are taken and combined with mechanisms to solve localization based on such maps. As users move through the building, their location data are estimated through Radial Basis Function Networks (RBF). All smart objects are assigned to a security zone. If a user has been granted access to a security zone, and they make an access request, their credentials are evaluated before access is granted. Credentials are attached in the access request as access capabilities, as defined in the CapBAC model [27].

4.4   *SEAC* (Sensor Enhanced Access Control)

The *SEAC* [6] approach is focused on a single physical space such as a room and identifies that logical access control is restricted by physical security. For example, a sensitive financial report is physically rendered by e.g. displaying it on a screen or printing it as a document. The access to this report is constrained by physical security as a user without read access, located in the same room, may view the report as it is being printed. The granularity of physical access control, such as the boundaries of a room consequently defines the context for logical access control. The constraints imposed by physical security may thus override that of logical security. By using sensors, the current context in the room can be established and adapted. Sensors are placed at physical end-points such as at screens, speaker systems, or printers and are managed by a sensor server. Simple web cameras used in combination with motion detection determines whether a user enters or leaves a room. The context of the user's situation and the location of the user may be able to provide constraints to support logical access control.

The access control policy supports authorization and visibility zones. Authorization zones are established using location based services and visibility zones are defined for output devices. The continuous enforcement of access control is done based on context. A simple mandatory access control model is supported based on the Bell and LaPadula model [28], enforcing the no-read-up and no-write-down rules. Security labels are associated with all files and processes that access files. Events are issued by a visibility manager when a user enters or leaves a visibility zone. The visibility manager uses the clearance level of a user and the window levels on a screen to enforce a no-view-up rule to ensure that users only view content that they have been granted access to. For example, if a window level is greater than the clearance level of a user, the window is unmapped. All users in a visibility zone need to be considered at the same time.

4.5   SC (Spatial Connector: Mapping Access Control Models for Pervasive Computing and Cloud Environments)

The *SC* model [22] is based on a real-world physical model where pervasive services are activated/deactivated in accordance with changes that occur in the real world. A bridge is defined between context-centric access control for services and devices in proximity of a user, and the access the user has to services in the cloud at that time and in a specific location. This requires interaction between the pervasive processes in the user's proximity and cloud infrastructures. RBAC is the most prevalent access control mechanism for restricting access to resources in the cloud. Due to the fact that context aware services cannot effectively make use of subject-based access control, RBAC cannot be considered when a user is changing the lights in a room. In this case, the context of the user is more relevant to consider. The concept of the *spatial connector* is introduced to bind the pervasive processes around the user with cloud services, thereby bridging context-aware and subject-based access control with each other. A containment relationship between spaces is used to organize physical spaces. The positions of entities and spaces are virtually bound, and as they change processes are deployed accordingly. The framework contains a location model, which is maintained by RFID sensors, that identifies spaces, entities, and computing devices in a tree structure. A virtual counterpart of the physical world provides all details such as user profiles and network addresses. Finally, a spatial connector connects a virtual counterpart with one or more services. For example, when a user enters a room with his smart phone, a virtual counterpart is migrated to the corresponding room. The spatial connector ensures that a physical entity such as a user is able to make local use of cloud services within a physical space.

The next section discusses their evaluation against a set of criteria.

4.6   Evaluation of Current Research Approaches

The evaluation of the five approaches is now summarized by considering how physical and logical access control is represented, access control, information and location models, and the use of sensors, context and their integration. A selection of the evaluation criteria is shown in Table 1.

Physical and Logical Convergence of Access Control Entities: To enable physical and logical access control convergence, physical and logical entities need to be represented logically in a single model. In most cases, a subject is the physical human who moves about in the real world while trying to gain access to a physical space, physical assets or logical information contained within a physical asset. All models make use of tokens or credentials to represent physical users, with the exception of *SEAC* that uses identity and clearance levels. At the one end of the spectrum, *TAAC* addresses physical access control to enable authorized users to walk through physical spaces containing physical and cyber assets, enabled by logical representations and decision making. Each physical object is given a logical representation, and access control is physically enforced when the user arrives at a door. At the other end of the spectrum, the *SC* model only considers access to logical services to be executed, depending on the location of a user. *SEAC* uniquely considers the fact that logical objects are rendered into physical objects that required more protection due to the physical space they are delivered into.

Access Control Models: Due to the fact that large buildings are being protected, the use of role-based access control combined with attributes, as shown in Table 1 is relevant. Another appropriate model to use is context-based access control where permissions are associated to contexts. *SCLAC* makes use of a distributed CapBAC model that utilizes capabilities. *SEAC* makes use of the mandatory access control model to ensure strict access control for sensitive information.

Spatial Models: To be able to converge physical and logical access control, it is appropriate to have a spatial data model such as a building information model as shown in Table 1. Such a model should be standards-based to ensure interoperability between the systems of an organization. Spatial data is thus stored in a separate model, and referenced by access control policies. With the exception of *TAAC* and *AFBIM*, none of the models employ a standards-based spatial model such as BIMs. *TAAC*, *SC*, and *AFBIM* structure physical spaces using containment relationships to show the relationships between spaces. All models limit a physical space by its physical boundaries, where a room is the smallest space to be considered. *SCLAC* can limit its space to a smaller range of 2.9 m due to the magnetic sensor on the phone.

Table 1. Evaluation

Model	AC model	Spatial model	Spatial awareness	Context	Arch	Sensors	Wearable sensor	Accuracy
AFBIM	RBAC ABAC	BIM	Containment, connectivity, accessibility	Location, time, building layout, status	C	CCTV, lights, smoke sensors, doors	N	Room
TAAC	RBAC ABAC	BIM-SEC	Reachability	Location, building layout, status	C	CCTV, ultra-wideband	N	Room
SCLAC	CapBAC	Magnetic field map	Location of subject and object	Magnetic field values, location	D	Magnetic field sensors	Phone	~2.9 m
SEAC	Mandatory	None	Sensor range, auth zone, visibility zone	Location, time, motion, temperature, file status	C	Camera, radio, noise, temperature	N	Room
SC	CBAC RBAC	Virtual counterpart	Changing location of subjects and objects	Location	C	RFID, Wi-Fi	Phone	Room, 2 m, 1–20 m

Spatial Awareness: Spatial awareness and spatial reasoning shown in Table 1 can intelligently prevent a highly sensitive area from being indirectly accessed via an area without security. A spatial reasoning module should be able to analyze the possibility of how access can be enabled between two spaces such as two rooms. The use of spatial attributes in access control policies is not new, however, the use of three-dimensional spatial data in access control has not been explored extensively. In the *SC* model, the positions of subject, objects and their related locations are spatially bound in a virtual counterpart. As they move through the physical world, their counterparts are deployed at identified locations. When physical entities and object move around in physical spaces, their movements should be detected by location-sensing techniques to change their containment relationship.

Context: As shown in Table 1, a variety of context data is sourced from sensors in the environment such as location, time, temperature, status of physical and cyber subjects and objects.

Sensors and Wearable Sensors: The information collected on physical entities are collected through sensors that transform physical observations into logical signals to form the context that is used in access control decisions. The nature of a sensors may require that they are placed on persons and objects to better their accuracy. Some are only used to determine which room a subject is in, while others are more precise to an order of meters, or direct line of sight. Some models pose no restriction on how to use sensors. More sensors equate to greater density. Some models can operate with a single sensor collecting context while others require each user to carry one such as a mobile phone. Even though more types of context are better to base access decisions on, this would require additional computing power. Ideally, a high context yield and low sensor density is ideal.

The *TAAC* and *AFBIM* models follow a traditional physical access control route by using CCTV cameras and other sensors to enable subjects to enter rooms resulting in a low level of context information gathering. The *SCLAC* model yields the least context information as it is purely location-based. The model is also inexpensive as it uses sensors built into most smartphones. This however does lead to a high density of sensors as each employee needs to have a mobile phone with them.

The *SC* model is more expensive as the industry-grade positioning systems employed are expensive, while still collecting a low amount of context. The *SEAC* model yields a high amount of contextual information due to the assortment of sensors, but each sensor must be placed at each end-point which results in a higher cost and higher sensor density. Figure 1(A) below summarizes the number of contexts vs sensor density. The y-axis indicates a low to high number of context gathered and the x-axis indicates a low to high density.

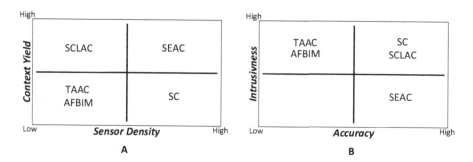

Fig. 1. Sensor context and accuracy

Figure 1(B) sensor intrusiveness verse accuracy. Intrusiveness is an arbitrary measurement that indicates the required effort by users of the system to utilize the sensors. For example, observation by camera takes no effort on the user's part, but the wearing of active RFID tags or passive RFID tokens is more intrusive. The accuracy measurement is considered high if sensor accuracy can place a user within an order of meters, and low if a user can only be placed in a particular room. A low intrusiveness and high accuracy are ideal in this comparison.

SEAC is an ideal model in this comparison as it is not intrusive and provides a high level of accuracy due to line-of-sight of the camera sensor.

Due to the RFID approaches used by *TAAC* and *AFBIM*, they both yield low accuracy while being intrusive which makes them the least ideal.

SC and *SCLAC* are in the middle ground as they are both intrusive but are accurate.

5 Access Control Requirements for Physical Spaces Protected by Virtual Perimeters

Based on research question *Q1* identified in the scenario, and the evaluation presented above, this research proceeds to propose a set of access control requirements following the approach defined by Haley et al. [29]. Such requirements should meet the access control goal of protecting both physical and logical assets found within a virtual perimeter. Functionally, a physical space exists where e.g. employees have gained legitimate access to an office space for a meeting. The space is defined by the boundaries of the rooms by walls and doors. Both logical assets found on Alice's laptop, as well as logical services on the smart devices of the visiting employees, such as cameras needs to be protected. For protection of high-assurance to be enforced in these spaces, the logical and physical domains need to be converged and viewed in a unified manner in a single access control model.

The following access control requirements are presented to satisfy the scenario's access control goals.

5.1 Representation of Physical and Cyber Spaces and Access Control Information Must Be Comprehensive

Security relevant contextual information can be provided by having a representation of the topology of cyber and physical assets in order to understand their relationships and structure.

- The topology of the physical space can provide information on rooms and equipment and their relations with regards to containment and connectivity.
- The topology of the cyber space can capture how digital assets and services are configured, how they are contained and connected to each other.

The representation of physical subjects and objects needs to be defined logically by ensuring a tight coupling between the physical entity and the state of the logical representation.

- The representation of physical subjects such as users can be implemented with tokens and credentials.
- The representation of physical objects such as a laptop can be defined logically by its e.g. identity, location and image.
- The rendering of a logical object into a physical object needs to be represented in the access control policy due to the fact that the physical spaces in which it is rendered does not provide protection.

The representation of a physical location needs to be carefully implemented. When using location indoors, it is not important to know the real geographical position of an object or subject. It is rather more important to understand their relative position to their environment. For this research, virtual coordinates can be used to identify a specific location by using a three-point coordinate systems as the spatial base.

5.2   Continuous Authentication Needs to Be Enforced

In physical cyber security convergence, a physical access control policy of a building could have many points of authentication where a user presents his access token. The repetitive re-authentication of a user should be avoided, but the user should rather be tracked using sensors from where authentication is done to where access control is enforced. Similarly, physical objects that are moved around need to be continuously tracked to ensure their integrity and safety.

5.3   A Spatial Data Model and Spatial Awareness Needs to Be Supported

To be able to protect resources in a cyber-physical world, a spatial data model can be of importance as it provides a vocabulary to represent location data that is needed to express subjects and objects in access control policies. A spatial data model can represent objects to ensure that object representations are removed from access control policies to better manage changes. Changes to spaces that are represented by spatial coordinates in access control policies would require a change to all rules that reference a space. The BIM data model described previously can be used by large organizations. Other approaches such as the ISDM (Indoor Spatial Data Model) can be used to support 3D indoor locations [30].

Due to the fact that access control decisions need to be able to interpret user location and object location from a spatial data model, spatial functions are required to assist with this decision making. The spatial data model and any spatial reasoning components should support spatial functions such as the containment of spaces, the connectivity between spaces and the accessibility of spaces.

5.4   Virtual Boundaries Need to Be Enforced

The protection provided by physical walls should be extended from the physical to the cyber domain. For this research, a virtual boundary is defined as a "virtual perimeter". The level of protection provided by a virtual perimeter can be determined by the sensitivity of resources to be protected. For example, either no access or read access can be provided.

A virtual perimeter should be placed around a real-world physical space, where it is assumed that the space is atomic in nature. For example, Alice can specify a virtual perimeter around her desk in the office, so that all resources would be protected if unauthorized persons should come within 2 m of her desk. A virtual perimeter thus belongs to the owner of the physical space to protect all resources owned by them.

To be able to implement virtual perimeters, various technologies such as geofences [31] can be used, as they are used as virtual perimeter for real-world indoor areas. Approaches such as FloGeo [32] provide a floatable 3D geofence model that can move around with objects.

5.5   Sensors Should Accurately Identify, Locate and Track Physical and Cyber Entities

Current research indicates that resources are protected within a space such as a room, where sensor technology can determine that they have moved into or out of a room. The accuracy of commonly used sensors does not have the ability of measure the movement of a person 2 m from a desk to right in front of the desk. If sensors do have this ability, they are normally used invasively in a manner that may prompt users to circumvent their use.

It is shown that CCTV cameras and radio sensors can successfully track persons as they move around in a building. In [6] a simple web camera sensor identified persons that came into a space without the person wearing a token. A limitation of these cameras is that they are subject to inaccuracies such as occlusion and manage 2D images that cannot support measurement of the distance between objects.

In this regard, depth sensing cameras may be an important new type of sensor to add the set of sensors to be used. Depth sensing cameras are inexpensive and have the ability to evaluate the distances between a generic point in space and multiple objects in the environment. They return a rich set of information via a single camera. A common approach for estimating distances makes use of a point cloud obtained by projecting a depth image in a Cartesian space which is a three-dimensional coordinate that represents the distances between points. Using a single camera in the corner of the office, the distance between an uninvited employee and Alice's desk can be determined to understand if a virtual perimeter has been crossed. Such a configuration of sensors may result in a high context yield and low sensor density.

As the location and context information produced by sensors may be considered invasive by employees, their privacy needs to be considered. Every effort must be made to use location sensing and context information only for authentication or access control purposes and to protect it from unauthorized persons. For example, one may limit the viewing of location information or feeds from sensors until an irregularity is identified by the system [33].

5.6   Logical Access Control Should Be Enforced in a Physical Space

Access control should be extended to not only protect logical entities, but also logical entities that have been rendered into a physical representation [6]. Logical services within the bounds of a virtual perimeter should be detected and managed to ensure the protection of resources within the virtual perimeter. For example, the camera and microphone on the smart device of an employee should be switched off while inside a virtual perimeter. The movement of the laptop to a meeting room should result in similar physical protections in the logical domain.

6 Conclusion

This research identifies the need for a virtual perimeter in a physical space to protect both logical and physical entities by using an example. An extensive evaluation is performed of five recent approaches where physical and logical access control was converged in some manner. The evaluation provides insight into recent access control design aspects such as spatial data models and spatial awareness, logical and physical representations of location and topology, and the limitation when considering physical spaces as almost all models make use of the boundaries of a space such as a room.

To address research gaps that were identified, this research proposes a set of six access control requirements for physical spaces that need to provide better protection to physical and logical entities. The main contribution of this research is the identification of the lack of effective positioning systems for access control to be adequately performed. Camera systems are not popular to solve these problems as they suffer from inaccuracies when monocular image processing is performed. To date, not much research has been performed using stereovision camera systems to accurately determine topology information. The next research aims to explore the use of advanced stereovision imaging to support depth perception, positional tracking, and 3D mapping to better access control for use in physical spaces.

References

1. Plank, H., Steinbaeck, J., Druml, N., Steger, C., Holweg, G.: Localization and context determination for cyber-physical systems based on 3D imaging (Chap. 1). In: Solutions for Cyber-Physical Systems Ubiquity, pp. 1–26. IGI-Global (2018)
2. Alarifi, A., et al.: Ultra wideband indoor positioning technologies: analysis and recent advances. Sensors **16**(5), 707 (2016)
3. Tsigkanos, C., Pasquale, L., Ghezzi, C., Nuseibeh, B.: On the interplay between cyber and physical spaces for adaptive security. IEEE Trans. Depend. Secur. Comput. **15**(3), 466–480 (2016)
4. Gao, C., Yu, Z., Wei, Y., Russell, S., Guan, Y.: A statistical indoor localization method for supporting location-based access control. Mob. Netw. Appl. **14**(2), 253–263 (2009)
5. Marakkannu, S.P., Sivakumar, B.B., Joseph, V., Honeywell International Inc.: Physical and logical threat analysis in access control systems using BIM. U.S. Patent 9,799,208 (2017)
6. Jensen, C.D., Geneser, K., Willemoes-Wissing, I.C.: Sensor enhanced access control: extending traditional access control models with context-awareness. In: Fernández-Gago, C., Martinelli, F., Pearson, S., Agudo, I. (eds.) IFIPTM 2013. IAICT, vol. 401, pp. 177–192. Springer, Heidelberg (2013). https://doi.org/10.1007/978-3-642-38323-6_13
7. Sandhu, R.S., Samarati, P.: Access control: principle and practice. IEEE Commun. Mag. **32**(9), 40–48 (1994)
8. Matyáš, V., Říha, Z.: Biometric authentication—security and usability. In: Jerman-Blažič, B., Klobučar, T. (eds.) Advanced Communications and Multimedia Security. ITIFIP, vol. 100, pp. 227–239. Springer, Boston, MA (2002). https://doi.org/10.1007/978-0-387-35612-9_17
9. Sandhu, R., Samarati, P.: Authentication, access control, and audit. ACM Comput. Surv. (CSUR) **28**(1), 241–243 (1996)

10. Sandhu, R.S.: Lattice-based access control models. Computer **26**(11), 9–19 (1993)
11. Cardenas, A., Amin, S., Sinopoli, B., Giani, A., Perrig, A., Sastry, S.: Challenges for securing cyber physical systems. In: Workshop on Future Directions in Cyber-physical Systems Security, vol. 5, July 2009
12. Cerullo, G., Coppolino, L., D'Antonio, S., Formicola, V., Papale, G., Ragucci, B.: Enabling convergence of physical and logical security through intelligent event correlation. In: Novais, P., Camacho, D., Analide, C., El Fallah Seghrouchni, A., Badica, C. (eds.) Intelligent Distributed Computing IX. SCI, vol. 616, pp. 427–437. Springer, Cham (2016). https://doi.org/10.1007/978-3-319-25017-5_40
13. Rainham, D., McDowell, I., Krewski, D., Sawada, M.: Conceptualizing the healthscape: contributions of time geography, location technologies and spatial ecology to place and health research. Soc. Sci. Med. **70**(5), 668–676 (2010)
14. Fallah, N., Apostolopoulos, I., Bekris, K., Folmer, E.: Indoor human navigation systems: a survey. Interact. Comput. **25**, 21–33 (2013)
15. Duque Domingo, J., Cerrada, C., Valero, E., Cerrada, J.: Indoor positioning system using depth maps and wireless networks. J. Sens. **2016**, 8 (2016)
16. Duque Domingo, J., Cerrada, C., Valero, E., Cerrada, J.A.: An improved indoor positioning system using RGB-D cameras and wireless networks for use in complex environments. Sensors **17**(10), 2391 (2017)
17. Mautz, R., Tilch, S.: Survey of optical indoor positioning systems. In: Proceedings of the 2011 International Conference on Indoor Positioning and Indoor Navigation (IPIN), Guimaraes, Portugal, 21–23 September 2011, pp. 1–7 (2011)
18. Petersen, K., Feldt, R., Mujtaba, S., Mattsson, M.: Systematic mapping studies in software engineering. In: EASE, vol. 8, pp. 68–77, June 2008
19. Skandhakumar, N., Reid, J., Dawson, E., Drogemuller, R., Salim, F.: An authorization framework using building information models. Comput. J. **55**(10), 1244–1264 (2012)
20. Pasquale, L., et al.: Topology-aware access control of smart spaces. Computer **50**(7), 54–63 (2017)
21. Hernández, J.L., Moreno, M.V., Jara, A.J., Skarmeta, A.F.: A soft computing based location-aware access control for smart buildings. Soft. Comput. **18**(9), 1659–1674 (2014)
22. Satoh, I.: Spatial connector: mapping access control models for pervasive computing and cloud computing. Procedia Comput. Sci. **110**, 174–181 (2017)
23. Gu, N., Singh, V., Taylor, C., London, K., Brankovic, L.: BIM adoption: expectations across disciplines. In: Handbook of Research on Building Information Modeling and Construction Informatics: Concepts and Technologies, pp. 501–520. IGI Global (2010)
24. ISO 16739:2013. https://www.iso.org/standard/51622.html
25. OASIS XACML Technical Committee. eXtensible access control markup language (XACML) Version 3.0. Oasis Standard, OASIS (2013)
26. Kandala, S., Sandhu, R., Bhamidipati, V.: An attribute based framework for risk-adaptive access control models. In: 2011 Sixth International Conference on Availability, Reliability and Security (ARES), pp. 236–241. IEEE, August 2011
27. Hernández-Ramos, J.L., Jara, A.J., Marin, L., Skarmeta, A.F.: Distributed capability-based access control for the internet of things. J. Internet Serv. Inf. Secur. (JISIS) **3**(3/4), 1–16 (2013)
28. Elliott Bell, D.: Bell–La Padula model. In: van Tilborg, H.C.A., Jajodia, S. (eds.) Encyclopedia of Cryptography and Security, pp. 74–79. Springer, Boston (2011). https://doi.org/10.1007/978-1-4419-5906-5_811
29. Haley, C.B., Laney, R., Moffett, J.D., Nuseibeh, B.: Security requirements engineering: a framework for representation and analysis. IEEE Trans. Softw. Eng. **34**(1), 133–153 (2008)

30. Kim, Y.J., Kang, H.Y., Lee, J.: Development of indoor spatial data model using CityGML ADE. ISPRS-Int. Arch. Photogramm. Remote Sens. Spat. Inf. Sci. **1**(2), 41–45 (2013)

31. Namiot, D., Sneps-Sneppe, M.: Geofence and network proximity. In: Balandin, S., Andreev, S., Koucheryavy, Y. (eds.) NEW2AN/ruSMART -2013. LNCS, vol. 8121, pp. 117–127. Springer, Heidelberg (2013). https://doi.org/10.1007/978-3-642-40316-3_11

32. Young-Hyun, E., Young-Keun, C., Cho, S., Jeon, B.: FloGeo: a floatable three-dimensional geofence with mobility for the internet of things. J. Adv. Res. Dyn. Control Syst. 08-Special Issue, 114–120 (2017)

33. Rajpoot, Q.M., Jensen, C.D.: Video surveillance: privacy issues and legal compliance. In: Promoting Social Change and Democracy Through Information Technology, p. 69 (2015)

Towards the Definition of a Security Incident Response Modelling Language

Myrsini Athinaiou[1(✉)], Haralambos Mouratidis[1(✉)], Theo Fotis[1(✉)],
Michalis Pavlidis[1(✉)], and Emmanouil Panaousis[2(✉)]

[1] Centre for Secure, Intelligent and Usable Systems, University of Brighton,
Brighton, UK
{M.Athinaiou,H.Mouratidis,T.Fotis,M.Pavlidis}@brighton.ac.uk
[2] Surrey Centre for Cyber Security, University of Surrey, Guildford, UK
e.panaousis@surrey.ac.uk

Abstract. This paper presents a cyber-physical systems modelling language for capturing and describing health-based critical infrastructures. Following this practice incident response plan developers are able to model and reason about security and recovery issues in medical cyber-physical systems from a security requirements engineering perspective. Our work builds upon concepts from the Secure Tropos methodology, where in this paper we introduce novel cyber-physical concepts, relationships and properties in order to carry out analysis of incident response plans based on security requirements. We illustrate our concepts through a case study of a radiological department's medical cyber-physical systems that have been infected with the WannaCry ransomware. Finally, we discuss how our modelling language enriches security models with incident response concepts, guiding plan developers of health-based critical infrastructures in understanding cyber-physical systems vulnerabilities and support decision making at a tactical and a strategic level, through semi-automated secure recovery analysis.

Keywords: Cyber-physical systems modelling language
Meta-model · Incident response · Security requirements engineering

1 Introduction

In this paper we present a Security Incident Response Modelling Language (SIRML) to capture incident response (IR) concepts. When a hacker is able to damage medical equipment by taking control of devices, the best a health care organization can hope for is that the cyber-physical attack will be identified early, the medical systems will shut down without causing further damages/harm and normal operation will be restored in short-time. When attacks have occurred, decisions cannot be made on the go. There is a need for a structured approach to thwart adversarial attempts making changes to systems and their components. Because, once the security perimeter of the corporate infrastructure is penetrated, the industrial systems are exposed to attacks that will be

© Springer Nature Switzerland AG 2018
S. Furnell et al. (Eds.): TrustBus 2018, LNCS 11033, pp. 198–212, 2018.
https://doi.org/10.1007/978-3-319-98385-1_14

generated from inside an organization. Incident response planning is also important to become more automated and dynamic, as attackers can use common responses as triggers for further attacks [5].

This work builds upon the Secure Tropos [18] modelling language and extends concepts, attributes and relationships to allow the cyber-physical aspect to be represented along with the view of IR as integral part of security. The SIRML is part of a broader research effort to create a methodology which will allow the modelling of health-based IR, supporting safety and security constraints, prioritizing to protect patients. This paper contributes to the current body of knowledge by **(C1)** providing a meta-model for cyber-physical systems (CPS), aligning concepts of security and IR, **(C2)** defining concepts, attributes and relationships to model at an operational, tactical and strategic level secure IR plans and **(C3)** presenting the graphical notation that can be used to instantiate the SIRML in order to facilitate further analysis, common understanding and assessment of recovery plans from heterogeneous incident response teams (IRTs), which can consist of managers, medical equipment technicians, engineers, IT sub-teams and security experts.

The remaining of the paper is structured as follows. Section 2 introduces the secure recovery meta-model and explains in more detail the newly introduced concepts, relationships and notation. In Sect. 3 a case study is discussed to demonstrate how the SIRML can be utilized. In Sect. 4 the related work is briefly presented. Finally, while Sect. 5 concludes the paper by summarizing its content and contributions, it also discussing language limitations and future research directions.

2 The Secure Incident Response Modelling Language

In this section the SIRML, that enables the modelling of CPS IR plans from a security requirements engineering point of view, is presented. Firstly, the meta-model of the secure recovery language is introduced, which extends and builds upon the Secure Tropos modelling language [18]. The current version of the SIRML meta-model is shown in Fig. 1. To distinguish the inherited from Secure Tropos concepts from those newly introduced, colours are used. The concepts of the model that are white are used as in Secure Tropos and their definitions can be found in [18], unless specified otherwise. On the other hand, the novel secure recovery concepts are coloured with green (bronze), grey (silver) and yellow (gold). The different colours indicate the recovery stage that a plan refers to and range from operational to tactical and strategic.

2.1 SIRML Introduced Concepts and Attributes

We now present our security IR extensions, highlighting each addition of a concept through a definition, description and explanation of the main reason that needs to be introduced at a metamodelling level. Furthermore, in this subsection we present attributes in order to describe an instance of a concept in more

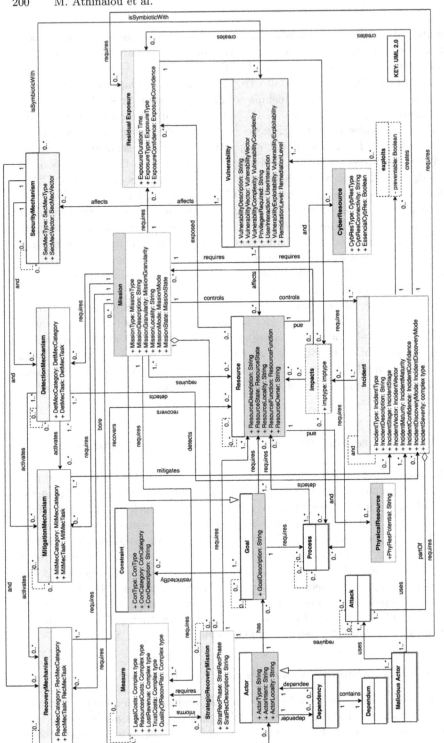

Fig. 1. The secure incident response language meta-model. (Color figure online)

detail. Attributes allows the IRT to provide both abstract and technical details to instances of a concept, therefore supporting varying degrees of granularity when describing the system or/and infrastructure under design. The range of values of the attributes of the SIRML concepts are shown in Fig. 2.

Cyber Resource is a digital entity that is part of an infrastructures function that includes different types of software (i.e. operational system, forensic toolkits and digital badges). At a detection level, it can indicate the source of an attack precisely. It is a necessary concept for the designation of duties to IT subteam. *Mission* represents a sub-goal that cannot fail during an attack due to its criticality for a CI. This concept is helpful for an IRT to prioritize resources at a tactical recovery stage. *Physical Resource* stands for the kinetic aspect of a system which can include controllers, switches, actuators, timers, field devices, active medical devices, meters and similar entities. At a detection level it can assist the inspections planning of the engineering sub-team of an IRT. This concept is necessary for the designation of duties to engineering sub-teams with different areas of specialization e.g. mechanical, electrical, biomedical.

Incident stands for the intentional unauthorized access to a system, service or resource of a CI or the compromise of a system's security properties (i.e. CIA triad, CO2 triad). This concept differentiates an event and a threat clarifying that an incident is successful and has malicious intent. Aggregates one or more *attacks* as attempts to exploit a vulnerability and together they can constitute an incident. From there, the planning can face the particular aspects of an incident and examine its possible propagation in order to identify the root cause and predict any propagation attempts and cascading effects. *Detection Mechanism* includes the security means used primarily from an infrastructure within a particular threat scenario for detection purposes. It allows IRTs to design how they are going to collect information for a possible attack in order to support management decisions. *Mitigation Mechanism* is used for security means that are utilized primarily from an infrastructure within a particular threat scenario for mitigation purposes. It enables IRTs to plan relocation, isolation of resources, conducting impact assessment and signing to each resource a priority towards the stabilization of an attack. *Recovery Mechanism* is for security means used primarily from an infrastructure within a particular threat scenario for recovery purposes. It permits IRTs to model the uncontaminated, replaced, reintegrated resources and the means needed for those action to be achievable.

2.2   SIRML Introduced and Extended Relationships

In this subsection we outline the relationships linking together concepts from recovery and security requirements engineering domains. We now define the relationships in our modelling language by building upon the meta-model in the previous section.

Specialization of Mission: A *mission* is a critical part of an *activity* that needs to be protected even when an incident in the form of a cyber-physical attack has been successful. When recovery for an individual responder is designed this *mission* can become more fine-grained. This becomes particularly important in the long term planning and the concept of *strategic mission*. Based on this concept *activities* and relocation of resources can be modelled along with other decisions and specifying the actors that will perform them, showing the different time interval for the applicability of such recovery plans, focused on security. Hence, the specialization of a mission is represented with an inheritance relationship.

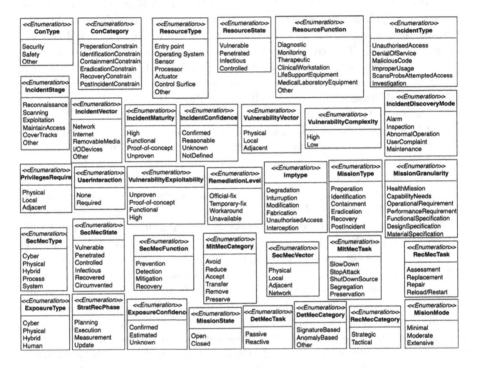

Fig. 2. The secure IR concepts' attributes.

Specialization of a Security Mechanism: A *security mechanism* can be decomposed to *detection mechanism, mitigation mechanism* and *recovery mechanism*. These subcategories of *security mechanisms* have different functions within an incident response plan and its phases. These phases are commonly referred as preparation, identification, containment, eradication, recovery, lessons learned and should not be confused with the different child concepts of security mechanism. To indicate this sharing of common behaviours among detection, mitigation, recovery and security mechanisms we depict there relationships using the inheritance arrow.

Resource Reflexive Association: The reflexive association among resources occur as the *resource* class can perform different tasks and forms various associations among concepts of the same class, as well as other classes. For example, a medical device, which is a form of resource, works in a hospital and can be an X-ray scanner, a defibrillator, an anesthetic machine, a medical laser or a medical image storage device. If the X-ray scanner is storing images in a medical image storage device then there relationship could be modelled as two instances of the same class that communicate with each other.

Incident Reflexive Association: Incidents are referring to cyber-physical attacks that commonly described as been wrapped, usually inside exploit kits. The execution of one attack triggers a series of other attacks. In some cases they multiply and spread. In order for the modelling language to able to show that an *incident* can associate, encapsulate, support or generate another *incident*, the reflexive association is used. For instance, a ransomware replicates itself in crucial locations of a system as for instance when it reboots and displays the ransom message. In this case the incident reflexive association will be used to connect the ransomware.exe with its copies in AppData, Start menu and root directory.

Exploits: The exploits relationship indicates that the *incident* concept connects with a *vulnerability* through this form of relationship. This relationship can specify if the actual attack is preventable. A *vulnerability* can be the target of one or more *incidents* due to the existence of relationships from a range of attacks, indicating that an *incident* aims to exploit a vulnerability and this attempts are expressed through the relationship *exploitss*. For instance, the WannaCry attack was exploiting with the EternalBlue exploit tool the vulnerability CVE-2017-0144 and with the DoublePulsar attack with related vulnerabilities CVE-2017-0143, CVE-2017-0144, CVE-2017-0145, CVE-2017-0146, CVE-2017-0147 and CVE-2017-0148.

2.3   SIRML Graphical and Textual Notation

In this section we present the visual notation of the modelling language. The diagramming notation is considered an important aspect of the modelling language as it can facilitate communication and assist problem solving [9]. The graphical notation is visualized using a set of diagrammatic components, where each concept in the modelling language is mapped to an unique visual vocabulary in the form of a notation. The shapes of the visual vocabulary were chosen based on the theory of the "physics" of notation [17]. The instance syntax is further discussed as it offers a textual encoding of the concrete syntax which provides an one-to-one mapping of a concept from our meta-model to an instance of a concept. The purpose of the instance syntax is to provide a formal representation of concept instances, in a machine readable format in order to perform analysis on recovery models through tool support. Thus, the instance syntax allows the unambiguous encoding of concepts in a textual format, which describes the instantiated concepts from a secure recovery model to facilitate security analysis within the context of recovery. The visual notation of the SIRML is shown in Fig. 3.

Starting from the parent concept of *mission* and its child the *strategic recovery mission*, both are represented diagrammatically with the same shape, shown in Fig. 3, but the child differentiate from the parent concept with the

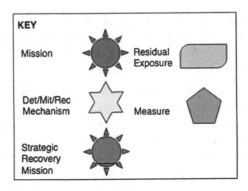

Fig. 3. Key of graphical notation extensions

use of a line as part of the shape. Here another important difference can be noticed in the instance syntax. The *mission* description can take the form *MIS(DES, GR, TER,MOD,ST)*. In the instance notation DES gives the description of a mission, GR clarifies the granularity, TER specified the terrain or deferently the area/aspect analyzed, MOD specifies the mode of the mission and ST explicitly states the state of a mission. For example, a DES can be mitigation of ransomware attack, GR operational requirement, TER hospital, MOD extensive and ST open. This can be expressed from an instance syntax as *MIS(ransomware attack mitigation, operational requirement, hospital, extensive, open)*. In a similar manner the concept *strategic recovery mission* can be expressed in the form of an instance syntax as *STRMIS(PH,DES)*. Here the PH denotes the phase of a particular recovery mission and the DES describes in more detail the strategic recovery mission context. For instance, a strategic recovery mission can be at the PH of planning and in more detail its DES can be among the lines of patch vulnerability planning. This will generate an instance syntax *STRMIS(planning, patch vulnerability planning)*.

Another important concept in the modelling language is that of security mechanisms, borrowed from Secure Tropos and extended to the specialized detection, mitigation and recovery mechanisms. These types of mechanisms are useful at different stages of security that relate directly with the broader scope of incident response. The graphical syntax is presented in Fig. 3 and their generic instance syntax can be described as *SECMEC(CAT,TYP,DES,NAM,ST,VEC,FUN,COS)*. Based on this syntax CAT stands for the category, TYP for the type of the security mechanism, DES for the description as in the rest of the concepts that have been explored, NAM for the name of the specific mechanism, ST for the state that the mechanism is assessed to be while under conditions of a cyber-physical attack, VEC is referring to the vector and FUN to the function that a mechanism primarily performs. Whereas this instance syntax take the form of *RECMEC(DES,TYP,CAT,NAM,VEC,FUN)* for the recovery mechanism and remains pretty similar for the rest of the security mechanisms.

Secure Tropos does not use risk as one of its concepts. However, a recovery plan needs to incorporate the concept of risk. This takes the form of the *residual exposure*. As a recovery plan attempts to face risks deriving from a cyber-physical attack, even after planning an IRT needs to be aware of what are the remaining areas of exposure for a system/infrastructure that is examined. In instance syntax terms this concept takes the form *RE(DUR, TYP, CON)*, where DUR stands for the estimated duration that this exposure remains, TYP is the type of the exposure and CON denotes the confidence that such an attack will take place. The graphical representation is a blue rectangle with sharp and rounded corners. An example can be remaining malware code that was in the system for sixteen hours before detection. The type of threat is cyber as it has the form of software and there is actual confirmation that this exposure has occurred. In an instance syntax the same concept will be expressed as *RE(16 hours, Cyber, Confirmed)*.

The final concept that is modelled is the *measure*. The measure has as instantiation syntax *MET(LEGC,RESC,LREV,TRC,QREC)*. All the attributes represent complex types that are specified in the reasoning support of the framework that due to space limitations is not included in this paper. LEGC stands for the legal costs, RESC for the costs of the resources used or planned to be used, the LREV for the revenue that has been lost due to recovery processes, TRC for the trust that has been lost due to the cyber-physical attack including the employees of the CI and QREC for the quality assessment of an incident response plan. The graphical representation of the *measure* concept is shown in Fig. 3.

3   Wannacry Case Study

In this paper we present a case study based on the WannaCry ransomware attack, which in 2017 affected CIs at a global scale [16]. According to the National Audit Office [20] *"at least 81 out of the 236 trusts across England"* were affected either because the attacked had infected them or because they disconnected/shut down resources to prevent a possible exploitation or aggravation of the attack [20]. As a result, *"603 primary care and other NHS organisations were also infected, including 595 GP practices."* It is important here to stress that this attack was not targeting health-care. Still the implications were disruptions of health-based CI's normal operational workflow that resulted to cancelled appointments for patients and the necessity to redirect ambulances [16]. This attacks have the capabilities to impact MCPS when looking for specific targets like unpatched legacy operating system devices.

Based on this attack, a fictional scenario is examined where a hospital's network has been hit from a datalocker ransomware attack. The attack was detected when a hospital employee who saw a pop-up message in a hospital's workstation, warning him/her that the computer is encrypted and a ransom needs to be paid before a timer expires. The hospital is cyber-aware and does not by its policy pay ransom. However, the hospital is conscious of the need to recover from the ransom-ware attack. SIRML approaches recovery at three levels, generating interconnected but different views of an event/incident. These views are: (a) **Operational Secure Recovery View (OSRV):** It instantiates the preventive measures that a CI uses along with processes, tools and mechanisms to identify that an event/incident is occurring. (b) **Tactical Secure Recovery View (TSRV):** It models the defensive posture of a CI in order to contain an attack and/or eradicate it. (c) **Strategic Secure Recovery View (SSRV):** It models the after incident activities that take place in order to restore and recover from an attack. Moreover, it initiates a lessons learned process that feedback the OSRV and TSRV.

Due to space limitations, we have modelled partially the SSRV of the *mission* to recover from ransomware attack. The SSRV instance in Fig. 5, was generated using the SIRML proposed in this paper. The strategic aspect of recovery consists of the longer planning and execution; it is supported by measures of events/incidents/attacks and improves with feedback the overall recovery plan. Firstly, we describe actors and their roles, such as *"IRT"* who plays a substantial role for the achievement of the overarching strategic recovery mission of managing operating systems through their life-cycle and in particular in terms of patching activities and bugfixes that relate even closer to security. We model the vulnerable resources identified individually in the TSRV within sets of resources that share common characteristics relevant to a long-term recovery plan. An example resource set, in our case study (see Fig. 5), contains *"legacy Windows operating systems"*.

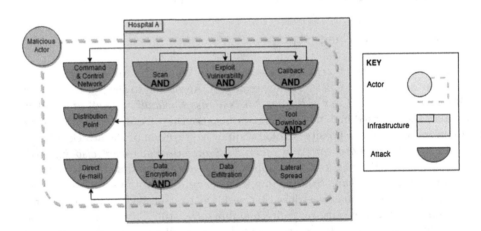

Fig. 4. General ransomware TIRV

For a longer time frame of planning recovery activities and assessment of applied recovery plans, measures can guide the overall process. These measures can exist at an actor level, like the timelines of bugfixes and at an infrastructure level, such as quality measures for ransomware tactical recovery, which is affected from the effectiveness with which the IRT has collaborated with external to the Hospital H third parties, that were presented at the OSRV. But, a secure

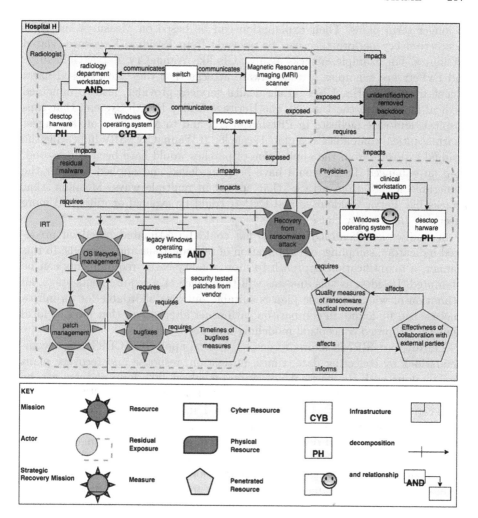

Fig. 5. WannaCry partial strategic secure-recovery view

recovery needs also to consider the residual exposure from an attack. In the case of WannaCry, malware might be still within the hospitals network. Additionally, backdoors might persist in medical equipment. This can iteratively feedback the secure TSRV that can be enhanced to incorporate these newly identified residual threats in its containment policy and defensive posture. A representation of the ransomware is given in Fig. 4 as part of the TSRV.

The contribution here is that by associating recovery properties related to cyber-physical attacks with security concepts, we are able to refine the specific recovery needs of each resource and resource set including their dependencies at a modelling level. Thus, the benefit is three-fold: firstly, by using the SSRV, the recovery team can debrief, argue and reason about their decisions that relate to longer term plans. Their explanation can be based on Measures and their secure recovery performance can be assessed from Residual Exposure related attributes. For example, attacks against CIs like WannaCry, Petya/GoldenEye and ExPetr are examples of ransomware attacks that they have caused harm except from the NHS, UK's public health services provider, also to unnamed medical facilities in the U.S. [8], the Heritage Valley Health System, that runs hospitals and care facilities in Pittsburgh [10] and to Merck one of the largest pharmaceutical companies at a global scale [6]. If WannaCry SSRV indicating the residual exposure from the application of patches would have been understood, then an enhanced TSRV would have been modelled and applied to cover the vulnerable MCPS from attacks that spread in multiple ways. Meaning, that attacks like Petya/GoldenEye and ExPetr could be avoided or mitigated more effectively before they cause damage.

Secondly, the *OualityOfRecoveryPlan* could be estimated based on prede-fined indicators, sampling and application of relevant tools and methods. In this manner, a quantification approach to more quality-based requirements can be attempted. Besides, as this analysis will take place at a requirements stage, an estimation of which strategic plan is suitable but also affordable for an infras-tructure can be found, in comparison with other alternatives that have as focal point the proposed conceptual modelling language.

Thirdly, our SIRML allows forensic teams to apply ICS-CERT [23] recom-mendations by collecting date, times, mitigation, response and recovery plans applied along with the particular resources involved. The forensic team can be in a position to decide based on these concepts from what active CPS data have to be captured before a tactical plan is applied and how to shut down a CPS to preserve forensic evidences. It also supports then to co-examine heterogeneous security mechanisms and decide when such a mechanism can change the envi-ronment of forensic interest in a way that will impede discovery. For example an anti-virus run might cause such modifications. Moreover, changes in other resources can have the same effect at a hardware, software and firmware level. By creating a recovery plan, IRTs can consult forensic investigators at a design level as of what actions might hinder a forensic inquire and identify those recov-ery processes that need to be supported from human resources with forensic expertise.

Overall by using all three views we are able to model in detail the data required for secure recovery at an organizational, tactical and strategic level, how the data permeates through the physical components of an MCPS, the jurisdiction due to the geographical location, and the specific information of the enabling cyber components including networking and communications. Based on the information elicited through these concepts, we are then able to model the secure recovery concepts such as vulnerabilities in an MCPS along with threats, security constraints and detection, response and recovery plans through security mechanisms and recovery activities, derived from health-based goals and activities. Thus, our work provides a secure recovery modelling language for health-based CIs enabling IRTs to express and model MCPS recovery needs, understanding the close interconnection between MCPS and a patient's care.

4   Related Work

Many security requirements engineering (SRE) methodologies have been proposed with increasing intensity the last fifteen years. A number of these methodologies use as fundamental components the concepts of assets and their associated risks. Mead et al. published the Security Quality Requirements Engineering (SQUARE) methodology that utilises a broad spectrum of artefacts, such as use cases, misuse cases and attack trees [12]. The work of Mellado et al. proposed the Security Requirements Engineering Process (SREP) using the Common Criteria (ISO/IEC 15408) for the software life-cycle [14]. Mouratidis and Giorgini introduced the Secure Tropos approach for security and trust [18]. Compagna et al. connected the legal requirements with security and privacy, identifying patterns [4] and examined the relation of security with safety requirements [7]. Other researchers extended Secure Tropos for risk management [11]. Threat modelling was also used for security requirements with an orientation towards the role of attacker as an actor [21]. Other researchers developed methodologies driven by misuse cases [25] and reuse cases [24]. Yu et al. has also proposed a social ontology to connect software engineering with security [28]. MITRE's knowledge base and model, abbreviated as ATT&CK^{TM} expresses attack phases [15] and STIX^{TM} is a language to gather intelligence regarding an attack, such as suspected compromise and perpetrators, courses of actions and legitimate resources used for malicious purposes [19]. These approaches are indeed very important and focus on the elicitation and analysis of security requirements and analysis, they do not explicitly consider recovery concepts which can range from detection to mitigation and actual recovery. The lack of clearly incorporating security requirements with recovery limits the scope and coverage of the multidimensional character of security. Our approach attempts to provide an alignment of recovery with security that will enable IRTs to be more versatile and ready to face cyber-physical attacks, which initiate and propagate from the cyber domain, but are impacting and are triggered from the physical world.

The literature also provides a large body of resources from the domain of recovery engineering. A sustainable amount of works relevant to recovery are concerned with the traceability of code to requirements documentation [1,27]. Business process languages have been used to analyze the relevant concepts and identify potential gaps [22]. The disaster management meta-model (DMM) proposed by Othman and Beydoum, follows the NIST segmentation of recovery stages [21]. Bareiss et al. introduced a model for failure recovery in order to minimize downtime of manufacturing systems [2]. Chen et al. have examined path-based failures [3] and Zhu et al. have used mathematical models to analyze failure and recovery strategies [29]. Mead proposed an approach for survivable systems separating their usage into legitimate and intrusive [13]. Hwang et. al. have presented work for failure handling of grid work-flow [26]. These works mainly provide advances related to safety requirements from hazards rather than security issues related to attacks. Therefore, they have limited role in supporting the identification of recovery requirements as part of a security-based design. Although, in some cases, they might combine safety with security at a quantitative, qualitative requirements base, they do not express how security can be an attack vector nor how recovery can assist an attack to aggravate. Also, although these methodologies are useful for the generation of specifications for cyber-physical systems they usually do not consider the human factor in the loop, that might be needed when everything else has failed and can also be the one initiating the security failures.

5   Conclusion

The proposed secure recovery modelling language in this paper enables IRTs to plan as part of their normal operations, in long and short time-frames, how they can securely recover under attack conditions, without causing more harm. We have defined a security modelling language to capture recovery and cyber-physical systems concepts (C1 and C2). The detailed relationships and attributes give to the language representational capabilities. By using the graphical notation (C3) in the case study, a shared understanding of a CPS and how it can recover can be designed and shared. The textual notation that underpins the graphical syntax allows decision-support with semi-formal representation of the language components towards automation, providing models in a machine-readable format. Reflecting on the current stage of this work, current limitations are the health-care focus and cyber-physical attacks modelling. This though does not mean that the modeling language is not suitable for other critical infrastructures, as its specialization is mainly at the level of attributes. From a social engineering attacks point of view, they can be modeled currently under the concept *Attack* as in the case study with the direct e-mail, along with other types of attacks. The focus remains though on the cyber-physical incidents. It is also necessary to provide in the future a systematic analysis that will structure the currently undefined implementation and usage of the language. Future work will emphasize on the semi-automated analysis and the formation of a process that will generate through instances of the SIRML optimal secure recovery plans for given CPS, threat circumstances and constraints. There one of the main challenges is expected to be the practical implementation of the language, which will possibly be supported through a tool.

Acknowledgments. The authors would like to thank the Engineering and Physical Sciences Research Council (EPSRC) for their support.

References

1. Antoniol, G., Canfora, G., Casazza, G., De Lucia, A., Merlo, E.: Recovering trace-ability links between code and documentation. IEEE Trans. Softw. Eng. **28**(10), 970–983 (2002)
2. Bareiss, P., Schutz, D., Priego, R., Marcos, M., Vogel-Heuser, B.: A model-based failure recovery approach for automated production systems combining SysML and industrial standards, pp. 1–7. IEEE, September 2016
3. Chen, P., Scown, C., Matthews, H.S., Garrett, J.H., Hendrickson, C.: Managing critical infrastructure interdependence through economic input-output methods. J. Infrastruct. Syst. **15**(3), 200–210 (2009)
4. Compagna, L., El Khoury, P., Krausov, A., Massacci, F., Zannone, N.: How to integrate legal requirements into a requirements engineering methodology for the development of security and privacy patterns. Artif. Intell. Law **17**(1), 1–30 (2009)
5. Crane, S., Larsen, P., Brunthaler, S., Franz, M.: Booby trapping software, pp. 95–106. ACM Press (2013)
6. Filipov, D., Roth, A., Nakashima, E.: Companies struggle to recover after massive cyberattack with ransom demands. The Washington Post, June 2017
7. Firesmith, D.G.: Engineering safety and security related requirements for software intensive systems, p. 169. IEEE, May 2007
8. Fox-Brewster, T.: Medical Devices Hit by Ransomware for the First Time in US Hospitals. Forbes, May 2017
9. Harel, D.: On visual formalisms. Commun. ACM **31**(5), 514–530 (1988)
10. Henley, J., Solon, O.: 'Petya' ransomware attack strikes companies across Europe and US. The Guardian, June 2017
11. Matulevicius, R., Mouratidis, H., Mayer, N., Dubois, E., Heymans, P.: Syntactic and semantic extensions to secure tropos to support security risk management. J. Univers. Comput. Sci. **18**(6), 816–844 (2012)
12. Mead, N.R.: Requirements engineering for survivable systems. Technical report CMU/SEI-2003-TN-013, Carnegie Mellon University, September 2003
13. Mead, N.R., Stehney, T.: Security quality requirements engineering (SQUARE) methodology. ACM SIGSOFT Softw. Eng. Notes **30**(4), 1 (2005)
14. Mellado, D., Fernndez-Medina, E., Piattini, M.: A common criteria based security requirements engineering process for the development of secure information systems. Comput. Stand. Interfaces **29**(2), 244–253 (2007)
15. MITRE. Adversarial Tactics, Techniques & Common Knowledge. https://attack.mitre.org/wiki/Main_page. Accessed 30 May 2018
16. Mohurle, S., Patil, M.: A brief study of WannaCry threat: ransomware attack 2017. Int. J. Adv. Res. Comput. Sci. **8**(5), 1938–1940 (2017)
17. Moody, D.: The physics of notations: toward a scientific basis for constructing visual notations in software engineering. IEEE Trans. Softw. Eng. **35**(6), 756–779 (2009)
18. Mouratidis, H., Giorgini, P.: Secure tropos: a security-oriented extension of the tropos methodology. Int. J. Softw. Eng. Knowl. Eng. **17**(02), 285–309 (2007)
19. OASIS. Structured Threat Information Expression. https://oasis-open.github.io/cti-documentation/stix/intro. Accessed 30 May 2018
20. National Audit Office. Investigation: WannaCry cyber attack and the NHS. Department of Health Report HC414, National Audit Office, October 2017

21. Othman, S.H., Beydoun, G.: A disaster management metamodel (DMM) validated. In: Kang, B.-H., Richards, D. (eds.) PKAW 2010. LNCS (LNAI), vol. 6232, pp. 111–125. Springer, Heidelberg (2010). https://doi.org/10.1007/978-3-642-15037-1_11

22. Recker, J., Indulska, M., Rosemann, M., Green, P.: Business process modeling - a comparative analysis. J. Assoc. Inf. Syst. 10(4), 333–363 (2009)

23. Homeland Security. Recommended Practice: Improving Industrial Control System Cybersecurity with Defense-in-Depth Strategies. Technical report, Department of Homeland Security (DHS) National Cybersecurity, Communications Integration Center (NCCIC) and Industrial Control Systems Cyber Emergency Response Team (ICS-CERT), September 2016

24. Sindre, G., Firesmith, D.G., Opdahl, A.L.: A reuse-based approach to determining security requirements. Requir. Eng. 10, 34–44 (2004)

25. Sindre, G., Opdahl, A.L.: Eliciting security requirements with misuse cases. Requir. Eng. 10(1), 34–44 (2005)

26. Hwang, S., Kesselman, C.: Grid workflow: a flexible failure handling framework for the grid, pp. 126–137. IEEE Computer Society (2003)

27. Winkler, S., von Pilgrim, J.: A survey of traceability in requirements engineering and model-driven development. Softw. Syst. Model. 9(4), 529–565 (2010)

28. Yu, E., Liu, L., Mylopoulos, J.: A social ontology for integrating security and software engineering. In: Integrating Security and Software Engineering: Advances and Future Visions, pp. 70–106 (2007)

29. Zhu, Z., Sivakumar, K., Parasuraman, A.: A mathematical model of service failure and recovery strategies. Decis. Sci. 35(3), 493–525 (2004)

An Enhanced Cyber Attack Attribution Framework

Nikolaos Pitropakis[1(✉)], Emmanouil Panaousis[2], Alkiviadis Giannakoulias[3],
George Kalpakis[4], Rodrigo Diaz Rodriguez[5], and Panayiotis Sarigiannidis[6]

[1] Edinburgh Napier University, Edinburgh, UK
n.pitropakis@napier.ac.uk
[2] Surrey Centre for Cyber Security, University of Surrey, Guildford, UK
[3] European Dynamics SA, Athens, Greece
[4] Information Technologies Institute, Centre for Research and Technology Hellas,
Thermi, Greece
[5] Atos Spain SA, Madrid, Spain
[6] University of Western Macedonia, Kozani, Greece

Abstract. Advanced Persistent Threats (APTs) are considered as the
threats that are the most challenging to detect and defend against. As
APTs use sophisticated attack methods, cyber situational awareness and
especially cyber attack attribution are necessary for the preservation of
security of cyber infrastructures. Recent challenges faced by organizations in the light of APT proliferation are related to the: collection of
APT knowledge; monitoring of APT activities; detection and classification of APTs; and correlation of all these to result in the attribution
of the malicious parties that orchestrated an attack. We propose the
Enhanced Cyber Attack Attribution (NEON) Framework, which performs attribution of malicious parties behind APT campaigns. NEON
is designed to increase societal resiliency to APTs. NEON combines the
following functionalities: (i) data collection from APT campaigns; (ii) collection of publicly available data from social media; (iii) honeypots and
virtual personas; (iv) network and system behavioural monitoring; (v)
incident detection and classification; (vi) network forensics; (vii) dynamic
response based on game theory; and (viii) adversarial machine learning;
all designed with privacy considerations in mind.

1 Introduction

The financial crisis made Information Technology (IT) infrastructures around the
world divert their business plans and often reduce expenditures. Although these
reductions have not been reflected on the productivity line, they did however,
affect cybersecurity. At the same time, malicious parties have advanced their
technology and have managed to be one step ahead of those who try to defend
their infrastructures. In 2010, Stuxnet's identification totally reshaped the cybersecurity landscape along with the perception about cyber threats. Advanced Persistent Threats (APTs) had already made a statement, and they stood up to their

© Springer Nature Switzerland AG 2018
S. Furnell et al. (Eds.): TrustBus 2018, LNCS 11033, pp. 213–228, 2018.
https://doi.org/10.1007/978-3-319-98385-1_15

name with Duqu in 2011, Flame in 2012, Red October in 2012 and MiniDuke in 2013. All of those attacks impacted critical infrastructures.

During the past decade, large-scale and well-organized cyber attacks have become more frequent. In 2017, the Shadow Brokers hacking group came up with a Windows platform exploit named as EternalBlue. This was later used as a part of the WannaCry ransomware that affected numerous countries around the world and their critical infrastructures such as the UK's National Health System (NHS), where it proved to have devastating and life threatening effects, resulting in delays of treatments of patients who were suffering from long term illnesses.

Motivation. Although, the cybersecurity and scientific communities have developed several defensive mechanisms against APTs, there is a number of different challenges that have not been fully addressed. First of all, there is scattered information about APT campaigns, hidden in technical reports as well as in scientific publications that has neither been collected nor visualized in order to facilitate a potential exchange of intelligence. In detail, the sources contain lots of valuable information e.g., domain names, IPs and malware hexes, which have been used in each APT campaign. The same sources contain useful elements that can lead to the detection of a lot of social engineering attacks of which their main target is the human factor. The latter has not been taken into consideration yet when it comes to augment the capabilities of honeypots [1]. In addition to that, malicious parties often reveal information about their activities through social media, which can contribute another valuable source of information.

Conventional incident detection and classification mechanisms have to face a new threat that of adversaries who aims to harm defending mechanisms that use machine learning introducing a new field of research called adversarial machine learning [2]. As malicious parties become aware of the machine learning techniques used in defensive strategies they become elusive, lowering the accuracy rate of all detection capabilities. All of those identified issues are immediately connected with two pillars on which cybersecurity community should depend on; *attribution* and *cybersecurity situational awareness*. The first reflects the need to identify who (i.e., cyber attacker) is responsible for the orchestration of a cyber attack. Like police processes use every piece of evidence coming from investigation and forensic science to understand who are responsible for an incident and their motivating factors, cybersecurity science has exactly the same need. The identification of the malicious parties who have orchestrated large-scale cyber attacks and their correlation with former activities can greatly impact the timing and efficiency of their detection. Additionally, as social engineering attacks take advantage of the human factor, which is referred as the weakest link [3], cybersecurity situational awareness must increase towards protecting cyber infrastructures.

Our Contribution. We introduce the Enhanced Cyber Attack Attribution (NEON) Framework, illustrated in Fig. 1, which is designed to accommodate components that address the aforesaid challenges. NEON leads to a user-centric automated cybersecurity platform that gathers heterogeneous data coming from

APT reports and publicly available information from social media. By using this material as ground truth, NEON correlates this with other data collected from network and system behavioural monitoring components. To increase defence against social engineering attacks, NEON uses honeypots that attract the attention of potential attackers through the creation and management of virtual personas [1]. The virtual personas accelerate the manifestation of the attacks in contained environments, drawing at the same time valuable information about the adversaries. As part of dynamic response against APTs, NEON uses a game theoretic approach to propose optimal cybersecurity actions against them. All the above result in an integrated system of early detection, classification, optimal response and attribution of APTs. To the best of our knowledge, *NEON is the first framework that has been designed with the ultimate goal to perform enhanced attribution of APT campaigns.* We envisage that the implementation of NEON will have great impact to the situational awareness of cyber infrastructures against sophisticated cyber attacks.

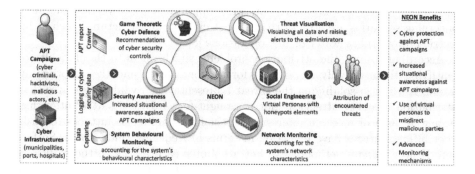

Fig. 1. NEON approach.

Outline. The rest of the paper is organized as follows: Sect. 2 offers some background information about APTs; Sect. 3 provides a related literature review; Sect. 4 introduces the NEON framework and briefly describes its components; Sect. 5 describes NEON's operation in a healthcare usecase; and finally, Sect. 5 draws the conclusions giving some pointers for future work.

2   Background

After 2010 and Stuxnet's identification a new terminology was introduced by cybersecurity experts, that of Advanced Persistent Threat (APT) [4]. Advanced, because the adversary is conversant with computer intrusion tools and techniques and is capable of developing custom exploits; Persistent, because the adversary intends to accomplish a mission. They receive directives and work towards specific goals; Threats, because the adversary is organized, funded and motivated.

An APT is a multi-step attack designed to infiltrate a system and remain there undetected for a long period of time to obtain high-value information. A characteristic of APTs is that they may spend a significant interval of time between different attack stages. In addition, an APT may combine different attacks types, e.g., zero-day attacks (exploitation of unpatched vulnerabilities) and advanced social engineering attacks. In 2009, when Stuxnet was created, multiple APT campaigns have been identified, e.g., Duqu in 2011, Flame in 2012, Red October in 2012 and MiniDuke in 2013. From 2013 on-wards, the frequency of identified APTs has greatly increased. This is reflected on the posts of major security software companies that have published numerous reports regarding these threats [5–7].

APTs' number one target has always been organizations with high value assets hence the reason behind the persistency of those attacks. The information obtained from APTs can be used for an active (i.e., with immediate disruption) or passive (i.e., reconnaissance) malicious action. APTs usually cause major data breaches or they are part of cyber-espionage to cripple critical cyber-physical infrastructures. While APTs can impact political agendas, military plans, and government operations as well as enterprise operations and revenues, the most concerning scenarios are attacks that impact critical infrastructures, such as an electric power grid or water or fuel operations [8].

According to [9], "the attribution problem, which refers to the difficulty of identifying those initially responsible for a cyber attack and their motivating factors, is a key in solidifying the threat representation", while [10] states that "attribution of cyber attacks is not a straight-forward task". Attribution has become an area of research interest the past few years as the attacks towards cyber infrastructures have increased in terms of frequency and impact. So far, there is no concrete methodology that attributes each attack to the malicious parties who launched it. Additionally, no methodology takes into consideration past knowledge of APT campaigns and both network and system behavioural data.

3   Related Work

Advanced Persistent Threats. Several attempts to track, disable or counter APTs have been proposed. Giura et al. [11] propose a Context-Based Detection Framework that introduces the attack pyramid model and takes into account all events occurred in an organization. Specifically, their methodology correlates all relevant events across all pyramid planes, to detect an APT within a specific context as initially collected events are classified into contexts. Virvilis and Gritzalis [12] dive deeper into the technical reports of Stuxnet, Flame and Red October proposing potential countermeasures and defences against APT campaigns. They discuss patch management, strong network access control and monitoring, the importance of Domain Name System related to Command and Control (C&C) servers, protocol-aware security, and usability of Host Based Intrusion Detection Systems along with honeypots. Jasek et al. [13] elaborate on the honeypot use and propose solutions that lead to the detection of APTs as honeypots can outperform ordinary solutions contributing to the identification of zero-day exploits.

By performing a study in APTs, Chen et al. [14] refer to potential counter-measures that besides traditional defense mechanisms, advanced malware detection, event anomaly detection and data loss prevention, they point out the need for security awareness and training and intelligence-driven defense. They also discuss the usability of the proposed countermeasures. In [15], Friedberg et al. propose an anomaly detection technique for APTs based on both network and system behaviour while Marchetti et al. [16] narrowed down the problem of detecting APT activities through network monitoring by making use of high volumes of network traffic and ranking the most suspicious internal hosts, which allows security specialists to focus their analyses on a small set of hosts out of the thousands of machines that typically characterize large organizations.

From another point of view [17], Hu et al. consider the joint threats from APT attacker and the insiders, and characterize the interplay as a two-layer game model, i.e., a defense/attack game between defender and APT attacker and an information-trading game among insiders. Consequently, they use game theoretic models to identify the best response strategies for each player and prove the existence of Nash Equilibria in both games. Very recently, Zhu and Rass [18] propose a general framework that divides a general APT into three major temporal phases, and fits an individual game model to each phase, connecting the games at the transition points between the phases.

Bhatt et al. [19] propose a framework that models multi-stage attacks. Their intuition is to model behaviors using an Intrusion Kill-Chain attack model and defense patterns. The implementation of their framework is made by using Apache Hadoop. In a similar way, Giura et al. [20] use a large-scale distributed computing framework, such as MapReduce to consider all possible events coming from the monitoring process and process all possible contexts where the attack can take place.

Cyber Attack Attribution. In 2003, Wheeler published techniques for cyber attack attribution [21] while in 2008, Hunker et al. [22] highlighted the importance of cyber attack attribution and they present its challenges. Bou-Harb et al. [23] proposed an architecture that provides insights and inferences that help in attribution. Their architecture investigates attacks against cyber-physical systems. Qamar et al. [24] proposed a methodology that creates groups of threats based on their similarities in order to aid decision making; they also use ontologies. The importance and timeliness of enhanced cyber attribution is also pronounced by the fact that in 2016 USA Defense Advanced Research Projects Agency (DARPA) created a call which aims for the identification of the malicious parties responsible for the cyber attacks [25]. In the same year, the US Department of Defense awarded Georgia Institute of Technology a large research contract, to enable the development of the capability to quickly, objectively and positively identify the virtual actors responsible for cyber attacks [26].

DARPA [27] splits the attribution process in three distinct phases which run in parallel. First is the "Activity Tracking and Summarization" where ground truth is being formed through the collection of information from multiple sources (e.g., Ops desktop, mobile phone, IoT, captured C2 nodes, network infrastructure). Second phase is "Data Fusion and Activity Prediction" where some points of interest are picked from the previous phase and predictive profiles are being developed and ambiguous data associations are being captured across diverse data set. Third phase is "Validation & Enrichment" where adversary mistakes and externally observable indicators (e.g., Open-source intelligence, Commercial Threat Feeds, Network IDS/analytics etc.) are being identified.

NEON's Novelty. The NEON framework takes into consideration all other approaches of APT detection proposed in the literature but it also introduces mechanisms that cope with rising challenges. NEON follows the DARPA guideline [27] to first build a ground truth of APT campaigns' related data through intelligence gathering. Then, it correlates collected data and uses honeypots to create points of interest that will allow the detection of zero-day exploits and novel attack techniques. During that process, it takes into consideration the challenge of adversarial machine learning to ensure that optimal decisions are taken, even in the presence of attacks aiming at disrupting defences that us machine learning. NEON also uses game theory to help in the arms race between the attacker and the defender by devising optimal defending strategies. Its final step is not only to pronounce the situational awareness, but also to contribute to the attribution of attackers.

4   Proposed Framework

In this section we discuss the various components of NEON, which are also illustrated in Fig. 2.

4.1   APT Collector and Analyzer

To the best of our knowledge NEON APT Collector & Analyzer is the first of its kind to collect, sanitize and link different APT reports along with publicly available information on social media. There are a lot of APT repositories and crawlers which usually extract segments of the content of each report. The APT Collector & Analyzer is implemented by the following components [28].

Content Crawler. The various APT reports published by industry and academia are written in various ways making crawling a challenge. The NEON Content Crawler (CC) monitors a number of crawling points corresponding to repositories and social media sources with diverse content in an automatic and continuous fashion, with the goal to discover and collect APT reports and any other information related to them. CC is based on a crawling infrastructure capable of selectively collecting and scraping content related to APTs from Web resources by estimating (e.g., by using a distance function) their relevance to the

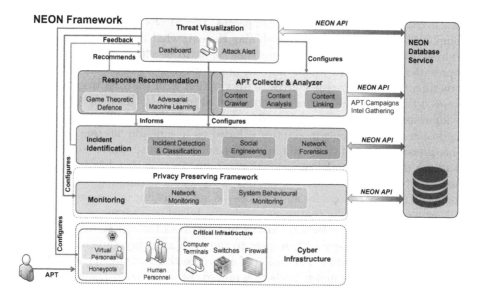

Fig. 2. NEON architecture.

topic of interest. This is based on an adaptive approach [29], which employs a semi-supervised methodology using unlabelled data within a supervised learning framework [30]. The crawling process is carried out using open source tools, such as Apache Nutch.

Content Analysis. The gathered APT related information is delivered to the NEON Content Analysis (CA) component for further processing. This extracts the named entities and concepts of interest (e.g., names of malware groups, APT names, temporal expressions, number expressions, domains used and their respective IP addresses) from the collected APT reports and from the other social media related sources. The collected information then subjects to linguistic analysis and is processed through a series of steps employing a pipeline of tools in the following order: sentence-breaking, tokenization, lexicons, part of speech tagging, text normalization, and eventually parsing [31]. Experiments are performed (i) with supervised/semi-supervised techniques and active learning techniques for parsing into shallow semantic structures as well as, (ii) with a dependency parser to generate deep syntactic structures. NEON then utilizes established linguistic approaches to named entity recognition (NER) and further enhances them by implementing machine learning techniques [32]. Furthermore, NEON integrates linguistic dependencies information, searches for the semantic types of relations used for the identification of candidate senses, and checks the overall semantic consistency of the resulting disambiguate structures.

Content Linking. Many different organizations, companies and research labs have analyzed the same APT campaigns. However, each research team gives a different name to the same campaign. In addition, the social media collected data is not directly linked to APT campaigns. The NEON Content Linking (CL) component solves this issue by combining the extracted APT concepts (e.g., ip address, campaign name), a process that needs to be efficient and scalable to cope with the large data volume and the highly heterogeneous nature of the data structure. CL fuses several sources of information with the goal to create links between the APT related information retrieved from CA. Given an APT report as input and using its meta-data and extracted concepts as multiple modalities, the fusion of all available modalities is based on a semantic filtering stage [33]. This process filters out the non-relevant results in a progressive way starting from the dominant modality, i.e., the attribute/concept that has been proven most effective in uni-modal APT-to-APT comparison. Comparing the similarity among all pairs of objects for all modalities is not a scalable process and involves at least a quadratic computational complexity. Based on a vector representation of the query and the collection, NEON first retrieves the top k_m-results which are relevant to the query with respect to the m-th modality and computes the corresponding similarities. The fusion of all progressively obtained similarities is a graph-based process and it leads to a ranked list of retrieved results.

4.2   Monitoring

Network Monitoring. NEON supports network forensic activities by using an efficient component to retrieve relevant data that allows the ulterior processing, detection and classification of anomalies. Many, if not most, security breaches in an organization are facilitated or conducted through a network. Monitoring the network traffic the primary mechanism for detecting attacks. At key network points, the Network Monitoring (NM) component collects data for each network flow and for each network packet individually, utilizing technologies of Deep Packet Inspection (DPI), towards detection and classification of anomalies and intrusions. NM sends information about suspicious network activities to the NEON Incident Detection & Classification (IDC) component, described later on.

System Behavioural Monitoring. The detection of usage patterns, based on the knowledge of the normal system behaviour, becomes prominent for the detection of anomalies with respect to the normal behaviour of users and devices and the network traffic [34]. The System Behavioural Monitoring (SBM) component inspects network traffic in real-time and assesses the behaviour of systems nodes and their deviations from "standard" behaviour. It is dynamic in nature, meaning that it can adapt to changing environments. For instance, the input to the network sensors can be any systems or network communications feature, making it possible to detect a wide range threats.

Furthermore, situational awareness techniques are used for a context-based detection of anomalies when a holistic view of the whole cyber infrastructure is required, including the knowledge of interactions among participants (either human or physical devices) and their inter-dependencies. SBM incorporates supervised and unsupervised machine learning algorithms that may operate as standalone modules or as an ensemble that produces more accurate results but also requires more computational resources. The unsupervised component is capable of detecting anomalies within a system up to a point where the number of anomalous nodes exceeds the number of normal behaviour nodes and raise alarms displaying the anomalous node details using the Attack Alert (AAlrt) component, described later on. The supervised module supports two algorithms: (i) Support Vector Machines and (ii) Logistic Regression, which are capable of working in an online setting and can be reconfigured in real-time based on feedback from the system, environment or operator.

4.3   Incident Identification

Social Engineering. The Social Engineering (SE) component consists of two elements; the Virtual Personas (VPs) and the Honeypots.

Virtual Personas. A versatile set of VPs is utilized for making active and attractive to the cyber attackers [1]. Both genders are present while the most frequent identities of personas will be determined and used within honeypots, described later in this section. The creation of VPs is based on real-world employees and their daily routines. Each VP becomes a unique prey to APTs and it appears to work in a different part of a cyber infrastructure, having different privileges. VPs are being continuously attended and updated according to the cyber infrastructures real workload so as to maximize the resemblance along with the realism. VPs' goal is to attract attacks promptly acquiring the appropriate knowledge, which contribute towards the attribution of the attacker.

Honeypots. These act as beacons of interest for the malicious parties throughout their lifetime, as VPs will appear more unaware of security procedures than other employees offering themselves to be exploited. The malicious actions will be recorded and continuously feed the collection process. The real-world data collected from those attacks supports the existing background knowledge on APT campaigns when correlated with network traces and system behavioural data, as well as APT reports. Consequently, SE is able to collect information from new APT campaigns before their manifestation, thus minimizing their impact. SE calculates a set of thresholds that will trigger the defending organisation to involve a human operator in the honeypot process. After this point, live operation monitoring helps to extract more information about the attacker by introducing controlled human errors that will accelerate the manifestation of the attack.

Incident Detection and Classification. The Incident Detection & Classification (IDC) component provides the capabilities of a Security Information and Event Management (SIEM) solution with the advantage of being able to handle large volumes of data and raise security alerts. A suitable correlation among the different types of information is paramount for discovering ongoing incidents that may lead to a serious compromise of the cyber infrastructure. Network and system behavioural data, data from honeypots, virtual personas logs, data from past incidents and data stored in the NEON database have to be correlated for the *identification of current incidents* or *estimation of future incidents*.

Machine learning techniques, such as clustering methodologies or decision trees, combined with usage behaviour patterns, are being used to predict potential malicious events threatening cyber infrastructures. IDC performs real-time collection and analysis of security events; prioritization, filtering and normalization of the data gathered from different sources; consolidation and correlation of the security events to carry out a risk assessment and generation of alarms by the NEON Attack Alert (AAlrt) component.

Network Forensics. To enable collection of necessary forensic information that can be used as legal evidence in court, towards the attribution of cyber attackers, the Network Forensics (NF) component leverages an investigation methodology and relevant network forensic tools to analyze the collected network traffic. Using the OSCAR (Obtain information, Strategize, Collect evidence, Analyze, Report) methodology [35] we ensure that necessary forensic information is collected and can be used as legal evidence. The collection of evidence is achieved through the NM and BM components. NF consist of the following parts: (i) *Obtain information*: gather general information about the incident itself (date and time of the incident, persons and systems involved, what initially happened, what actions have been taken since then, who's in charge, etc.) and the environment (company, organisation) where it took place, that usually changes over time and go or change positions while at the same time equipment is phased out or replaced, new equipment is being added and configurations are changed; (ii) *Strategize*: since network data is very volatile, NF prioritizes forensic data acquisition according to the volatility of the sources, the potential value to the investigation and the effort needed to obtain them; (iii) *Collect evidence*: to allow collection of evidence all actions taken and all systems accessed should be logged, while the log should be safely stored and should include time, source of the evidence, acquisition method and the investigator(s) involved. Two major sources of network evidence exist: (a) network traffic captures, (b) log files that can be either collected at the generating system or a central log host; (iv) *Analyze*: different tools are used to recover evidence material; and (v) *Report*: NF provides a detailed forensic report as the final product of any forensic investigation. The report can be read by non-experts and it is in accordance with general forensic principles.

4.4   Response Recommendation

Game Theoretic Defence. Conventional defences against APTs are often deployed in an ad-hoc manner. NEON aims to take into account the understanding of the attackers' goals and the objectives of the infrastructure under attack. It then utilizes the Game Theoretic Defence (GTD) component to propose optimal cybersecurity actions against the APT attacker. GTD is called when signs of the adversary are confirmed and mitigation must take place. GTD ensures that optimal defending strategies, in the form of security tasks (e.g., security configurations, manual human actions), are undertaken. The response includes both the set of controls that are used to mitigate the attack actions as well as the way the tasks of a system administrator are prioritized to maximize their efficiency. GTD is based on the representation of the system under-attack in the form of a graph with different states, including both exploited and recovery states. GTD is based on a zero-sum game between the defender, which is the organisation that NEON protects and the APT attacker. The defender chooses among different cybersecurity portfolios and the attackers have a set of targets to exploit in system/network they have gained access to [36–38].

Adversarial Machine Learning. Adversarial machine learning (AML) is the study of robust machine (or statistical) learning techniques to an adversarial opponent, who aims to disrupt the learning (causative attacks) or the classification (exploratory attacks) and hence any subsequent decision making process with malicious intent [2]. For example, AML can make innocent data input to be classified as malicious and vice versa. NEON uses AML defences to prevent erroneous behaviour of security-related classifiers. In this way, NEON guarantees data trustworthiness thus increasing trust to the systems involved in undertaking cyber security related actions, such as intrusion detection. For example, NEON shall compute "optimal" thresholds for retraining a classifier as a result of a concept drift [39]. A first set of experiments have been undertaken as part of [40] to assess the performance of various classifiers in presence of adversarial samples of varied volume.

4.5   Threat Visualization

Dashboard. Given the heterogeneity and complexity of any data related to APTs, the visual analysis is done through a simple intuitive interface allowing for effective representation of the identified data patterns. NEON employs an interactive user-friendly visualization dashboard displaying real-time information acquired from NM, SBM, IDC, and GTD components, as well as from the APT Campaign Database. This is done by the NEON Dashboard (DsB) component. This offers visual analytics with several security-oriented data transformations and representations, including but not limited to network intrusion graphs, traffic histographs, temporal charts, location maps, and 3D visualizations, in an effort to simplify the highly complex data and provide a meaningful threat analysis. The main goal is to provide a highly customizable environment for users, attempting to balance between automation and control. DsB is built upon a tier-based architecture, where the higher-level tiers present a general overview of the data and the lower-level tiers display more detailed representations, allowing users to pull up information and drill down into specific details when needed. Finally, the graphical user interfaces built for the configuration of the NEON components provides users with the opportunity to handle and manage the operation of the NEON framework.

Attack Alert. Incidents threatening a cyber infrastructure can affect the system in different ways. Certain threats may not have great impact to the system when they compromise devices with no connections to the critical assets. Other threats may have greater impact on critical systems that, depending on the type of infrastructure, can even impact human lives (i.e., temperature sensors in nuclear plants). The Attack Alert (AAlrt) component interfaces with IDC to provide system administrators with localized and situated notifications. AAlrt delivers visual and audio notifications to the users through the dashboard aiming at increasing the user understanding and situational awareness. The alerts refer to the potential infection risks when a suspicious activity is detected by IDC.

As the component uses the results of classification to alert administrators about various current and future incidents, it allows prioritizing potential reactions against threats, depending on the foreseen effect in the infrastructure. To this end, assessment techniques are carried out in order to estimate the risk associated to a threat. Aspects such as the criticality of the system affected by a threat and the cost (either monetary or in term of resources consumption) of dealing with it or the speed of "threat propagation" across the system, may determine the appropriateness of mitigating certain threats in an effort to allocate limited resources in an optimal way. All these criteria are used to classify incidents, giving system administrators valuable information for an efficient and trustworthy management of cyber infrastructures.

5   Healthcare Use Case of NEON

Every established national healthcare system handles medical data and other sensitive data (insurance, payment, etc.). Additionally, it possesses a lot of other mechanisms which help the treatment process and in case a minimum delay appears in the process, it may even result in human casualties. In the chosen scenario, illustrated in Fig. 3, a healthcare system is being attacked. The attack takes place through phishing using social media and valuable information from a malicious insider. The latter provides the attacker with necessary information (**1. Gives Information**) to approach a real person, thus ignoring the honey-farm establishment. Because the specific person has been recruited recently and has not taken the training session, falls for the phishing attack (**2. Phishing Attack**). Consequently, the newly recruited employee clicks the malicious file sent through social media, which installs a binary that takes advantage of a zero-day vulnerability (**3. Executes**). It then hides itself by attaching its executable to a legitimate process in the deployed system. The attacker's final goal is to infect the whole healthcare system and break the electronic health service.

The attacker has managed to overcome NEON's implemented honey-farm establishment due to the help of the malicious insider. However, the execution of the malware from the untrained employee will produce system behavioural data (**4. System Behavioural Monitoring**). The recorded data populates the existing APT-related database, which stores data collected from APT reports and social media sources handled by the APT Collector & Analyzer components (CC, CA, CL) and the Network Monitoring component. All this data will be correlated with former known attacks (**5. Incident Detection and Classification**). The detection is supported by the Adversarial Machine Learning (AdvML) component as the adversary may use evasion techniques. As soon as the NEON database is updated with new APT data (**6. Data Update**),

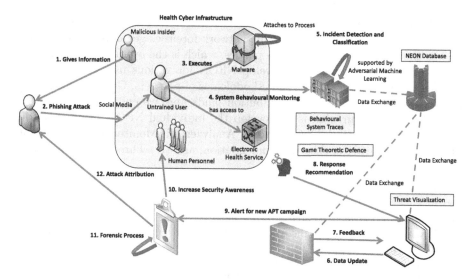

Fig. 3. Healthcare use case of NEON.

it will be possible to identify parts of known attacks in APT campaigns enabling their attribution and triggering attack alerts (AAlrt component) (**7. Feedback**). The Game Theoretic Defence component (**8. Response Recommendation**) will propose optimal security responses. Consequently, any well-hidden or hibernated mechanism will be revealed and generated alerts (**9. Alert for known APT campaign**) will notify organization employees and increase their security awareness about the new threat (**10. Increase Security Awareness**). After the infrastructure has gained resistance against the APT campaign and it has collected evidence that includes network traces, system behavioural patterns, IPs and domain names, the Network Forensics component (**11. Forensic Process**), will deliver a report that is factual and defensible in detail in a court of law, in order for the law prosecution process to be initiated (**12. Attack Attribution**).

6   Conclusions

Enhanced attack attribution frameworks are in their infancy. At the same time APT becomes the most prominent threat paradigm. To address challenges that emerge from the above, this paper proposes the NEON framework. Its primary target is the collection and representation of intelligence about APT campaigns and then the correlation with monitoring activities. In NEON, honeypots with the help of virtual personas improve the detection capabilities of zero-day exploits and social engineering attacks. Game theoretic defences are incorporated into NEON to mitigate the actions of sophisticated APT attackers. Furthermore, adversarial machine learning supports data trustworthiness thus facilitating accurate APT detection and attribution and a threat management console visualizes and pronounces the situational awareness of people and critical infrastructures in NEON. Finally, network forensics generate evidence that lead to the attribution of malicious parties, which is the overall aim of NEON.

As future work, we aim to develop NEON for various use cases based on existing software tools and novel methodologies of partners. Given the complexity of the APT detection and attribution landscape, we envisage this to be a challenging task. Our plan is to develop the individual NEON components in the following order: (i) APT Collector & Analyzer, (ii) Monitoring, (iii) Incident Identification, (iii) Response Recommendation, and (iv) Threat Visualization.

References

1. Farinholt, B., et al.: To catch a ratter: monitoring the behavior of amateur Dark-Comet RAT operators in the wild. In: IEEE Symposium on Security and Privacy, pp. 770–787. IEEE (2017)
2. Huang, L., Joseph, A.D., Nelson, B., Rubinstein, B.I., Tygar, J.: Adversarial machine learning. In: 4th ACM Workshop on Security and Artificial Intelligence, pp. 43–58. ACM (2011)
3. Pfleeger, S.L., Sasse, M.A., Furnham, A.: From weakest link to security hero: transforming staff security behavior. J. Homel. Secur. Emerg. Manag. 11(4), 489–510 (2014)
4. Langner, R.: Stuxnet: dissecting a cyberwarfare weapon. IEEE Secur. Priv. 9(3), 49–51 (2011)
5. Kaspersky: Targeted cyber attacks logbook. https://apt.securelist.com/. Accessed 09 Feb 2018
6. Symantec: Advanced persistent threats: a symantec perspective. https://www.symantec.com/content/en/us/enterprise/white_papers/b-advanced_persistent_threats_WP_21215957.en-us.pdf. Accessed 09 Feb 2018
7. ITU: Targeted attack trends. https://www.itu.int/en/ITU-D/Cybersecurity/Documents/2H_2013_Targeted_Attack_Campaign_Report.pdf. Accessed 09 Feb 2018
8. King, S.: Apt (advanced persistent threat) - what you need to know. https://www.netswitch.net/apt-advanced-persistent-threat-what-you-need-to-know/. Accessed 09 Feb 2018
9. Cavelty, M.D.: Cyber-security and Threat Politics: US Efforts to Secure the Information Age. Routledge, Abingdon (2007)
10. Choo, K.K.R.: The cyber threat landscape: challenges and future research directions. Comput. Secur. 30(8), 719–731 (2011)
11. Giura, P., Wang, W.: A context-based detection framework for advanced persistent threats. In: International Conference on Cyber Security, pp. 69–74. IEEE (2012)
12. Virvilis, N., Gritzalis, D.: The big four-what we did wrong in advanced persistent threat detection? In: 8th International Conference on Availability, Reliability and Security, pp. 248–254. IEEE (2013)
13. Jasek, R., Kolarik, M., Vymola, T.: APT detection system using honeypots. In: 13th International Conference on Applied Informatics and Communications, pp. 25–29. (2013)
14. Chen, P., Desmet, L., Huygens, C.: A study on advanced persistent threats. In: De Decker, B., Zúquete, A. (eds.) CMS 2014. LNCS, vol. 8735, pp. 63–72. Springer, Heidelberg (2014). https://doi.org/10.1007/978-3-662-44885-4_5

15. Friedberg, I., Skopik, F., Settanni, G., Fiedler, R.: Combating advanced persistent threats: from network event correlation to incident detection. Comput. Secur. **48**, 35–57 (2015)
16. Marchetti, M., Pierazzi, F., Colajanni, M., Guido, A.: Analysis of high volumes of network traffic for advanced persistent threat detection. Comput. Netw. **109**, 127–141 (2016)
17. Hu, P., Li, H., Fu, H., Cansever, D., Mohapatra, P.: Dynamic defense strategy against advanced persistent threat with insiders. In: IEEE Conference on Computer Communications, pp. 747–755. IEEE (2015)
18. Zhu, Q., Rass, S.: On multi-phase and multi-stage game-theoretic modeling of advanced persistent threats. IEEE Access **6**, 13958–13971 (2018)
19. Bhatt, P., Yano, E.T., Gustavsson, P.: Towards a framework to detect multi-stage advanced persistent threats attacks. In: 2014 IEEE 8th International Symposium on Service Oriented System Engineering (SOSE), pp. 390–395. IEEE (2014)
20. Giura, P., Wang, W.: Using large scale distributed computing to unveil advanced persistent threats. Sci. J. **1**(3), 93–105 (2012)
21. Wheeler, D.A., Larsen, G.N.: Techniques for cyber attack attribution. Technical report, Institute for Defense Analyses, Alexandria, VA (2003)
22. Hunker, J., Hutchinson, B., Margulies, J.: Role and challenges for sufficient cyber-attack attribution. Institute for Information Infrastructure Protection, pp. 5–10 (2008)
23. Bou-Harb, E., Lucia, W., Forti, N., Weerakkody, S., Ghani, N., Sinopoli, B.: Cyber meets control: a novel federated approach for resilient CPS leveraging real cyber threat intelligence. IEEE Commun. Mag. **55**(5), 198–204 (2017)
24. Qamar, S., Anwar, Z., Rahman, M.A., Al-Shaer, E., Chu, B.T.: Data-driven analytics for cyber-threat intelligence and information sharing. Comput. Secur. **67**, 35–58 (2017)
25. DARPA: Enhanced attribution federal project. https://govtribe.com/project/enhanced-attribution. Accessed 09 Feb 2018
26. Kintis, P., et al.: Hiding in plain sight: a longitudinal study of combosquatting abuse. In: ACM Conference on Computer and Communications Security, pp. 569–586. ACM (2017)
27. Keromytis, A.: Enhanced attribution. https://www.enisa.europa.eu/events/cti-eu-event/cti-eu-event-presentations/enhanced-attribution/. Accessed 09 Feb 2018
28. David Westcott, K.B.: Aptnotes. https://github.com/aptnotes/data. Accessed 09 Feb 2018
29. Meusel, R., Mika, P., Blanco, R.: Focused crawling for structured data. In: 23rd ACM International Conference on Conference on Information and Knowledge Management, pp. 1039–1048. ACM (2014)
30. Triguero, I., García, S., Herrera, F.: Self-labeled techniques for semi-supervised learning: taxonomy, software and empirical study. Knowl. Inf. Syst. **42**(2), 245–284 (2015)
31. Olston, C., Najork, M.: Web crawling. Found. Trends Inf. Retr. **4**(3), 175–246 (2010)
32. Cimiano, P.: Ontology learning from text. In: Cimiano, P. (ed.) Ontology Learning and Population from Text: Algorithms, Evaluation and Applications, pp. 19–34. Springer, Boston (2006). https://doi.org/10.1007/978-0-387-39252-3_3
33. Gialampoukidis, I., Moumtzidou, A., Tsikrika, T., Vrochidis, S., Kompatsiaris, I.: Retrieval of multimedia objects by fusing multiple modalities. In: ACM on International Conference on Multimedia Retrieval, pp. 359–362. ACM (2016)

34. Pitropakis, N., Pikrakis, A., Lambrinoudakis, C.: Behaviour reflects personality: detecting co-residence attacks on Xen-based cloud environments. Int. J. Inf. Secur. **14**(4), 299–305 (2015)
35. Davidoff, S., Ham, J.: Network Forensics: Tracking Hackers Through Cyberspace, vol. 2014. Prentice Hall, Upper Saddle River (2012)
36. Fielder, A., Panaousis, E., Malacaria, P., Hankin, C., Smeraldi, F.: Decision support approaches for cyber security investment. Decis. Support Syst. **86**, 13–23 (2016)
37. Fielder, A., Panaousis, E., Malacaria, P., Hankin, C., Smeraldi, F.: Game theory meets information security management. In: Cuppens-Boulahia, N., Cuppens, F., Jajodia, S., Abou El Kalam, A., Sans, T. (eds.) SEC 2014. IAICT, vol. 428, pp. 15–29. Springer, Heidelberg (2014). https://doi.org/10.1007/978-3-642-55415-5_2
38. Fielder, A., Konig, S., Panaousis, E., Schauer, S., Rass, S.: Uncertainty in cyber security investments. arXiv preprint arXiv:1712.05893 (2017)
39. Widmer, G., Kubat, M.: Learning in the presence of concept drift and hidden contexts. Mach. Learn. **23**(1), 69–101 (1996)
40. Nikhi, B., Giannetsos, T., Panaousis, E., Took, C.C.: Unsupervised learning for trustworthy IoT. In: IEEE International Conference on Fuzzy Systems (FUZZ-IEEE) (2018)

A Comprehensive Methodology for Deploying IoT Honeypots

Antonio Acien$^{(\boxtimes)}$, Ana Nieto, Gerardo Fernandez, and Javier Lopez

Network, Information and Computer Security (NICS) Lab, Lenguajes y Ciencias de la Computación, Universidad de Málaga, Málaga, Spain
{acien,nieto,gerardo,jlm}@lcc.uma.es

Abstract. Recent news have raised concern regarding the security on the IoT field. Vulnerabilities in devices are arising and honeypots are an excellent way to cope with this problem. In this work, current solutions for honeypots in the IoT context, and other solutions adaptable to it are analyzed in order to set the basis for a methodology that allows deployment of IoT honeypots. This methodology aims to cover all the aspects needed, including which devices are interesting, how can attackers be attracted to the honeypot, and how to obtain useful info from the deployment.

Keywords: IoT · Honeypot · Security · Methodology

1 Introduction

The *Internet of Things* (IoT) has initiated a technological revolution that affects both the public and private sector. One major concern is that users are delegating in their personal objects an important part of their daily routine without being really protected against malicious attacks.

In fact, the number of connected devices is expected to exceed twenty billion in 2020 (being prudent) [1]. This is a problem due the obvious density of devices sharing the same spectrum, but it also means that there will be even more platforms and services deployed independently and within a too short time interval. Security solutions need time to be deployed prior this deployment of networks and devices and it will be materially impossible to do that. Furthermore, even considering that security mechanisms and services are deployed in some way, nowadays it is impossible to accurately predict the effect that a targeted attack can have on the current infrastructure network.

In particular, IoT devices are a succulent call for attackers which intend to cause enormous damage, precisely given (i) the user's dependence on their devices, and (ii) the power of decision that we give to these devices (e.g. relying on an automatic vehicle to drive for us).

It would be unrealistic to think that attacks will not occur, so we must promote measures to detect threats as early as possible, understand them and

© Springer Nature Switzerland AG 2018
S. Furnell et al. (Eds.): TrustBus 2018, LNCS 11033, pp. 229–243, 2018.
https://doi.org/10.1007/978-3-319-98385-1_16

analyze them in a safe environment, prepared to receive them. In other words, it is necessary to attract attacks against trap nodes or networks in order to obtain malicious code that can be analyzed safely. These attractive hooks for cyberattackers are known as honeypots and honeynets. The simulation and emulation of these services would also allow the deployment of trap services dynamically as the analysis platform requires. Moreover, these honeypots are useful when it comes to monitoring and logging attacks that usually erase their traces, and are affordable both economically and on processing power, since they allow to use simulated systems instead of real devices.

Although the security on IoT devices was considered back as far as 2011 due to attacks on routers and other embedded devices [2], it was the amount of botnets (networks of bots) that started appearing what raised serious concern. After some botnet attacks (Tsunami, Gafgyt, BrickerBot), the one that caused major disruption was Mirai in 2016, which taking advantage of vulnerabilities in IoT devices, launched a distributed denial of service attack that took down websites such as Amazon, Twitter or GitHub [3]. As the worry about these attacks increases, the amount of malware targeted to IoT platforms does too, as well as the budget destined to IoT security [4].

This article is focused on one of the major concerns in the deployment of IoT honeypots. Specifically, we propose a methodology to deploy *relevant* honeypots in IoT environments, considering aspects as the *ranking popularity* of the chosen devices and the requirement for avoiding the detection of our *trap nodes* as honeypots by some of the most popular IoT scanners. Although the methodology proposed could be adapted to generic honeypots we focus on IoT honeypots due to the concern they represent nowadays.

2   Related Work

Although there have been revent and exhaustive surveys about honeypots which include classifications, maintenance and focus [5], to the best of our knowledge, there is no work regarding the deployment of IoT honeypots with a whole methodology behind.

The existing surveys do not analyze the specific requirements that are needed in order to deploy honeypots in IoT environments. This is the main focus of this paper; to properly and clearly identify a set of steps and procedures to successfully deploy honeypots in IoT environments avoiding to be detected as honeypots by web search engine tools and, at the same time, be attractive to the attackers, looking as real devices.

There is some work done in the field of IoT honeypots, with some interesting deployments and architecture, but due to the novelty of the field, the amount is very limited. Some IoT honeypots deployment architectures, such as IoTPOT [6], SIPHON [7] or IoTCandyJar [8] are quite interesting, since they have advantages such as redirecting low-interaction honeypots to high-interaction ones (making the whole system look more real to an attacker without a high cost), connecting the honeypots to cloud servers to make them look distributed all around the world, or using the responses of real IoT devices connected to the internet. Some other works are improved implementations of these ones, such as [9], which is an improved open-source version of IoTPOT.

There are also honeypots that are not focused on architecture, but worth mentioning, such as Wificam or Honeypot Camera [5], which impersonate webcams, MTPot [10] and ThingPot [11], which act as a IoT devices with certain vulnerabilities (Mirai and TR-064 respectively), or others that focus on personal area networks (PAN) [12]. Some honeypots specialize in industrial environments, such as Conpot [13]. Both categories, honeypots architectures and standalone ones, are detailed in Table 1.

Table 1. IoT honeypots

Honeypot	Characteristics				Viability of emulation		
	Scope	Type	Protocol	Architecture	HW	Downl.	Maintenance
IoTPOT	Industrial, home, personal	High	Telnet	MIPS, ARM, PPC	No	No	Article: May 2015
SIPHON	Profesional, personal	High	SSH,HTTP	Cloud-based	Yes	No	Article: Jan. 2017
Multi-purpose IoT honeypot	Industrial, home, personal	High	HTTP, SSH, TR-064, Telnet	MIPS, ARM, PPC	No	Yes	Article: May 2017
Conpot	Industrial	Medium	Modbus(TCP), SNMP	ICS, SCADA, BACNet, HVAC	No	Yes	Article: Sep. 2016 [13]
IoTCandyJar	Industrial, home, personal	*Intelligent*	HTTP, SSH, Telnet, TR-064, XMPP, MQTT, UPnP, CoAP, MS-RDP	MIPS, ARM, PPC	No	No	Article: July 2017
ThingPot	Household	Medium	HTTP, XMPP	Philips Hue lights	No	No	Last commit: Aug. 2017
HoneyThing	Routers	Low	TR-064	-	No	Yes	Last commit: Mar. 2016
ZigBee Honeypot	Personal	Medium	ZigBee	-	No	No	Last commit: June 2017
Honeypot-camera	Profesional, personal	Low	HTTP	-	No	Yes	Last commit: June 2015
MTPot	Mirai	Low	Telnet	-	No	Yes	Last commit: Nov. 2016
Wificam	Profesional, personal	Low	HTTP	-	No	Yes	Last commit: Apr. 2017

3   Methodology

Figure 1 shows the steps in the H-IoT methodology. We separate this methodology in five main blocks: (1) IoT search, (2) build honeypot, (3) training, (4) public deployment and (5) visualization and evaluation. Note that this last block can be executed in parallel to the training and the public deployment.

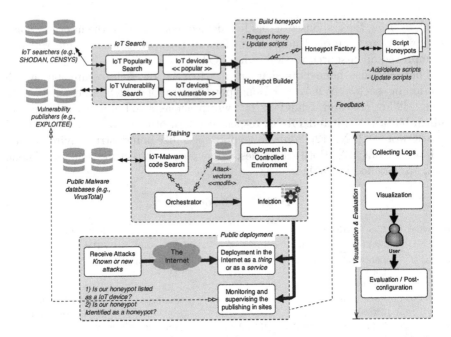

Fig. 1. Methodology

3.1   IoT Search

The two first challenges to be faced are (i) making the honeypot attractive for attackers and (ii) making the set of deployed honeypots representative of the general IoT context. This last one is crucial, due to the wide variety of devices which can be attacked. The usefulness of the results will depend on how rich the selected sample is. The related works are too specific or can become obsolete too soon if they don't satisfy (i) and (ii).

The first phase of the analysis aims to face both challenges. In this phase, IoT devices which can be used as honeypots are analyzed first. This, the searches are performed keeping in mind two basic attributes: popularity and vulnerability. These are not mutually exclusive, since popular devices may not be vulnerable to attacks, and vulnerable devices could be not widely used.

Next, the particularities of each search criterion are described. Some devices, such as those matching both criteria, or those in charge of a highly critical infrastructure, can be considered as high risk. Therefore, there must be a balance between the relevance of these attributes, which will depend on the context of the devices.

Popularity-Based Search In order to carry out a search by popularity, search engines specialized in IoT were consulted, searching for tags using manufacturers, models and types of devices. The search engines where the results were obtained from are the following:

Table 2. Popular IoT devices (data retrieved on 16/02/2018)

Device type	Model	Selling ranking	Search engine ranking
Routers	TP-Link TL-WR841N	1 (Amazon Spain, category: routers)	3 (Shodan, tags:router)-47K results
	TP-Link TL-WR740N		2 (Shodan, tags: router) - 78K results
	TP-Link TL-WR741ND		5 (Shodan, tags: router) - 11K results
	Linksys E2500		2 (Shodan, tags: linksys) - 3K results
	Netgear WNR1000v3		3 (Shodan, tags: netgear) - 3K results
	Linksys E1500	12 (Amazon USA, category: routers)	
	T-Mobile/ASUS AC1900	1 (Amazon USA, category: routers)	
	Netgear R6700	3 (Amazon USA, category: routers)	
	TP-Link N540	5 (Amazon USA, category: routers)	
	Linksys WRT54GL	2 (Amazon USA, category: routers)	
	Linksys E2500	4 (Amazon USA, category: routers)	2 (Shodan, tags: linksys) -1.8K results
	Linksys E4200	8 (Amazon USA, category: routers)	4 (Shodan, tags: linksys) - 500 results
IP cameras	DLink DCS-932L	17 (Amazon Spain, category: security cameras)	
	DLink DCS-5300		Censys, tags: "dcs-5300" - 73 results
	Sony SNC-RZ25		Censys, tags: "snc-rz25" - 798 results
	Axis M1054		Censys, tags: "axis m1054" - 401 results
	Axis 2100		Censys, tags: "axis 2100" - 350 results
DVRs and NVRs	Sony NSR-500	5 (Network Webcams)	Censys, tags: "nsr-500"- 3 resultados
	Axis Companion Recorder	1 (Network Webcams)	Censys, tags: "axis companion" - 10 results
	Hikvision DS 7604/7608/7616	3 (Network Webcams)	
	UniFi NVR		2 (Shodan, tags: nvr - 357 results)
	Zmodo NVR (ZMD-DT-SCN8)		5 (Shodan, tags: dvr - 450 results)

(*continued*)

Table 2. (*continued*)

Device type	Model	Selling ranking	Search engine ranking
Antennas	Ubiquiti AirGrid M AG-HP-5G27		4 (Shodan, tags: router-13K results)
Smart TVs	TiVo Series2 Firmware		2 (Shodan, tags: dvr-3'6K results)
Industrial devices	Schneider Electric BMX P34 2020		1 (Shodan, tags: Schneider electric-608 results)
	Schneider Electric BMX NOE 0100		2 (Shodan, tags: Schneider electric - 289 results)
	Schneider Electric SAS TSXETY4103		3 (Shodan, tags: Schneider electric - 169 results)
	Schneider Electric TM221CE40T		4 (Shodan, tags: Schneider electric - 117 results)
	Schneider Electric TM221CE40R		5 (Shodan, tags: Schneider electric - 60 results)
	Omron CJ2M		Censys, tags: "omron cj2m"-4256 results, Shodan, tags: "omron cj2m"-521 results
Drones and UAVs	DJI Phantom 3	9 (Amazon USA, category: hobby RC)	
	UDI U818A	8 (Amazon USA, category: hobby RC)	
	Holy Stone S160	1 (Amazon USA, category: hobby RC)	

- **SHODAN**: Search engine for IoT devices directly connected to the internet. Features filtering, banners, location and several other details. Also features HoneyScore, a parameter indicating the probability of a host being a honeypot.
- **Censys**: Searches the IPv4 namespace with ZMap. It can filter by protocol or words in the banner. Uses semantic search.
- **Reposify**: Thought with the goal of improving security, detecting bad settings (default credentials, open ports, obsolete firmware...).
- **Thingful**: Geographical search engine which categorizes the different IoT devices that it finds.
- **Wigle**: Searches networks by their SSID, which allows the user to find some devices that set up networks with a default name.

Moreover, general and specialized sellers were also used. To this respect, Table 2 shows a preliminar list of results of popular devices following both aforementioned criteria.

Vulnerability-Based Search. The second criterion to select devices as honeypots is based on known vulnerabilities. Furthermore, it is very important to have an updated database with the most relevant vulnerabilities classified by the type of device and context, and the estimated impact of the vulnerability. The relevant vulnerable devices found are listed in Table 3.

Websites specialized in device vulnerabilities were used for this research. The most used are listed here, altough some papers and journals were also used. These are cited when needed.

- **Exploitee.rs**: Website listing vulnerable devices and their exploits.
- **CVE Details**: Database containing all the CVE (Common Vulnerabilites and Exposures) entries, detailing which brands, models, versions of firmware are affected, and links to the exploits if available.
- **Exploit database (exploit.db)**: Website which contains usable exploits and proofs of concepts about some vulnerabilites.

3.2 Build Honeypot

This step in the methodology focuses in building honeypots considering both inputs from the previous phase, which are (i) IoT devices with known vulnerabilities and (ii) popular IoT devices. Sometimes both aspects may coincide. During this step, the viability to design and implement each honeypot is carefully analyzed in order to establish implementation priorities.

Although the implementation of the honeypots can depend of many factors (e.g., type of honeypot to be deployed, their dependency on hardware, etc.), in order to improve the efficiency of the system, it is very important to maintain a repository of solutions previously implemented. This would allow the deployment of honeypots which are similar to the already used ones in a fast and efficient manner, reusing some aspects such as parameters and settings. This is a likely scenario, since the output of the later phases will be used as feedback for this one, which will allow fine-tuning the deployed honeypots.

To classify and catalog these solutions based on the context, during this phase it is recommended to use a Honeypot Factory. This additional component will be used to control the access and modifications of a rich set of scripts, which describe the configuration of honeypots for the different application domains.

In addition, the deployment of honeypots will be much more efficient if these can be generated on-demand. This may happen, for example, if during the attack the honeypot gets corrupted, stuck, disabled or *broken*.

In the proof of concept presented in this paper, the infection of the virtual machine is manual, so this phase does not have as much weight as it would in a further developed deployment. However, future works are directed to develop specific IoT honeypots following this methodology.

Table 3. Vulneratble IoT devices

Device type	Model	Known vulnerability
Routers	TP-Link TL-WR841N	Directory traversal Cross-site scripting
	TP-Link TL-WR740N	Denial of service through httpd crash
	TP-Link TL-WR741ND	Malicious code injection in SSID field
	Linksys E2500	Code injection in URLs
	Netgear WNR1000v3	Password recovery credential disclosure
	Linksys E1500	Code injection in URLs
	Zyxel AMG1302 and P-660HN	TR-064 vulnerability [14]
	Sagecom Livebox	Denial of service filling the IPv6 routing table
	T-Mobile/ASUS AC1900	Remote code injection
	Netgear R6700	Remote code injection
	Linksys WRT54GL	Code injection Denial of service Buffer overflow Authentication bypassing
	Linksys E4200	Remote password stealing
IP cameras	DLink DCS-932L	Cross-site request forgery Remote password stealing
	DLink DCS-930L	Cross-site request forgery
	Sony SNC-RZ25	Heap-based buffer overflow
Industrial devices	Schneider Electric BMX P34 2020	Stack-based buffer overflow
	Schneider Electric Modicon M340	Buffer overflow through web server login
	Schneider Electric Homelynk (LSS100100)	Cross-site scripting
	Schneider Electric TSEXTG3000	Stack-based buffer overflow
	Omron CJ2M	Passwords transmitted in clear [15]
Drones and UAVs	DJI Phantom 3	GPS spoofing GPS jamming [16]
	Parrot AR 2.0	GPS spoofing [17]
	UDI U818A	Remote unauthenticated controlling [18]
Home appliances	iKettle	Password stored in clear [19]
	Samsung RF28HMELBSR Fridge	Man-in-the-middle attack through SSL vulnerability [20]
	FitBit Aria Scale	Password stored in clear [21]
	Miele PG 8528 Dishwasher	Directory traversal vulnerability
	Philips Hue Lights	Vulnerability in firmware verification [22]
Miscellanea	CloudPets	Unencrypted cloud database [23]

3.3   Testing

During the *training* phase, the deployment of the honeypots is carried on in a controlled environment in order to test it. In order to do that, the honeypot is infected using, for example, known malware code downloaded from the Internet. In some cases the infection of a device is not trivial at all. One of the purposes of this step in the methodology is also to evaluate the viability of a honeypot for being infected. Note that, in some cases, it will be desirable that the honeypot will be the most vulnerable possible (e.g., to record lazy, opportunistic and automated attacks) but in other cases the honeypot should represent a challenge for a persistent attacker that might suspect of the victim if it has not a minimum security level.

3.4   Public Deployment

The most useful feedback to the system implementing this methodology will be obtained from the phase of *public deployment*. During this step the selected honeypot is finally deployed with direct access to the Internet.

Paradoxically, although it is known that connecting IoT devices directly to the Internet exposes them to several threats, this is precisely what motivates the work. Due to the high density of devices, our honeypots can go unnoticed to the attackers, or even works, be identified as honeypots (alerting other attackers about it). The measures taken in the previous phases regarding the viability and interest of the honeypots try to prevent this.

Moreover, some factors, such as *marketing* will be needed, in order to make our devices listed by the relevant IoT search engines, and the places where the attacker get their targets from. Second, websites where devices are identified as honeypots must be checked to know if ours have been detected. Thus, a continuous monitoring is mandatory.

Last but not least, the deployment of the honeypot must be realistic. The technical complexity might depend for example on the dependencies of the solution with other theoretically *real* components in a productive environment. For example, PLCs in a SCADA system might require to interchange command controls with a controller. To reproduce all this behavior is very complex, furthermore considering that in some cases the protocols are proprietary.

3.5   Evaluation and Validation

The phase of *visualization and evaluation* is parallel to both the *training* and *public deployment* phases. However, the results achieved from both phases must be clearly separated and classified. This will contribute to know if the expected results prior the public deployment correspond with the real results obtained after the deployment.

In particular, this phase is directed to make the solution usable to an administrator or investigator, depending on the user profile of the resultant system where the methodology is being implemented.

We must emphasize that logs can be collected in different formats. This may represent a problem during the visualization step. Some tools for the interpretation of logs expect to receive them in a specific format. Therefore how to translate these logs to extract useful information must be considered during the implementation.

The methodology also considers the user feedback to improve/configure the honeypot platform. This is a feature that is needed in order to allow the improvement of the solution and enlarge its maintenance as far as possible.

4   Preliminary Results

In October of 2016, a malware specifically targeted to IoT devices called Mirai, caused a denial of service attack on the DNS provider Dyn. The magnitude of this attack was unprecedented, rendering services such as Spotify, Twitter, Netflix and Amazon unavailable. It was performed through thousands of vulnerable IoT devices, which were made part of a botnet, sending requests to the target. Most of these devices were simply left with the default credentials by the manufacturer, which allowed an automated attack to log and modify their behavior.

Recently, the malware has jumped to Windows platform, behaving in a slightly different way. Previously, only the IoT devices directly exposed to the Internet were vulnerable. Now, if a Windows computer is infected with its Mirai version, it will scan the local network, searching for vulnerable devices to make

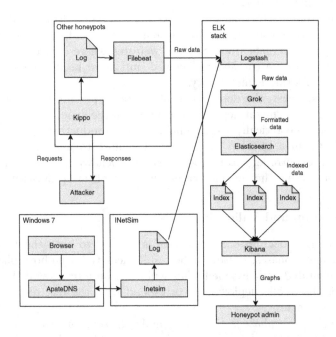

Fig. 2. Relationships between infected machines and ELK

them part of the botnet. This makes devices in private networks or located behind a firewall vulnerable [24].

Due to the novelty, repercussion, strength, and challenging aspects of this particular attack, it has been used in the proof of concept presented in this paper, which displays an infection with Mirai in a Windows computer inside of a controlled testing environment. Some other honeypots have been deployed in the very same environment, in order to run some tests that are beyond of the scope of this paper (environment preparation and checking, for example).

The malware samples have been downloaded from VirusTotal and Malwr, and the infection procedure has been carried out as detailed in a Securelist guide.

4.1 Environment

The environment where the proof of concept is run is vCloud, which allows virtualization, network definition, and snapshot restoration, which are useful tools. Moreover, it also provides isolation, in order to prevent the deployed attacks from spreading outside of the environment.

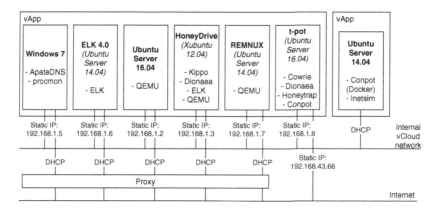

Fig. 3. Deployment in a controlled environment

The honeypots deployed and their connections are shown in Fig. 3. Most of them have been used merely for testing and achieving a better understanding of the environment, so they are not relevant when it comes to the results. It can be seen how they are connected to an internal network which does not have access to the Internet. In this configuration, a machine is dedicated to centralizing the logs for the evaluation and validation phase. This part of the methodology was implemented using the ELK stack. This stack is a solution which combines three services: ElasticSearch, Logstash and Kibana. The reasons why these technologies were chosen are their comprehensibility and the wide amount of plugins available, which simplify many tasks. The interactions between the are pretty simple: Logstash imports the logs from other machines, ElasticSearch indexes them, and Kibana retrieves the results from the indexes, showing them in simple and easy to understand graphs. Some of the plugins used are Filebeat, to send the logs from the honeypots to the stack, and Grok, to parse them into intelligible fields for the users. The interaction of the ELK stack with the system can be seen in Fig. 2.

Once the honeypots are connected to the ELK stack, in order to save the logs and obtain useful information from them, and the environment is properly set to prevent the infection from spreading, the infection can be carried out.

The proof of concept does not fully show the potential of the methodology, since it just covers the most important phases. Nonetheless, it aims to provide enough evidence of the strength and versatility of the methodology, whereas the phases left out will be further developed as future work.

4.2 Infection

Since the first step of the infection is to download a malicious executable file, and the machines do not have an Internet connection, a fake HTTP server has been set up inside the Windows machine with INetSim. The files needed for the infection are put there, and the requests to the URLs where Mirai is stored are redirected to the fake server through ApateDNS. Thus, the Windows machine downloads the files as if it were connected to the Internet.

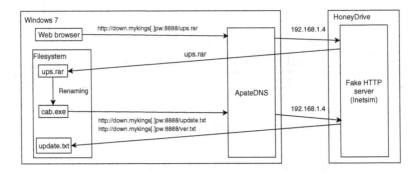

Fig. 4. Mirai infection process

Once the first file is obtained, it is renamed an executed, just as the infection guide details. If this execution is made with administrator privileges, it changes the DNS addresses of the machine (and does nothing, otherwise) to 114.114.114.114 and 8.8.8.8.

The process tries then to connect again to URLs from the same domain where the executable was located, in order to download *ver.txt* and *update.txt*. The first is available, but the second has not been found on the malware sample databases that were accessible, so the console output is *DNS set ok. ver different web:1.0.0.7 local:, needs update..* Since *update.txt* is missing, the execution aborts.

If the executable tries to download the files without Apatedns running and without Internet connection, the message shown is *get file list failed, exit*, just before it aborts as well.

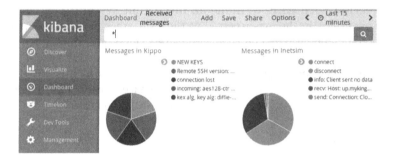

Fig. 5. Visualization of results in Kibana

In order to log the executions, the events were sent to the ELK stack. The messages were parsed with Grok, split into understandable fields and indexed, and then visualized. The messages were separated from the rest of honeypots with Kibana indexes, in order to differentiate Mirai from other attacks.

Also, the traffic generated in the request and response of files by the Mirai executable was captured and analyzed with Wireshark, where the IP redirection and the delivery of the files can be seen.

5 Discussion and Future Work

The defined methodology covers more cases than those shown in the proof of concept. A fundamental step would be the definition of specific honeypots for IoT following the criterion discussed in this work. The decision on deploying a honeypot for Mirai was based on its recent impact, but defining a set of IoT honeypots in order to capture unknown attacks is a goal to be achieved in future work. Although this is already being worked on, these details cannot be shared until obtaining substantial results from attacks, since the results could be compromised if specific details of the implementation are known.

The training phase is essential before considering the deployment of honeypots, thus it has been the focus of this work. Nonetheless, other points not considered in the present paper are very interesting, such as the following.

- **Infection from a Mirai botnet:** Instead of manually downloading the firmware and performing the spread, it would be interesting to cause the machine to be copromised from an already existing botnet. This approack would allow seeing how the honyepot would be indexed by the monitorizing mechanisms of the Mirai-infected devices. This is not easy, since it would mean to expose the honeypot directly to attacks, and maybe participating in its spread.

- **Infection to IoT devices in a network through Windows:** Creating a honeynet for this specifica scenario, in which the Windows machine is connected to IoT devices in the same local network, and see how they are infected and how they act.
- **Connection with ELK to make an intelligent system:** This consists on detecting events in the logs received at the ELK stack as signs of a potential infection happening based on their parameters (messages, timing, requests...) and taking the appropriate security measures.
- **Hajime infection:** Hajime is an anti-Mirai botnet, which is based on the same principle [25]. It logs on to vulnerable devices with default credentials, but blocks the access to the ports that Mirai usually checks.

6 Conclusions

Throughout the paper, it has been detailed how the IoT landscape is new, challenging and real. The average Internet daily user has one or several IoT devices, and will interact with more of them in a single day, often even without being aware of it. These devices have not been designed with enough security measures, and they are performing important and sensible roles in our lifes, regarding our privacy and security. The resulting scenario is one with vulnerable devices carrying out sensible tasks.

The difficulty of getting malware samples of IoT attacks, the possibility of simulating and emulating platforms without having real devices, the isolation layer honeypots provide, their logging of events (since IoT attacks usually erase their traces) and other particularities of IoT attacks, make honeypots the perfect tool for this work.

A methodology for this deployment is needed, because although the tools are available, it must be studied which honeypots should be deployed, how they can attract attackers, and how they can be improved based on the information obtained. This is where the proposed methodology comes into play. Every phase is thoroughly detailed, and has justified relevance in all the process. This is demonstrated by carrying out a proof of concept where one of the most worrying IoT attacks is deployed in a controlled environment, and the data obtained from this test is shown, detailing how it was carried out following the methodology.

Acknowledgement. This work has been financed by Ministerio de Economía y Competitividad through the projects IoTest (TIN2015-72634-EXP) and SMOG (TIN2016-79095-C2-1-R). The second author has been financed by INCIBE through the grant program for excellency in advanced cybersecurity research teams.

References

1. Danova, T.: 75 billion devices will be connected to the internet of things by 2020. Business Insider, vol. 2 (2013)
2. Roman, R., Najera, P., Lopez, J.: Securing the internet of things. Computer **44**(9), 51–58 (2011)

3. Kambourakis, G., Kolias, C., Stavrou, A.: The mirai botnet and the IoT zombie armies. In: Military Communications Conference (MILCOM) MILCOM 2017 IEEE, pp. 267–272. IEEE (2017)
4. Business Insider: This one chart explains why cybersecurity is so important. Retriev. August **16**, 2016 (2016)
5. Nawrocki, M., Wählisch, M., Schmidt, T.C., Keil, C., Schönfelder, J.: A survey on honeypot software and data analysis, arXiv preprint arXiv:1608.06249 (2016)
6. Pa, Y.M.P., Suzuki, S., Yoshioka, K., Matsumoto, T., Kasama, T., Rossow, C.: IOTPOT: analysing the rise of IOT compromises. EMU **9**, 1 (2015)
7. Guarnizo, J.D., et al.: SIPHON: Towards scalable high-interaction physical honeypots. In: Proceedings of the 3rd ACM Workshop on Cyber-Physical System Security, pp. 57–68. ACM (2017)
8. Luo, T., Xu, Z., Jin, X., Jia, Y., Ouyang, X.: IoTCandyJar: towards an intelligent-interaction honeypot for IoT devices. Black Hat (2017)
9. Krishnaprasad, P.: Capturing attacks on IoT devices with a multi-purpose IoT honeypot. Ph.D. dissertation, Indian Institute of Technology Kanpur (2017)
10. Radice, A.: Playing with a mirai honeypot: Mtpot (2017)
11. Wang, M., Santillan, J., Kuipers, F.: ThingPot: an interactive Internet-of-Things honeypot (2017)
12. Dowling, S., Schukat, M., Melvin, H.: A ZigBee honeypot to assess IoT cyberattack behaviour. In: Signals and Systems Conference (ISSC) : 28th Irish IEEE 2017, pp. 1–6 (2017)
13. Jicha, A., Patton, M., Chen, H.: SCADA honeypots: an in-depth analysis of Conpot. In: Intelligence and Security Informatics (ISI) IEEE Conference on 2016, pp. 196–198. IEEE (2016)
14. Singh, J.P., Chauhan, A.: Detection and prevention of non-pc Botnets
15. Wardak, H., Zhioua, S., Almulhem, A.: PLC access control: a security analysis. In: World Congress on 2016 Industrial Control Systems Security (WCICSS), pp. 1–6. IEEE (2016)
16. Trujano, G.B.R.R.F., Chan, B., Beams, G., Rivera, R.: Security analysis of DJI phantom 3 standard. Mass. Inst. Technol. (2016)
17. Szabo, M.: Drone hacking (2017)
18. Fox-Brewster, T.: Watch a very vulnerable USD140 Quadcopter drone get hacked out of the sky (2017)
19. Hughes, M.: Why the iKettle hack should worry you (even if you don't own one) (2015)
20. PenTestPartners: Hacking defcon 23's IoT village samsung fridge (2015)
21. Munro, K.: Extracting your WPA-PSK from bathroom scales (2015)
22. Ronen, E., Shamir, A., Weingarten, A.-O., O'Flynn, C.: IoT goes nuclear: creating a ZigBee chain reaction. In: IEEE Symposium on 2017 Security and Privacy (SP), pp. 195–212. IEEE (2017)
23. Hern, A.: CloudPets stuffed toys leak details of half a million users (2017)
24. Lab, K.: A windows-based spreader for MIRAI malware has been discovered (2017)
25. Edwards, S., Profetis, I.: Hajime: analysis of a decentralized internet worm for IoT devices. Rapidity Netw. 16 (2016)

Trustworthiness Cases – Toward Preparation for the Trustworthiness Certification

Nazila Gol Mohammadi[✉], Nelufar Ulfat-Bunyadi, and Maritta Heisel

paluno - The Ruhr Institute for Software Technology,
University of Duisburg-Essen, Essen, Germany
{nazila.golmohammadi,nelufar.ulfat-bunyadi,maritta.heisel}@uni-due.de

Abstract. The trustworthiness of cyber-physical systems that support complex collaborative business processes is an emergent property. In order to address users' trust concerns, trustworthiness requirements of systems must be assured. In this paper, we discuss the challenges of evidence-based trustworthiness assurance in order to tackle the problem of neglecting trustworthiness requirements while developing systems. To achieve this, we propose an approach that considers trustworthiness requirements using so-called trustworthiness cases. Our trustworthiness cases will guide the system development process toward evidence-based assurance of trustworthiness. Trustworthiness cases are based on assurance cases that have been successfully applied in safety- and security-related systems. We use an application example from the health care domain to demonstrate our approach.

Keywords: Trust · Trustworthiness · Requirements
Trustworthiness cases · Assurance cases for trustworthiness

1 Introduction

The adoption and acceptance of cyber-physical systems (CPS) by end-users are dependent on whether users have trust into these systems [4,8,25]. CPS comprise humans as well as software and hardware components, are distributed and connected via the Internet [4]. *Trust* is defined as "a bet about the future contingent actions of others" [31]. The components of this definition are belief and commitment. There is a belief that placing trust in a person or a system will lead to a good outcome. Then, there is a commitment to actually place trust and take an action to use this system based on this belief. *Trustworthiness* has become a more and more emergent property of CPS because of (a) ubiquity of the Internet makes it difficult to produce trustworthy systems in the first place, (b) the increasing general distrust into the Internet (e.g. related to Snowden's revelations[1]). Existing software life-cycle processes and approaches were not able to

---

[1] http://www.theguardian.com/us-news/the-nsa-files.

© Springer Nature Switzerland AG 2018
S. Furnell et al. (Eds.): TrustBus 2018, LNCS 11033, pp. 244–259, 2018.
https://doi.org/10.1007/978-3-319-98385-1_17

successfully address this important requirement. Despite different theoretic (e.g. automated proving, data flow analysis techniques etc.) and practical approaches (Common Criteria [20], Microsoft Security Development Lifecycle [29] etc.), we still often see that software either is not able to be (or remain) trustworthy, or that it is not used due to potential trust reasons, or both. The current software development methodologies and best practices need some improvement in order to successfully address the complex issue of delivering trustworthy systems. Therefore, we propose an approach to integrating trustworthiness into the development process by co-developing the cyber-physical system and its trustworthiness cases. This will enable trustworthiness requirements to influence the design, assessment, and operation of a critical system from the earliest stages.

Our idea of creating trustworthiness cases is based on the creation of assurance cases for certification. *Certification* generally refers to the process of assuring that a product (e.g. a system) or a process has certain specified properties, which are then recorded in a certificate [27]. In accordance to that, *assurance* is defined as justified confidence in a property of interest, and an *assurance case* attempts to demonstrate that sufficient assurance has been achieved [16]. Assurance cases have long been established in the safety domain, where they are called safety cases (although they are not restricted to that domain). The task of a *safety case* is to communicate a clear, comprehensible and defensible argument that a system is acceptably safe to operate in a particular context [23]. The explicit presentation of the argument is fundamental, since it is used to demonstrate why the reader should conclude that a system is acceptably safe from the evidence available. For presentation, the Goal Structuring Notation (GSN) [14] is frequently used.

The task of the *trustworthiness cases* that we introduce in this paper is to communicate a clear, comprehensible and defensible argument that a system is acceptably *trustworthy* to operate in a particular context. In previous work [12], we defined trustworthiness as a vector of relevant trustworthiness properties for a system. The reason is as follows. *Trust* is subjective and different from user to user, i.e. users have different *trust concerns*. These trust concerns are elicited during requirements engineering and manifest themselves as *trustworthiness requirements*. The trustworthiness requirements describe *trustworthiness properties* the system should possess, i.e. qualities that potentially influence trust of end users in a positive way. Note that trustworthiness is domain- and application-dependent. For instance, in health-care applications, the following trustworthiness properties are typically relevant: availability, confidentiality, integrity, maintainability, reliability and safety, but also performance and timeliness. In other application domains, another vector of properties might be relevant. For presentation of our trustworthiness cases, we also use GSN. However, we need to extend the notation of GSN.

Our contribution in this paper not only consists in the trustworthiness cases that we suggest. In previous work, we developed methods and techniques which support the development of a trustworthy system, i.e. *trustworthiness by design*. An important characteristic of these methods and techniques is that they do not prescribe a certain development process. They can be combined with any development process. They ensure that trustworthiness is considered as an important system quality right from the beginning and is realised in the system. Therefore, as a further contribution, we show how our trustworthiness-by-design methods and techniques can be used to generate the artefacts that are required for documentation in trustworthiness cases. Thus, our co-development approach supports evidence collection in different phases of the development process. This allows for guiding developers in building the to-be-expected trustworthiness, and thus to steer and manage development activities and correspondingly focus necessary efforts towards satisfying trustworthiness goals.

The remainder of this paper is structured as follows. In Sect. 2, we describe our trustworthiness cases and the artefacts that are required for documentation. In Sect. 3, we illustrate the creation of trustworthiness cases for an application example from the health-care domain. In Sect. 4, we present and discuss related work. In Sect. 5, we finally draw conclusions and provide an outlook on future work.

2   Trustworthiness Cases

Assessing a development process and the resulting system to identify its intrinsic qualities is not a trivial task. An assessment methodology must take into account multiple aspects and factors at the same time: some indications may come from an analysis starting from an observation of the activities conducted by developers, like for instance to assess whether risk assessment has been systematically conducted. Others may come from the generated developed system artefacts, for example, the measured availability of a service is 99.9% within a certain time frame. Therefore, the selection of the target for the assessment can be a complex task. For assessing a specific quality, typically two types of targets are defined: (1) definition of the target for the system under assessment and (2) definition of the target for the performed development activities.

In case of trustworthiness assessment, we also consider two types of targets: (1) trustworthiness goals or trustworthiness requirements that the system under development should satisfy in order to be trustworthy, (2) execution of certain trustworthiness enabling activities. The latter does not only have to be assessed with respect to whether they have been performed at all, but also how well they have been performed. However, defining product or process metrics is not the focus of this paper. Our prior work [7] focused on these aspects, but here, using trustworthiness cases, we aim at documenting the evidence that is produced during the development life cycle. Yet, both, product and process metrics, can be used to support the trustworthiness argument.

Evidence is presented by system providers or developers, and is verified by an evaluator. In the Common Criteria (CC), evidence is defined as "anything" that can prove the compliance with a mandatory CC requirement: evidence generally consists of documents, interviews as well as statements made by evaluators during the assessment. We adopt this definition of evidence in our trustworthiness cases. Performed development activities and observable trustworthiness properties of the system that are objectively measurable may serve as trustworthiness evidence.

In the following, we first describe the conceptual model of our trustworthiness cases. Then, we describe how a trustworthy-by-design development process (which uses the methods and techniques that we developed in previous work) can be aligned with the process of documenting trustworthiness cases.

2.1   The Conceptual Model for Trustworthiness Cases

Figure 1 shows the conceptual model of a trustworthiness case. We developed the conceptual model based on the highly accepted assurance cases and safety cases. In this subsection, we briefly describe the core elements and their relations. A detailed explanation will follow in the next subsection.

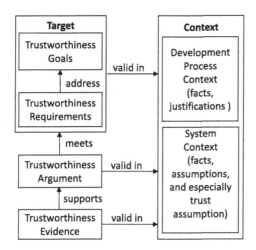

Fig. 1. Conceptual model of trustworthiness cases

The *trustworthiness goals and requirements* (describing the trustworthiness properties the system should possess) represent the target. The trustworthiness requirements must be addressed to assure the trustworthiness of the system under consideration. The *trustworthiness argument* logically states and convincingly demonstrates how and why trustworthiness requirements are met (by evidence). *Trustworthiness evidence* is information from the trustworthiness-by-design development process. This information supports the trustworthiness argument in order to demonstrate that the target is met. The *context* provides the basis for the whole trustworthiness case. We differentiate between two types of context: development process context and system context. The context of the development process includes facts and justifications about the performed development activities and the generated artefacts. The system context includes the

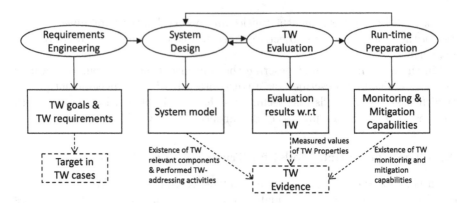

Fig. 2. Co-development of trustworthiness (TW) cases with the development process

general facts and assumptions about the system's (i.e. the CPS's) physical environment. We define trust assumptions as part of the system context information that should be included in trustworthiness cases, since the trustworthiness case will only be valid by consideration of the made trust assumptions.

For representing trustworthiness cases, we suggest using the GSN which is also used for assurance and safety cases. The notation is shown in Fig. 4. The purpose of the modelled goal structure is to show how goals (claims about the system) are broken down into subgoals, until eventually they can be supported by evidence (solutions). As part of this structure, the strategies (that are adopted for assuring that a goal is met) may be modelled as well, just as the rationale (assumptions and justifications) and the context in which the goals are stated. In order to be able to model trust assumptions explicitly, we extend GSN with a corresponding modelling element (TA) as shown in Fig. 4. Examples related to trust assumptions will be presented in Sect. 3.

2.2 Approach for Co-developing the CPS and Its Trustworthiness Cases

The amount and diversity of the information that flow into trustworthiness cases are high. As depicted in Fig. 2, we present an approach for co-developing trustworthiness cases and the CPS.

Requirements Engineering: A requirements engineering (RE) process must lead to a list of trustworthiness goals and requirements which can be included in the trustworthiness cases as target.

As an example of such an RE process, we have developed a method that supports the elicitation and documentation of trustworthiness requirements using goal and business process models [10,11]. This process is concerned with identifying the participants and initial context information. The goal model captures the major intentions of the involved participants/stakeholders. Trust concerns of end users and their dependencies on other participants in the business are identified. Based on trust concerns, the goal model is refined with the trustworthiness goals and their relations to the other goals (conflicts or positive influences). The trustworthiness goals include the purpose of building trustworthiness properties into the system under development. Then business process models are set up that include trustworthiness properties which fulfill the trustworthiness goals from the goal model.

System Design: The system design phase must lead to a system model. The system model must address the trustworthiness requirements (resulting from the RE phase).

Any design process can be selected to build the system model of the CPS. We recommend using a model-based method, since such a method will result in a system model. A further benefit of a model-based method is that model-based risk assessment approaches towards trustworthiness can then be used as well.

In previous work [9], we have developed a collection of methodologies, patterns, and practices which can be applied in order to achieve that the system under design is trustworthy. These trustworthiness-by-design methodologies ensure that trustworthiness is at the core of the software engineering practices so that the entire system and its individual components (standalone or chained) have high levels of trustworthiness through the implementation and maintenance of trustworthiness properties in the design process. The trustworthiness-by-design best practices can be adopted by any project. For example, risk-based design [26, 30] can be employed, and the result of this risk-based system design is the system model. The treatments to block threats compromising trustworthiness can be documented as evidence (solutions in GSN), and the use of such methods and best practices can be documented as arguments (strategies in GSN) in the trustworthiness cases.

Trustworthiness Evaluation of the System Model: The trustworthiness evaluation must lead to an evaluation result that includes measured values of trustworthiness properties for the CPS.

As an example of such methods, we have developed a technique [7] that objectively evaluates the trustworthiness of a whole system based on the evaluation of each of its components. This technique is based on computational methods (i.e. trustworthiness metrics) and aggregates trustworthiness measurements for the combined functionality of the components making up a system. In that method, we consider a trustworthiness vector for the whole CPS, whose values depend on the corresponding trustworthiness properties of its components. It is important to emphasize that our trustworthiness evaluation depends on the trustworthiness vector and also on the system structure, i.e. the way the components' functionalities interact. This latter factor is a complementary way to prevent threats becoming active by avoiding architectures that allow for groups of related components to be jointly affected by certain types of threats. Such structural issues should be captured in the design process and should be considered as a major parameter affecting the trustworthiness of the CPS.

Trustworthiness metrics must allow for comparing alternative system models. Alternative system models may result from the risk reduction practices performed in the design phase. For instance, designers may include a control to block a specific threat to trustworthiness, e.g. redundant components. The resulting modified system model represents an alternative to the previous system model. Evaluation of such alternative system models can give solid evidence as regards the question which of both is "more trustworthy", regardless of the method used to develop each one. We argue that a user should justifiably distrust the first one much more than the second one. Although the system is not running yet, we know that the second alternative has followed a better development process, which in turn is known to help avoiding vulnerabilities. Thus, we can say that the trustworthiness of systems (taking their development methodology itself as evidence) is dependent on the development process and methodology, and it can make the user confident to some extent.

Note that other trustworthiness evaluation methods can be used as well in this step, e.g. the method of Qiang [15] that focuses on trustworthiness measurement for workflow management systems.

The result of the trustworthiness evaluation can be documented as evidence (solutions in GSN), and the use of trustworthiness evaluation methods can be documented as arguments (strategy in GSN) in the trustworthiness cases.

Preparation for Run-Time Trustworthiness Maintenance: In cyber-physical systems, sub-optimal or incorrect functioning of the system may have detrimental effects. In addition to designing systems with trustworthiness in mind, maintaining trustworthiness at run-time is a critical task in order to identify issues that could negatively affect the trustworthiness of the CPS. To this end, monitoring and mitigation capabilities for the CPS must be provided. Including these capabilities and interfaces for monitoring and adaptation might change the system model. In prior work [8], we proposed business processes for monitoring, measuring, and managing trustworthiness, as well as mitigating trustworthiness issues at run-time. In that work, we provide a reference architecture for trustworthiness maintenance systems. When this reference architecture is realized, trustworthiness maintenance capabilities for monitoring and managing the CPS's trustworthiness properties in order to preserve the overall established trustworthiness during runtime exist. Hence, these capabilities and artefacts that realize such a solution can be documented as evidence (solutions in GSN), and the practices leading to such monitoring and maintenance capabilities are valid arguments (strategies in GSN) in trustworthiness cases.

3   Application Example

This section demonstrates our approach of documenting trustworthiness cases in a development process that uses the trustworthy-by-design methods and tech-

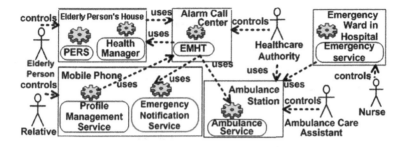

Fig. 3. Overview of an AAL system inspired by [7]

niques that we suggested in Sect. 2. The example stems partially from the experience that the first author gained during the OPTET project[2] on an ambient assisted living (AAL) system.

Motivating Scenario. A motivating scenario for the creation of trustworthiness cases can be the following. Suppose that we are responsible for designing and coordinating an AAL system. An overview of an exemplary AAL system with its services and apps is shown in Fig. 3.

Use-Case Scenario. The AAL system supports different use-case scenarios. We will focus on the following one: we want to assure that our end users, elderly people who are in need of urgent health-care service, can be transferred to a hospital in a reasonably short time. As part of the AAL, a *home monitoring system (HMS)* will be developed (not shown in Fig. 3). The HMS is responsible for incident detection and detection of abnormal situations to prevent emergency incidents. The HMS allows elderly people in their homes to call for help in case of emergency situations. Furthermore, the HMS analyzes the elderly person's health status for preventing incidents in the first place. The incidents are reported to an *Alarm Call Center* that, in turn, reacts, for example, by sending out ambulances or other medical caregivers, and notifying the elderly person's relatives. For preventing emergency situations, the vital signs of the elderly person are diagnosed in regular intervals to reduce hospital visits and falls. An elderly person can use a so-called *PERS device* (personal emergency response system) to call for help, which is then reported to the alarm call center that uses an *emergency monitoring and handling tool (EMHT)* for visualizing, organizing, and managing emergency incidents. The EMHT is a software service hosted by the alarm call center that, in turn, is operated by a health-care authority. *Emergency notification* and *Ambulance Service*, which run on mobile phones of relatives, or *Ambulance Stations* respectively, are called in order to require caregivers to provide help. An ambulance service is requested in case an ambulance should be sent to handle an emergency situation. The other case is that, based

---

[2] https://cordis.europa.eu/project/rcn/105733_en.html.

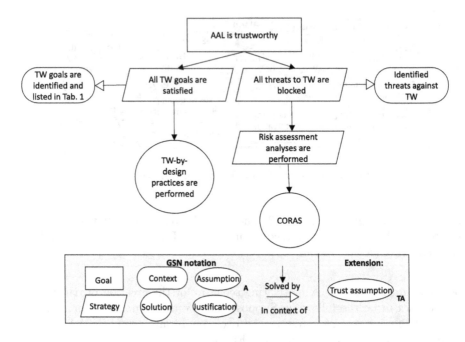

Fig. 4. Trustworthiness case for entire AAL

on analyzed information sent to the *EMHT*, an abnormal situation is detected and further diagnoses are necessary. Therefore, the elderly person will get an appointment and notifications for a tele-visit in her/his *Health Manager app*.

For this use-case scenario, we show in the following some simplified trustworthiness cases in the form of GSN diagrams. To recapitulate, there is the following mapping between the elements of our trustworthiness cases and GSN elements: trustworthiness goals and trustworthiness requirements map to GSN goals, trustworthiness evidence maps to GSN solutions, and trustworthiness arguments map to GSN strategies.

Figure 4 shows the top tier of the trustworthiness case for the AAL system. It starts with the top-level trustworthiness goal for the whole AAL system (i.e. the trustworthiness vector for the AAL system) and shows how this goal is achieved by a defensible trustworthiness argument. The high-level goal in this trustworthiness case is "AAL is trustworthy", which is refined into the two strategies "All TW goals are satisfied" and "All threats to TW are blocked". These strategies will assure that the "AAL is trustworthy" goal is met.

The strategy "All TW goals are satisfied" is solved by the solution "TW-by-design practices are performed". Figure 4 also illustrates the contributing factors to the trustworthiness of an AAL system. The "physical environment" has no impact on this level of abstraction, and therefore context information regarding the system context is not modelled. Yet, context information regarding the development process has to be considered. The context information related to the strategy "All TW goals are satisfied" is, that an appropriate requirements engineering method has been performed and the result of the requirements engineering method is a list of trustworthiness goals (and, to be specific, the trustworthiness requirements). Hence, the GSN model in Fig. 4 documents that the strategy "All TW goals are satisfied" is valid in the context that "TW goals are identified and listed in Table 1". Please note that here Table 1 is simply a fictitious reference to a table where the trustworthiness goals are listed. Due to space limitations, we do not provide a trustworthiness requirements specification. The strategy "All threats to TW are blocked" can be assured, for example, by using risk assessment approaches. This is modelled as the substrategy "Risk assessment analyses are performed". This substrategy is solved by performing the "CORAS" risk assessment methodology (see [26] for details on CORAS). The context information related to "All threats to TW are blocked" is that there is a list of "Identified threats against trustworthiness".

In Figs. 5 and 6, we present a breakdown of the abstract trustworthiness case goal presented in Fig. 4. Since the latter is a vector of trustworthiness properties, we can break it down into these properties (e.g. reliability, usability, etc.). The trustworthiness properties can be assigned to relevant parts of the CPS, and each part can then be analysed with respect to the trustworthiness properties from the vector that is relevant for that part. This trustworthiness goal breakdown structure represents the argument that is implicit in a trustworthiness refinement process. Specifically, it shows how the claims entailed by trustworthiness requirements can be developed and linked to the supporting evidence produced from the specified trustworthiness evaluation methods.

Figure 5 depicts the trustworthiness case for the trustworthiness property reliability of the AAL system. The goal "Reliability TW property is satisfied by AAL" is refined into three strategies: "Availability of emergency services", "Redundant sensors for incident detection", and "Correctness of medical treatments via service". As mentioned in the last section, it is important that, additionally to the context information regarding the development process, the operational or physical environment of the AAL is considered as well. Therefore, we documented a trust assumption as contributing factor to the strategy "Correctness of medical treatments via service". The elderly persons' perception of correctness is dependent on intuitively visualized treatment information.

The strategy "Redundant sensors for incident detection" is solved by "PERS + video sensor" as solution. This solution for the strategy shows how the trustworthiness case is co-developed with the AAL, because the design decision of adding an additional sensor is only made in order to increase the reliability of the AAL in case of incidents.

The strategy "Availability of emergency services" is refined to the substrategy "The emergency service is available in 99% of the time". This can be assessed by conventional verification techniques. Therefore, this substrategy is solved by "Trustworthiness evaluation" and "Log file analysis". The result of trustworthiness evaluation is, for example, that the service is available during 99.9% of the time.

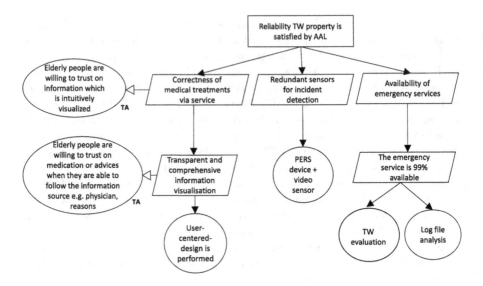

Fig. 5. Trustworthiness case for TW property reliability

Figure 6 shows the trustworthiness case for the trustworthiness property usability. The goal "Usability TW property is satisfied by AAL" is refined into three strategies that assure that this goal is met. These three strategies are: "Learnability", "Ease of use", and "Functioning indicators". For functioning indication, it is assumed that the elderly persons are willing to trust when they see explicit indications of service availability or functioning. This should, for example, be realized in the *Health Manager* app. These three strategies are solved by having reference manuals and handbooks, performing user-centred design, and including status indication with colour code.

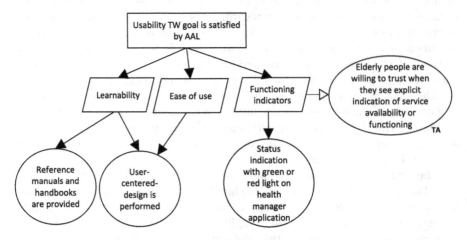

Fig. 6. Trustworthiness case for TW property usability

This application example is kept simple in order to exemplify the usage of the defined concepts. Moreover, a number of elements have been omitted for simplifying the graphical representation of the trustworthiness cases like, for example, the decomposition of the GSN models based on the trustworthiness vector elements and the composition of the system.

4 Related Work

We analysed related work from two perspectives: first, with regard to trustworthiness cases and, second, with regard to trustworthiness certification.

Trustworthiness cases are based on assurance and safety cases. Regarding assurance and safety cases, a lot of literature can be found. However, to the best of our knowledge, there are no existing approaches that define trustworthiness as a vector of trustworthiness properties (as we do) and create trustworthiness cases to demonstrate that a system is trustworthy. Nevertheless, we provide a short overview of important related work in the field of assurance and safety cases. Since assurance is defined as justified confidence in a property of interest [16–18], assurance cases are not restricted to a specific property and are thus more general. In contrast, safety cases focus on one property, namely safety. However, the use of assurance cases is not restricted to the safety domain. They are also used in the security domain [3,28,32] and in general for software-based systems [2,13].

Software certification can be used as a means to prove certain software product properties to potential consumers. There have been some efforts to automate the certification process, e.g. [1,24,25], to facilitate the adoption of these processes in service-oriented environments. Kaluvuri et al. propose the concept of descriptive digital certification that can capture information emanating from the certification process. This conceptual model has been realized by an XML-based approach [22]. The digital certificate contains information regarding the system that is being certified in a structured and machine-processable manner, thus providing transparency regarding the service architecture and implementation as well as its execution environment. However, in the above-mentioned works, the digital certificate concept is based on security certification schemes such as Common Criteria and, hence, have been used towards certification of security properties. Di Cerbo et al. [6] extend the concept of digital certificate in order to certify the trustworthiness of software. Their trustworthiness digital certification concept provides a data structure for capturing the information emanating from certification processes and, thus, does not prescribe the content of the certifications. Di Cerbo et al. realize the concept of trustworthiness digital certificate using linked data vocabulary [6]. In another paper, Di Cerbo et al. [5] propose an evidence-based trustworthiness approach through a controlled software development process. Similar to our work, the intention is to collect evidence for trustworthiness. However, their work does not aim at systematic generation and documentation of the evidence throughout the whole life cycle. Furthermore, the focus of their work is on evidence collected from coding, deployment, and operation phase.

All the above-mentioned approaches support post-design evaluation. Our trustworthiness cases cover the evidence generation and documentation in a co-development manner and cover the whole software development life cycle. They provide the content to the above-mentioned digital trustworthiness certificates, which - so far - do not include all the information that is provided in our trustworthiness cases.

5   Conclusions and Future Work

We have developed a new approach for assuring and documenting trustworthiness of cyber-physical systems in an evidence-based manner. We propose the co-development of trustworthiness cases along with the development of the CPS. Evidence that is documented in the trustworthiness cases is either product-oriented or process-oriented. Process-oriented evidence consists of the performed practices to build trustworthiness into the core of the CPS, e.g. by using a risk management method like CORAS. Product-oriented evidence includes the quantitatively evaluated results of trustworthiness metrics for a component or other types of qualitative evidence. One of the benefits of trustworthiness cases is that they provide well-structured arguments and evidence.

We have applied our approach in limited use cases and demonstrated its usefulness. As future work, feasibility studies must be performed by applying trustworthiness cases to larger real life examples and correspondingly improving them, for example, by defining useful metrics for assessment of trustworthiness. Furthermore, an evaluation and certification process must be developed to implement the independent validation of trustworthiness cases. To support an open market development, that process must be as open as possible.

Therefore, the certification process should allow different approaches in the following dimensions: (i) using different certification authorities (these are, in the language of certification processes according to ISO 17021 [19], the certification bodies as well as the owners of the trustworthiness cases and different involved stakeholders in the certification process), thus allowing all from self-signed certificates, industrial certification bodies, up to nation-level certification authorities/bodies, if deemed necessary, (ii) using different evaluation laboratories that perform the actual assessment or verification of the metrics values, thus allowing all from the manufacturers' own quality assurance department, industrially driven standards organizations, up to specialized accredited evaluation labs, (iii) using different scopes and context conditions as well as choice of metrics (and so evidence), thus allowing to adapt to different business and maybe also consumer scenarios in different verticals with different success factors and requirements for trustworthy CPS.

One important question that needs to be answered in an application of the above described scenario is the reliability of the overall process. We would recommend to stick to ISO 17021 [19] and to apply software quality measurement techniques as described in ISO 25021 [21], so as to benefit from the existing infrastructure for accreditation and certification that has been established and has proven to be successful in the market, for example, for quality management systems, information security management systems, and even Common Criteria certification schemes.

Acknowledgment. Research leading to these results received partially funding from the European Union's Horizon 2020 research and innovation programme under grant agreement number 731678 (RestAssured).

References

1. Anisetti, M., Ardagna, C.A., Gaudenzi, F., Damiani, E.: A certification framework for cloud-based services. In: Proceedings of the 31st Annual ACM Symposium on Applied Computing, SAC, NY, USA, pp. 440–447 (2016)
2. Bloomfield, R., Bishop, P.: Safety and assurance cases: past, present and possible future - an adelard perspective. In: Dale, C., Anderson, T. (eds.) Making Systems Safer, pp. 51–67. Springer, London (2010). https://doi.org/10.1007/978-1-84996-086-1_4
3. Bloomfield, R., Masera, M., Miller, A., Saydjari, O.S., Weinstock, C.B.: Assurance cases for security: the metrics challenge. In: A Report from a Workshop on Assurance Cases for Security, Edinburgh, UK (2007). http://ieeexplore.ieee.org/document/4273036/
4. Broy, M., Cengarle, M.V., Geisberger, E.: Cyber-physical systems: imminent challenges. In: Calinescu, R., Garlan, D. (eds.) Monterey Workshop 2012. LNCS, vol. 7539, pp. 1–28. Springer, Heidelberg (2012). https://doi.org/10.1007/978-3-642-34059-8_1
5. Di Cerbo, F., Gol Mohammadi, N., Paulus, S.: Evidence-based trustworthiness of internet-based services through controlled software development. In: Cleary, F., Felici, M. (eds.) Cyber Security and Privacy. CCIS, vol. 530, pp. 91–102. Springer, Cham (2015). https://doi.org/10.1007/978-3-319-25360-2_8
6. Di Cerbo, F., Kaluvuri, S.P., Motte, F., Nasser, B., Chen, W.X., Short, S.: Towards a linked data vocabulary for the certification of software properties. In: 10th International Conference on Signal-Image Technology and Internet-Based Systems, pp. 721–727 (2014)
7. Gol Mohammadi, N., Bandyszak, T., Kalogiros, C., Kanakakis, M., Weyer, T.: A framework for evaluating the end-to-end trustworthiness. In: Proceedings of the 14th IEEE International Conference on Trust, Security and Privacy in Computing and Communications (IEEE TrustCom) (2015)
8. Gol Mohammadi, N., et al.: Maintaining trustworthiness of socio-technical systems at run-time. In: Eckert, C., Katsikas, S.K., Pernul, G. (eds.) TrustBus 2014. LNCS, vol. 8647, pp. 1–12. Springer, Cham (2014). https://doi.org/10.1007/978-3-319-09770-1_1
9. Gol Mohammadi, N., Bandyszak, T., Paulus, S., Meland, P.H., Weyer, T., Pohl, K.: Extending software development methodologies to support trustworthiness-by-design. In: Proceedings of the CAiSE Forum at the 27th International Conference on Advanced Information Systems Engineering, Co-located with CAiSE, pp. 213–220 (2015)
10. Mohammadi, N.G., Heisel, M.: A framework for systematic analysis and modeling of trustworthiness requirements using i* and BPMN. In: Katsikas, S., Lambrinoudakis, C., Furnell, S. (eds.) TrustBus 2016. LNCS, vol. 9830, pp. 3–18. Springer, Cham (2016). https://doi.org/10.1007/978-3-319-44341-6_1

11. Gol Mohammadi, N., Heisel, M.: A framework for systematic refinement of trustworthiness requirements. Information **8**(2), 46 (2017)
12. Gol Mohammadi, N., et al.: Trustworthiness attributes and metrics for engineering trusted internet-based software systems. In: Helfert, M., Desprez, F., Ferguson, D., Leymann, F. (eds.) CLOSER 2013. CCIS, vol. 453, pp. 19–35. Springer, Cham (2014). https://doi.org/10.1007/978-3-319-11561-0_2
13. Graydon, P.J., Knight, J.C., Strunk, E.A.: Assurance based development of critical systems. In: 37th Annual IEEE/IFIP International Conference on Dependable Systems and Networks (DSN), pp. 347–357 (2007)
14. GSN Working Group. The 1st version of the Goal Structuring Notation (GSN) Standard, Version 1, November 2011. http://www.goalstructuringnotation.info/
15. Han, Q.: Trustworthiness measurement algorithm for TWfMS based on software behaviour entropy. Entropy, **20**(3) (2018). Article no. 195
16. Hawkins, R., Habli, I., Kelly, T., McDermid, J.: Assurance cases and prescriptive software safety certification: a comparative study. Saf. Sci. **59**, 55–71 (2013)
17. Hawkins, R., Kelly, T.: A structured approach to selecting and justifying software safety evidence. In: Proceedings of the 5th IET International Conference on System Safety, pp. 31–37 (2010)
18. Hawkins, R., Kelly, T.: A systematic approach for developing software safety arguments. J. Syst. Saf. Hazard Prev. **46**(4), 25 (2010)
19. ISO/IEC 17021-1. Conformity assessment - Requirements for bodies providing audit and certification of management systems - Part 1: Requirements - Requirements. Technical report (2015)
20. ISO/IEC 21827. Information technology, Security techniques, Systems Security Engineering - Capability Maturity Model (SSE-CMM). Technical report (2008)
21. ISO/IEC 25021. Systems and software engineering - Systems and software Quality Requirements and Evaluation (SQuaRE) - Quality measure elements. Technical report (2012)
22. Kaluvuri, S.P., Koshutanski, H., Cerbo, F.D., Mana, A.: Security assurance of services through digital security certificates. In: Proceeding of the 20th International Conference on Web Services (ICWS), pp. 98–102. IEEE (2013)
23. Kelly, T.P.: Arguing safety - a systematic approach to managing safety cases. Dissertation, Department of Computer Science, The University of York (1998)
24. Krotsiani, M., Spanoudakis, G., Mahbub, K.: Incremental certification of cloud services. In: 7th International Conference on Emerging Security Information, Systems and Technologie, SECURWARE (2018)
25. Lotz, V., Kaluvuri, S.P., Di Cerbo, F., Sabetta, A.: Towards security certification schemas for the internet of services. In: Proceedings of the 5th International Conference on New Technologies, Mobility and Security (NTMS), pp. 1–5 (2012)
26. Lund, M.S., Solhaug, B., Stølen, K.: Model-Driven Risk Analysis. The CORAS Approach. Springer, Heidelberg (2010). https://doi.org/10.1007/978-3-642-12323-8
27. National Research Council, Jackson, D., Martyn, T. (eds.): Software for Dependable Systems: Sufficient Evidence? Committee on Certifiably Dependable Software Systems, Computer Science and Telecommunications Board, The National Academies Press, Washington, D.C. (2007)
28. Patu, V., Yamamoto, S.: How to develop security case by combining real life security experiences (evidence) with d-case. Procedia Comput. Sci. **22**, 954–959 (2013). 17th International Conference in Knowledge Based and Intelligent Information and Engineering Systems - KES
29. Potter, B.: Threat modelling: Microsoft SDL threat modelling tool. Netw. Secur. **2009**(1), 15–18 (2009)

30. Surridge, M., Nasser, B.I., Chen, X., Chakravarthy, A., Melas, P.: Run-time risk management in adaptive ICT systems. In: International Conference on Availability, Reliability and Security, ARES, pp. 102–110. IEEE (2013)
31. Sztompka, P.: Trust: A Sociological Theory. Cambridge University Press, Cambridge (1999)
32. Weinstock, C.B., Lipson, H.F., Goodenough, J.: Arguing Security - Creating Security Assurance Cases (2007). https://resources.sei.cmu.edu/asset_files/WhitePaper/2013_019_001_293637.pdf

Author Index

Acien, Antonio   229
Aladawy, Dina   103
Alruban, Abdulrahman   135
Alshammari, Majed   85
Antunes, Luís   57
Athinaiou, Myrsini   198

Beckers, Kristian   103
Benenson, Zinaida   9
Bollwein, Ferdinand   23

Clarke, Nathan   135
Coetzee, Marijke   182

Fernandez, Gerardo   229
Fotis, Theo   198
Furnell, Steven   135

Gerber, Nina   119
Ghiglieri, Marco   119
Giannakoulias, Alkiviadis   213
Gol Mohammadi, Nazila   244
Grambow, Martin   39
Greaves, Brian   182
Gritzalis, Stefanos   150

Heisel, Maritta   244

Kalloniatis, Christos   150
Kalpakis, George   213
Kavroudakis, Dimitris   150
Kunz, Alexandra   119
Kunz, Michael   167

Lambrinoudakis, Costas   3
Leung, Wai Sze   182
Li, Fudong   135
Lopez, Javier   229

Mayer, Peter   119
Mazumdar, Subhasish   69
Mouratidis, Haralambos   198

Nieto, Ana   229
Nuss, Martin   167

Pallas, Frank   39
Panaousis, Emmanouil   198, 213
Pape, Sebastian   103
Paturi, Anand   69
Pavlidis, Michalis   198
Pitropakis, Nikolaos   213
Puchta, Alexander   167

Rack, Philipp   119
Reinfelder, Lena   9
Reinheimer, Benjamin   119
Renaud, Karen   119
Resende, João S.   57
Rodriguez, Rodrigo Diaz   213
Russ, Sophie   9

Sarigiannidis, Panayiotis   213
Schankin, Andrea   9
Simou, Stavros   150
Simpson, Andrew   85
Sousa, Patrícia R.   57

Troumpis, Ioannis   150

Ulfat-Bunyadi, Nelufar   244

Volkamer, Melanie   119

Wiese, Lena   23

Printed in the United States
By Bookmasters